The British army
and the
crisis of empire
1918–22

For Sally

Keith Jeffery

The British army
and the
crisis of empire
1918–22

Manchester
University Press

Copyright © Keith Jeffery 1984

Published by
Manchester University Press, Oxford Road, Manchester M13 9PL, England
and
51 Washington Street, Dover, N.H. 03820, USA

British Library cataloguing in publication data
Jeffery, Keith
    The British army and the crisis of empire
    1918–22.
    1. Great Britain—Military policy
    2. Great Britain—History, Military—
    20th century
    I. Titlw
    355′.0335′41   UA647

Library of Congress cataloging in publication data
Jeffrey, Keith.
    The British army and the crisis of empire, 1918–22.
    Bibliography: p. 187
    Includes index.
    1. Great Britain – Politics and government – 1910–1936.
2. Great Britain – Colonies – Administration.   3. Great
Britain – Military policy.   4. Great Britain. Army –
History – 20th century.   I. Title.
DA18.J42 1984 941.083   84–9729

ISBN 0–7190–1717–3

Photoset in Century Schoolbook by
Northern Phototypesetting Co., Bolton
Printed in Great Britain by
Butler & Tanner Ltd, Frome and London

Contents

Preface

This book deals with the period when Britain briefly possessed a 'military' empire and during which the empire experienced its greatest territorial extent. But a summit is also the moment of decline, and within a very few years Britain had begun to reduce the close military and political control she exercised, especially in the newly acquired Middle Eastern possessions. There were also signs of political retrenchment in the older empire: the Irish Free State gained 'dominion status', and a measure of self-government was conceded to India and Egypt. This study addresses itself to the question of why and how these concessions were made. It also deals with the specific problems of adjusting imperial and strategic policy to peacetime conditions after November 1918. During the First World War the empire became virtually a united and cohesive unit, but following the armistice the dominions and India – in marked contrast to their wartime attitude – refused to continue making substantial contributions to the empire's military effort. At the same time the empire was beset with an upsurge of nationalism and an unprecedented level of internal unrest. In the immediate aftermath of the war, the British government largely sought to solve these problems by military means – an extension of the 'war imperialism' which had characterised the years 1914–18. The book describes the failure of this policy and discusses the techniques employed thereafter to secure Britain's imperial interests.

In this book I hope to contribute towards our understanding of the major policy decisions made during the 1918–22 period. These were of considerable long-term importance. The modern history of India, Ireland and the Middle East, particularly regarding the post-imperial problems of partition and devolution of power, cannot be fully explained without an examination of the crucial years following the end of the First World War. The book also seeks to highlight the role which 'defence planners' play in British policy-making. It investigates problems of internal and external 'imperial defence' which still occur today, and, by concentrating on a critical period in the history of the empire, it also endeavours to illuminate the nature of twentieth-century British imperialism.

My study of imperial and military policy was conceived in Cambridge,

vi

most of the book was researched in London, much of it was written in Horgues and Royan – despite competition from more pleasurable pursuits – and it was completed in Belfast. In all these places there are people to whom I owe thanks. Above all, I owe an inexpressible debt of gratitude to the late Jack Gallagher, who first guided me towards a study of the post-war 'crisis of empire'. Dr Geoffrey Parker initiated me into the subtleties and style of scholarly history, while Tom Tomlinson introduced me to Commonwealth history, and also to Jack. Mr Brian Bond, Professor R. J. Gavin, Professor F. H. Hinsley, Professor M. E. Howard, Professor P. N. S. Mansergh, Professor A. J. A. Morris, Dr Philip Ollerenshaw, Dr Anil Seal and Professor D. C. Watt have all offered much helpful advice and criticism. John Murray-Browne provided a refuge in London; Brian and Odile Jeffery more than one in France. Dr J. G. Riddell administered the appropriate medicines and Mary Bell cheerfully coped with the typing. I must also thank my colleagues in the soon-to-be-disbanded School of Philosophy, Politics and History at the Ulster Polytechnic for providing such a stimulating atmosphere in which to work. My research has been assisted financially by the Northern Ireland Department of Education, the Master and Fellows of St John's College, Cambridge, and the Ulster Polytechnic, to all of whom I am most grateful.

Unpublished Crown-copyright material in the Public Record Office and in the India Office Records reproduced in this book appears by permission of the Controller of Her Majesty's Stationery Office. Quotation from other copyright material is made with the permission of the following: the University of Birmingham (Austen Chamberlain papers), Mrs Mary Bennett and the Bodleian Library, Oxford (H. A. L. Fisher diary), Mr J. P. A. Haldane of Foswell and the Trustees of the National Library of Scotland (Haldane papers), the Master, Fellows and Scholars of Churchill College in the University of Cambridge (Hankey papers), Lord Robertson and the Trustees of the Liddell Hart Centre for Military Archives (Robertson papers), and the Trustees of the Imperial War Museum (Sir Henry Wilson papers). My very considerable debt to all the institutions which have kindly granted access to collections of papers, and to the many authors whose work I have used, is recorded in the references and bibliography. Parts of my book draw on work first published elsewhere: in the *Journal of Imperial and Commonwealth History*, vol. V, no. 3, and *Modern Asian Studies*, vol. 15, part 3. I am grateful to the editors and publishers for permission to reprint this material here.

Finally I must thank my parents, who have supported and encouraged me from the very beginning, and Sally Visick, the least of whose contributions has been to draw the map.

Keith Jeffery
Belfast, January 1984

Abbreviations
used in the text and references

AG	Adjutant-General
CAB	Cabinet Office papers
CIGS	Chief of the Imperial General Staff
CinC	Commander-in-Chief
CO	Colonial Office
DMO	Director of Military Operations
FO	Foreign Office and Foreign Office papers
GHQ	General Headquarters
GOC(-in-C)	General Officer Commanding (-in-Chief)
IDCE	Inter-departmental Conference on Middle Eastern Affairs
IO	India Office
IOR	India Office Records
LG	Lloyd George
QMG	Quarter-Master-General
RIC	Royal Irish Constabulary
S. of S.	Secretary of State
WO	War Office and War Office papers

Chapter 1

The empire at war

The British empire reached its apogee at the end of the First World War. *Whitaker's Almanack* for 1922 recorded that the empire, enlarged by Britain's share of former German and Ottoman possessions, now occupied 'over one-quarter of the known surface of the globe, and its population exceeds one-quarter of the estimated number of the human race'. The Great War also represented an emotional imperial summit. 'Now it is all over', wrote one senior general in December 1918, 'and the Empire stands on a pinnacle built by her tenacity & courage – never did our reputation stand so high'.[1] And so it was, for even taking into account the hyperbole of victory, the empire had come closest in its history to being a coherent political, military and strategic unit. Australians had fought alongside Indians, Nigerians by South Africans, Canadians by Irishmen. Nearly one million white troops from the dominions had rallied to the flag during the war along with 1,400,000 Indian recruits.[2] At the highest level of decision-making – the 'Imperial War Cabinet' – the dominions had, in theory at any rate, shared with the United Kingdom in the direction of the war. At the 1921 imperial conference Lloyd George expressed popularly held sentiments in suitably fulsome terms. 'The War', he declared, 'demonstrated – I might say revealed – to the world, including ourselves, that the British Empire was not an abstraction but a living force to be reckoned with'.[3]

Nowhere is the wartime imperial effort better illustrated than in the Royal Colonial Institute's monumental history of the empire at war. Five substantial volumes were published between 1921 and 1926 with the declared aim of providing a complete record of the contribution made in the Great War 'by every unit of the Overseas Empire from the greatest to the smallest' and, in addition, to trace the growth of imperial military co-operation 'prior to the late war'.[4] During the half century or so leading up to the war, both the dominions and India made military contributions towards imperial defence and although these began on a very small scale, particularly in the case of the dominions, there is a discernible rise in the amount of imperial military co-operation during this period. For the dominions this trend was evinced more by administrative and organisational reforms than by manpower contributions. Dominion troops, nevertheless, fought in the South African War at the turn of the century and their chief value during the Great War, in Sir Charles Lucas's view, was that they were 'nurseries of fighting men of superb quality'.[5] The Indian Army, a more subordinate organisation than any dominion force, throughout much of the nineteenth century served as a sort of 'imperial fire brigade', provided colonial garrisons and, like the dominions in 1914–18, served as an enormous reservoir of men for the Allied cause. A brief review, therefore, of imperial military co-operation both before and during the war will serve to illustrate the assumption of British politicians and generals following the war that the empire could be relied upon to continue to share the burden of imperial defence with the United Kingdom.

India, as Lord Salisbury remarked in 1882, was traditionally regarded by many British politicians as 'an English barrack in the Oriental Seas from which we may draw any number of troops without paying for them',[6] and, indeed, Indian troops saw service in numerous colonial expeditions in the nineteenth century. Native Indian soldiers first fought outside India as early as 1792 when a force from Madras captured Manila in the Philippines. The most extensive use, however, of the Indian Army as an 'imperial' force did not come until after the 1857 Mutiny, when the armies of the East India Company were reformed as 'soldiers of the Queen', and from then until the war in 1914 Indian troops served in over a dozen different campaigns in places as far apart as China and Egypt.

From almost the very beginning, however, there was friction between the Indian and the British governments over the question of payment for Indian troops serving overseas. It was generally accepted that expeditions on the Frontier or in Burma should be borne upon the Indian establishment, but the position was much less clear in the case of operations in Africa or China. The despatch of Indian troops to reinforce the British garrison in Malta in 1878 raised the whole constitutional question of Indian Army service overseas and inflamed Liberal anti-imperialists in Parliament. W. E. Forster, from the opposition benches, questioned a policy which relied 'not upon the patriotism and spirit of our own people, but upon the power of our money bags, to get Gurkhas and Sikhs and Mussulmen to fight for us'.[7] Even the popular parodists had a word to say on the matter:

We don't want to fight; but, by Jingo, if we do,
We won't go to the front ourselves, but we'll send the
mild Hindoo.[8]

Imperial necessity, nevertheless, prevailed over tender Liberal consciences, for in 1882, after Gladstone had returned to power for his second administration, Indian troops were employed to reinforce British forces in Egypt. The financial question, however, continued to cause difficulties between Britain and India until in 1895 a Royal Commission was appointed to examine the problem. In April 1900 the Commission proposed a solution which was finally accepted by both governments in 1902. Apart from such 'special cases' as might arise, it was proposed that India should bear primary financial responsibility for those geographical regions in which she had a 'direct and substantial interest'. Included among such regions were Egypt 'so far as the security of the Suez Canal is affected', Persia, the Persian Gulf and Afghanistan.[9] Thus the matter rested until after the Great War when the Indian government once more began to question the financial basis upon which Indian troops were employed outside India.

Despite the extensive use of the Indian Army overseas during the later nineteenth century, it was not until 1898 that Indian troops were first employed in colonial garrisons. The strains which the South African War, a white man's war from which Indian troops were excluded, made upon the imperial military system confirmed these early arrangements and by 1914 the Indian Army was being regularly employed for garrisons in Egypt, the Indian Ocean, Singapore and China. There was, however, an older tradition of recruiting soldiers in India for service in special local forces in colonies and protectorates both in Asia and Africa. Sikh contingents saw service in the African protectorates and the Malay States Guides regiment was largely recruited in India. From 1892 to 1903 special service battalions were raised in India for service in Hong Kong and a battery of artillery was specially recruited for employment in both Hong Kong and Singapore. Although these special imperial units comprised only a very small part of India's total contribution to imperial defence, after the Great War the Indian government put up a scheme for colonial garrison regiments, to be raised separately from normal army recruitment. From the Indian point of view such an arrangement made rendering charges to the imperial exchequer, for 'imperial' rather than Indian defence, more straightforward than British proposals simply to continue seconding battalions from the Indian Army proper.

There were, however, no financial quibbles when the empire went to war in August 1914. Thanks to Lord Kitchener, who as Commander-in-Chief from 1902 to 1909 had reformed the Indian Army on the sensible grounds that the organisation of an army in peacetime should conform to the required organisation in time of war, the Indian government was in a position immediately to despatch troops to Europe, which is precisely what the Viceroy-in-Council did. By the end of October 1914 two Indian infantry divisions were fighting in Flanders. This was not simply a proconsular gesture by the Viceroy. Although it is impossible to assess the opinion of the mass of the Indian population, both the educated and princely classes, in 1914 at any rate, were enthusiastically behind the

United Kingdom. One of the Indian members of the Viceroy's Legislative Council went so far as to say that Indians were 'ready to meet any danger and render any sacrifices for the sake of the great and glorious Empire of which we are proud to call ourselves citizens'. On 7 September 1914 the Viceroy, Lord Hardinge, was able to give London details of offers of help and sympathy which he had received from nearly seven hundred Indian princes. Some nationalists, moreover, like their Irish counterparts, thought that to give assistance in time of need might advance their political purpose and even Gandhi offered his services and raised a Field Ambulance Corps.[10]

In addition to the troops sent to France in August 1914, India despatched six battalions to East Africa and a rather larger force to Egypt. In October 1914, foreshadowing India's major role in the Allied war effort, a brigade of troops was sent to the head of the Persian Gulf in order to secure British interests in the area, especially the Anglo-Persian Oil Company's installations in south-west Persia. With the declaration of war against Turkey at the end of the same month, this force was soon increased to a division. By the end of the war there were more than a quarter of a million Indian native troops in what became known as the Mesopotamian Command, covering Mesopotamia itself, Persia and the detachments in the Caucasus and Transcaspian regions of south Russia.[11] This figure was greater than the total number of Indian ranks serving at the outbreak of the war.

In addition to the Indian Army itself about 25,000 Imperial Service Troops – troops raised and financed by the native states – were put at the disposal of the government.[12] As well as providing manpower the Indian administration agreed early in the war to continue to bear 'the ordinary charges of the troops sent out of India which she would have had to pay had they remained in India', and subsequently also agreed to make a major contribution towards the 'ordinary' charges for the extra troops raised for the war. In 1917, moreover, India made an outright gift of £100 million towards wartime expenditure – 'nearly twice India's whole net revenue before the war'. Nor was this all, for during the war India proved to be a significant economic asset for the home government. As India's banker London was able to dispose of the large balances which accrued from her exports of war supplies and services, thus easing the difficulties faced by the British government in paying for the import of food and munitions, particularly from the United States of America.[13]

India's greatest part in the war was played in the Middle East. In October 1918 over half the troops in Mesopotamia were Indian and rather more than a third in Palestine. Throughout the war, moreover, India was exclusively responsible for providing all supplies and stores required by the troops, both British and Indian, in Mesopotamia.[14] But the Mesopotamian campaign also revealed serious administrative weaknesses in the Indian military machine. Kitchener's reform of the Indian Army a decade or so before the outbreak of war, while enormously improving the mobility of the army, had sacrificed administrative efficiency to this end, and nowhere was this more apparent than in Mesopotamia, which for the first two and a half years of the war was an exclusively Indian theatre of operations. From the beginning there were administrative difficulties and it was an almost total breakdown in support services which was in the most part responsible for the surrender of General Townshend's division at Kut in April 1917. Such was the Indian failure that for the rest of the war the control of military operations in Mesopotamia was transferred to the War Office. Thus, while India continued to supply much of the manpower and all of the *matériel* for Mesopotamia, the direction of military policy lay in London. In the aftermath of war this division of responsibility was to become a major source of friction between Delhi and London.

The dominions' contribution to imperial defence before the First World War was less consistent but, perhaps, more significant than that of India.[15] By the mid-1870s the British garrisons in Canada, Australia and New Zealand had been withdrawn and henceforth any dominion role in the defence of the empire depended largely on goodwill and consent on the dominion side, and persuasiveness of argument on the British. Throughout the second half of the nineteenth century, as Britain loosened the political ties binding her to the 'white' colonies, she also began to slough off some of her responsibilities for colonial defence. In March 1862 a House of Commons resolution ratifying the report of a Select Committee on Colonial Military Expenditure noted that not only should self-governing colonies be responsible for their own internal order but they also ought 'to assist in their own external defence'. The 'prosaic' business of the Imperial Conferences from 1887 onwards was to a great extent the business of Britain trying to squeeze contributions to imperial defence out of the dominions. This policy was not altogether without success, although actual dominion contributions were almost exclusively confined to the navy. Before the South African War (1899–1902) military aid was scanty. For a few years from 1858 a regiment was recruited in Canada for service abroad in the imperial interest, but this unit was organised and equipped at British expense and was never part of the Canadian military establishment. In 1884 Lord Wolseley recruited a force of 386 Canadian 'lumbermen and Caughnawaga Indians' to assist in the shipment of his expedition down the Nile to relieve Gordon at Khartoum.[16] His failure to do so, and the death of Gordon at the hands of the Mahdists, had such an effect on public opinion in Australia that the New South Wales' government immediately sent a force of 800 men which saw service in the Sudan during March and April 1885. 'It was the first time that the colonial troops of the British Empire had left their own territory to fight in a foreign war'.[17]

The first really significant demonstration of imperial military effort by the dominions came in the South African War when 31,000 troops from Canada, Australia and New Zealand fought alongside the British. Demonstrating, perhaps, incipient imperial need as well as dominion willingness to serve, the South African War presaged the Great War. Although one British general described the Australian troops under his command as 'a fat dammed lot of wasters',[18] on the whole the dominion troops served with distinction and encouraged the champions of increased dominion involvement in imperial defence.

At the 1902 colonial conference Joseph Chamberlain, the Colonial Secretary, appealed for aid in defence of the empire. 'The weary Titan staggers under the vast orb of his fate', he declared. 'We have borne the burden for many years. We think it is time that our children should assist us to support it'. The New Zealand Prime Minister, Seddon, was more than equal to the task and proposed to the conference the establishment of a joint colonial and imperial reserve force, but his suggestion fell on deaf ears and the scheme was dropped. Chamberlain had to be content with a declaration that Britain was 'perfectly satisfied with the results of voluntary, purely voluntary, and spontaneous offers. We trust entirely to them in the future'.[19] In the following years, however, a little progress was made. At the 1907 colonial conference there was unanimous approval for the establishment of an 'Imperial General Staff' on which the dominions would be represented and each dominion agreed to work towards the uniformity of organisation, equipment and doctrine of their respective armed forces with those of Britain. But the dominions would not commit themselves further and, led by Canada, they effectively blocked any advance towards closer imperial military co-ordination.[20]

With the coming of war, in 1914 the dominions responded quickly and enthusiastically to the needs of the Mother Country. The Australian Prime Minister, Sir Joseph Cook, declared at once that 'when the Empire is at war, so is Australia', and his Labour opponent, Andrew Fisher, claimed that Australia would defend England 'to our last man and our last shilling'.[21] On 1 August 1914 Sir Robert Borden telegraphed from Ottawa that Canada would make every sacrifice in the coming conflict, and Laurier, the French-Canadian Leader of the Opposition, proclaimed that 'all Canadians stand behind the mother country'.[22] Similar loyalty was expressed throughout the dominions and by the end of 1914 20,000 Australian, 30,000 Canadian and 7,000 New Zealand troops had been sent overseas. Even Newfoundland, with no military tradition at all, had supplied a contingent of 500 men to fight in France. For high imperialists perhaps the most satisfying contribution was that of South Africa. Her Prime Minister, General Botha, had led Boer forces against the British in the South African War. In August 1914, nevertheless, he too immediately offered aid to Britain. South Africa, having suppressed Afrikaner resistance to the war, conquered German South West Africa and sent troops to east Africa, still managed to provide an infantry brigade for France in August 1915. For one observer the contribution made by dominion troops, who served in every theatre of war, 'supplied a crowning proof that the British Empire is not an artificial creation of force . . . but a partnership'.[23]

Even so, it was not quite all plain sailing for the empire. There was opposition to the war in the three largest dominions, in each case concentrated within non-British minorities. From October 1914 until February 1915 the Union of South Africa faced an Afrikaner rebellion. Although it was a comparatively small-scale conflict, for a time it diverted the attention of South African forces from the conquest of South West Africa. General Botha, moreover, recognised the rising as being only an extreme manifestation of the reluctance of many Boers to support the war, a factor which to some extent circumscribed the South African contribution to the imperial military effort. The issue of conscription fired anti-war sentiment in both Australia and Canada. At the beginning of 1916 Great Britain adopted compulsory military service and in May New Zealand followed suit, but in October a referendum in Australia unexpectedly returned a small majority against the measure. In December 1916 Bonar Law, the Colonial Secretary, wrote to Lloyd George in some concern that 'things are not going too well in the Dominions and there is especially an ugly spirit in Australia'.[24] At the end of the same month the Australian Prime Minister telegraphed London to say that recruiting was 'practically at a standstill' and that the 'keystone' of opposition to the war lay in the Australian Irish community whose passions had been roused by the Easter Rising in Ireland eight months before. A settlement of the Irish question, he declared, would have a profound effect in Australia and would enable the government once more to prosecute a 'vigorous war policy'. Lloyd George had every sympathy for the Australian position but replied regretfully (and modestly) that 'it is not possible for me to settle the Irish question just as I please'.[25] In December 1917 a second referendum rejected conscription with an increased majority and there the matter lay for the rest of the war. By contrast in New Zealand, albeit with a much smaller Irish community, there was much excitement over the Irish question but little or no anti-war agitation.[26]

In Canada compulsory military service became law in August 1917 despite sustained opposition, chiefly from the francophone community. Conscription was not actually applied until after a violent general election in December which completely polarised opinion in the country. In the following spring, anti-conscription riots in Quebec, during which four people died, were sharply quelled by the government who, faced with demands for troops to meet the great German spring offensive, applied conscription with even greater rigour than hitherto.[27] Anti-war agitation in the dominions, however, was less a symptom of discontent with the imperial war effort *per se* as an expression of already existing domestic tensions. The impact of war served to translate latent discontent into lively, and sometimes violent, political conflict. In South Africa, for example, many Boers in 1914 still smarted bitterly from their defeat in the South African War and the hostilities in Europe tended only to stimulate a traditional sympathy with Germany. In Australia, the Irish, who constituted the bulk of the organised labour movement, had their own political objections to Hughes' rather centrist Labour administration which had little enough to do with the war, conscription, or even the situation in Ireland, while in Canada francophobe provincial governments used the war as an excuse to accelerate the introduction of discriminatory measures against French Canadians.

The colonial empire also played a significant part in the war. It would be rash to attempt to list the contributions of each and every one of Britain's scattered possessions. We may take Sir Charles Lucas's word for it that all units of the empire 'great and small alike, contributed in man power to the common cause in addition to contributions in money and in kind'. In tiny Tonga, for example, which because of 'a breakdown in the mails' did not learn of the outbreak of war until November 1914, nearly a fifth of the 250 British residents joined up and served overseas.[28] But the most interesting aspect of colonial military effort lies in the use of African native soldiers, which was to be one of the options investigated in the frantic quest for manpower following the war.

At the turn of the century the colonial authorities established two principal bodies of African troops: the West African Frontier Force and the King's African Rifles. The west African force, formally established in 1899, by 1914 maintained battalions in Nigeria, the Gold Coast and Sierra Leone along with a company in The Gambia. During the war the force proved 'of great value', particularly in east Africa. Over 10,000 combatants served in the campaign in German East Africa and, towards the end of the conflict two brigades were raised for service overseas which 'owing to the cessation of hostilities' were in the end not used. The King's African Rifles, organised in 1901 from several less formal local units, was rather smaller and maintained at the outbreak of war only one battalion in each of Kenya, Uganda and Nyasaland. After 1914, however, and with the stimulus of a local campaign, this was increased some sevenfold to 22 battalions comprising 32,000 men. The fighting in east Africa dragged on until late November 1918 when the able German commander, von Lettow-Vorbeck, finally learnt of the armistice in Europe. Von Lettow-Vorbeck himself had increased a pre-war German force of 4,600 African soldiers and police to some 16,000. By the end of the war in east Africa the British were employing over 83,000 native Africans in both combatant and non-combatant duties.[29]

The unity of purpose which the empire displayed during the war, particularly in contrast to the somewhat haphazard military co-operation of previous years, was a source of considerable satisfaction to imperial visionaries. In 1914 it was 'not Great Britain alone, but the whole – the heart-whole – British Empire',[30] which declared war against Germany. The French geographer, Albert Demangeon, described the dominions' contribution as offering 'an astonishing spectacle to the world: the whole of the British communities making common cause with the mother country and bringing her their wealth and their sons'. 'Never', he maintained, 'did the Empire seem more united and closeknit than during the Great War'.[31] Sir Douglas Haig believed that the old dream of imperial military unity had come true and that the war had created an 'Imperial Army', but this was only true to a certain extent. Although the direction of high military policy and strategy was centralised in the British War Office, dominion troops were organised in autonomous units and served *with*, rather than *in*, the British army.[32]

The war was at the same time both a dividing and a unifying factor in imperial development. As has been noted it provided a catalyst for domestic disaffection in the dominions. It also acted as a constitutional catalyst in the relations between the dominion governments and Westminster. At the 1911 imperial conference Asquith had declared that the United Kingdom could never share responsibility for foreign policy with the empire, but in 1917, with the establishment of the Imperial War Cabinet, the dominions were given a say in policy-making. At the peace conference in Paris following the war both the dominions and India were represented in their own right as well as being part of the British Empire Delegation. In somewhat florid terms it was afterwards claimed that the self-governing dominions 'completed their nationhood in the war'.[33] They were vigorously to assert this new status when the question of continued military co-coperation was raised after the armistice. In other parts of the empire the war had a similar catalytic effect. The accordance to India of full representation at the 1917 imperial conference, which the Colonial Secretary thought marked 'the greatest Imperial Development that has occurred',[34] was widely regarded as a reward for India's contribution to the war effort. Such constitutional sops, however, did little to assuage Indian national sentiment, growing as it was in the face of continual calls for sacrifice in the pursuit of the war. The declaration of post-war policy, made by the Secretary of State for India, Edwin Montagu, in August 1917, which promised 'the progressive realisation of responsible government in India as an integral part of the Empire', although a radical advance in British policy, merely served to quicken the pace of nationalist agitation. In India, moreover, where the bulk of the army was recruited from the Muslim population, loyalties were strained in the war with Turkey whose sultan was also the Kalifa, the titular leader of Islam.[35] Nearer home, England's extremity was, as ever, Ireland's opportunity. In Ireland, as in India, despite the hopes of many, home rule was scarcely advanced by generous co-operation in the war and there was a violent rising led by extreme nationalists at Easter 1916. The crude, but in the circumstances understandable, methods by which the rising was suppressed stimulated the beginnings of a decisive shift in Southern Irish public opinion towards Sinn Fein which was confirmed and accelerated by the threat of conscription in 1918.[36] In Egypt the rough derogation of domestic concerns to the war effort fuelled nationalist feeling to such an extent that open violence broke out in 1919.[37]

The First World War stimulated centrifugal as well as centripetal forces within the empire. During the conflict itself, however, the momentum of 'war imperialism'[38] was on the whole sufficient to carry the empire through in as united a condition as it had ever been. This imperialism was sustained by the compelling logic of both survival and conquest. It was, above all, a *military* imperialism, apparently fully vindicated by the comprehensive defeat of the empire's enemies in 1918. Writing on Armistice Day from the Western Front, General Sir Henry Rawlinson rejoiced in the imperial victory: 'It is really wonderful – we have now secured for the Empire a really firm foundation on which to build'.[39] He could hardly have been more wrong. With the coming of peace, and the relaxation of the enormous effort which the war had demanded, cracks in the imperial fabric were to become increasingly apparent. The bastard imperialism of 1914–18 could not long survive the armistice, but so profoundly were the minds of many British politicians and generals coloured by the experience of the war, that for a time it seemed to them as if this need not be the case. The high level of wartime imperial co-operation, they argued, could and should be continued. It was an impossible imperial dream, and the history of imperial defence in the aftermath of the Great War is very largely the history of how the structure of war imperialism was gradually but inexorably demolished.

Chapter 2

Weaknesses of the home base

Policy-making in any country with worldwide interests, such as the United Kingdom, always involves decisions about the relative allocation of national resources between internal and external needs. Since the protection of external interests in the last resort often depends on armed force, this process is sharply illustrated in questions of defence spending. The proportional commitment of resources to defence, while certainly depending on the degree of threat present at any given time, can be taken as at least a rough reflection of national priorities. In Britain's case the security of maritime communications and overseas trading interests has consistently been a very high priority, and in the nineteenth century considerable efforts were directed towards maintaining the Royal Navy as the strongest in the world. There was a similarly substantial commitment – although little of the cost of this fell on the British taxpayer – towards land forces in India, the greatest imperial possession of all. In the happy days of unequalled British prosperity, Palmerstonian self-confidence and overseas expansion, imperial defence needs were met with comparatively little strain. Not only was there an abundance of available resources, both material and moral, but the actual costs of protecting external interests were proportionally small. From about the 1890s, however, Britain's *relative* decline as a Great Power was accompanied by a rise in global defence costs. This was partly met by diplomatic initiatives – the Anglo-Japanese alliance, the agreement with Russia and *rapprochement* with France – but also by increased spending, especially on the navy.[1] At the same time, domestic political demands began to put significant pressure on the budget. Nevertheless, before the First World War the national economic cake was still large enough to provide both for a considerably expanded programme of naval construction and for Asquith's Liberal government to lay the foundations of the modern welfare state. Between 1914 and 1918 any debate there had been over the respective weight of domestic and external expenditure was largely suspended, and domestic needs understandably took second place to the prosecution of the war.

Such an ordering of priorities could not long survive the armistice. Nor did it. Indeed, a number of factors powerfully combined to circumscribe the military arm of external policy in the years following 1918. In the first place were the views of the war-weary British public who were undeniably attracted to the seductive notion that the recent conflict had been a 'war to end all wars'. Demands for domestic social reconstruction followed closely on the ending of hostilities and gained a ready response from many political leaders, notably Lloyd George, whose often misquoted assurance to provide 'a fit country for heroes to live in' simply reflected widespread public aspirations. Nineteen-eighteen also saw a significant increase in the importance and influence of public opinion in policy-making. With the extension of the franchise – increased almost three-fold by the Representation of the People Act, 1918 – Britain approached the ideal of a fully representative parliamentary democracy. One effect of this was to underscore the importance of domestic political considerations in the policy-making process. Another constraint on the military arm was finance. The unparalleled, and to contemporary observers appalling, economic cost of the war was instrumental in transforming Britain from a creditor to a debtor nation. In order both to pay off war debts and to finance national reconstruction it was thought imperative to cut government spending wherever possible. Chief among the areas looked to for savings were the armed forces who in the immediate post-war years (and indeed until the mid-1930s) had to fight a continual battle for funds with unsympathetic politicians and a more than usually parsimonious Treasury.

A novel constraint which emerged at the end of the war was fear of violent social upheaval within Great Britain itself. Until about mid-1921 widespread industrial unrest seemed to threaten the country with actual revolution, and intermittent fears continued to trouble the government until after the General Strike in 1926. Whether there was any real likelihood of revolution or not,[2] the apprehensions of many British leaders were real enough, and the overriding requirement, as Sir Henry Wilson (Chief of the Imperial General Staff) put it to Winston Churchill in January 1920, that 'we must secure our base first'[3] certainly limited the army's ability to provide military resources for external needs. In broad terms the years immediately following the First World War saw the emergence of a dilemma which was to become increasingly difficult for Britain's twentieth-century policy-makers: whether to devote national resources almost entirely to satisfying domestic requirements, but at the cost of securing external interests, or to meet the growing costs of Great Power status, especially in terms of maintaining armed forces throughout the world, but perhaps at the price of economic progress and social stability at home.[4] For the most part British governments have attempted with only qualified success to meet both objectives simultaneously.

The tension between domestic and external priorities emerged as soon as the war ended over the questions of demobilisation and domestic recruitment. In 1918 the CIGS faced greater military responsibilities than any of his predecessors had had to meet in peacetime. These responsibilities were not confined to the empire. In addition to imperial garrisons, now enlarged by acquisitions in the Middle East, in November 1918 there were British troops in France, Belgium, Germany, Italy, Greece, Austria-Hungary, Serbia, Bulgaria, the Ottoman Empire and Russia. To meet these military needs Sir Henry Wilson had at his disposal over three and a half million men.[5] But with the rapid demobilisation which followed the end of the war, that figure had been reduced in a year to just under 800,000 and in another year to 370,000 (November 1920).[6]

From the very beginning the War Office regarded these manpower reductions with some anxiety. Only two days after the armistice, the Secretary for War, Lord Milner, wrote to Lloyd George urging that some action be taken on the future of the army and complaining that 'without some sort of line to go on, we shall be paralysed at the War Office'. Milner acknowledged that ample and, he believed, workable preparations for demobilisation had been made, 'but', he warned ominously, 'unless some provision is made for recruiting or keeping men, you run the risk of finding yourself without any Army at all in 6 months!' Considering 'the disturbed state of Europe', and 'the revolutionary tendency, greater or less, in all countries', he added, 'it is as dangerous to have no Army as to have too big a one'.[7] While Milner, unusually for him, seems to have been sensitive to the strong public pressure for a quick demobilisation, underlying his concern was a realistic fear that the weary British soldier – conscript or volunteer – might not continue to serve unquestioningly now that the war was over. One possibility was to purchase loyalty, and he advised the Cabinet on 14 November that they would be 'courting complete failure' in asking men to extend their service, especially in India, unless the high wartime rates of army pay were for the time being retained.[8] It is also likely that Milner, who had been prominent in the pre-war campaign for compulsory military service in Britain, envisaged that continued conscription would be required to meet the military needs of the immediate post-war period. This was the view, certainly, of a strong lobby in the War Office. Wilson thought compulsion to be 'the only *fair* way of solving the problem'. Early in December he put forward a memorandum summarising the 'military commitments remaining after peace has been signed' in which he estimated that between 350,000 and 500,000 soldiers would be required to serve in armies of occupation 'for an unknown period after Peace has been signed. No machinery as yet exists for their provision', he concluded, 'since it would be unsafe to assume that they will be obtainable on a voluntary basis'.[9]

The Prime Minister, however, was not convinced that compulsion would be necessary. He told H. A. L. Fisher that 'if we get a good peace we shall not want conscription'[10] and during the general election campaign of December 1918 he promised in effect to end conscription as soon as possible. But Lloyd George's hopes for a speedy return to a volunteer army were quickly undermined by the immense British postwar military commitments. The difficulties facing the War Office, moreover, were compounded by widespread dissatisfaction in the army with the existing system of demobilisation which, although elaborately formulated by the Ministry of Labour in order to avoid mass unemployment, seemed to the longer-serving soldiers to be both slow and unfair in that it did not operate on a 'first in, first out' basis.[11] In these critical circumstances it soon became clear that Milner was not the best man to grapple with the problems besetting the War Office. His heart was not in the job and he rankled under the Prime Minister's impatient criticisms and continual interference in his departmental affairs. On 6 December, after a War Cabinet meeting during which Lloyd George had been particularly rude about the progress of demobilisation, Milner tendered his resignation, but the Prime Minister, anxious to maintain the unity of his government during the election campaign, persuaded him to stay on temporarily as a 'caretaker'.[12] In the meantime Lloyd George cast around for a suitably vigorous replacement. On 9 January 1919, Sir Henry Wilson learnt that his new master was to be Winston Churchill,[13] who was appointed Secretary for both War and Air.

Churchill, although he would have preferred the Admiralty to the War Office,[14] threw himself into his new task with his customary energy. The day after the appointment had been announced he told Wilson that he wanted to stop demobilisation altogether and on 17 January he proposed to a War Cabinet chaired by Bonar Law that compulsory military service be retained in order to provide for the armies of occupation.[15] On hearing of this proposal Lloyd George (in Paris for the peace conference) wrote immediately to Churchill to complain that he had not been consulted 'in the first instance' on such an important question 'of first class policy which may invoke grave political consequences'.[16] The fear that the extension of military service might kindle domestic unrest was effectively voiced by Christopher Addison, Minister for Reconstruction. Churchill's scheme, he thought, was 'open to the gravest objection . . . It would raise a storm of protest in the country', and its introduction at the present time 'would certainly be represented by not a few labour leaders as . . . partly because of industrial troubles'.[17] But Churchill did not waver. On 27 January he pointed out to the Prime Minister the urgent need for troops, both for the armies of occupation, and also in India and the Middle East. 'It is quite absurd', he wrote, 'to expect that these vitally necessary forces can be provided during the present year on a voluntary basis. They can only be provided on a compulsory basis pending the creation and organisation of voluntary forces, about which no time will be lost'.[18] Lloyd George reluctantly had to agree, and on 28 January the Cabinet approved 'the continuance of compulsion for the interim period'.[19] 'We shall get about a million men who will be compelled to serve for 12 mos:', commented Wilson, adding darkly, 'Of course if these men really refuse to serve we are done'.[20]

Wilson's fears were not entirely without foundation. At the beginning of 1919 there were several occasions when soldiers refused to return to France after being on leave at home. One of the most serious disturbances, involving some ten thousand men, occurred early in January at Folkestone.[21] On 6 January the military members of the Army Council resolved that the Prime Minister 'must make it clear to the country that the war is *not* over, that we are demobilizing quite fast enough ... If he does not do this the whole Army will turn into a rabble'.[22] The real difficulty, as Allenby was to point out from Egypt, was that 'nothing' would 'convince the troops that Military operations did not end on the signing of the Armistice'.[23] This was the rub, for both the generals and their men were correct. In terms of large scale action against major opponents, the war was indeed over, but in order to 'win the peace' and meet the post-war responsibilities accompanying Britain's new status as a great military land power, Wilson and his colleagues were again and again to stress the critical need for military manpower. In the end Lloyd George, while fully aware of public demands for a rapid scaling-down of the military machine, compromised and agreed to continue compulsory service for a strictly limited period.

The extension of conscription was given statutory effect in the 'Naval, Military and Air Force Service Act, 1919' which passed through parliament during March and provided for compulsion to be retained until 30 April 1920. Wilson, however, remained acutely unhappy about the numbers of troops available. In May 1919 Churchill circulated to the Cabinet a paper by Wilson on the subject. 'I feel compelled', wrote the CIGS, 'to bring to the notice of the War Cabinet the grave possibilities which confront us, and to draw attention to the serious shortage of troops with which we are threatened'. Although it had been agreed that approximately nine hundred thousand conscripts would be retained for the armies of occupation, Wilson asserted that this number now fell far short of his requirements. The original estimate, he declared, had been made in the 'illusory hope' that an early peace was possible 'and when no resumption of hostilities seemed probable'. Far from this being the case, 'numberless requests' for British troops were being received 'from every quarter of Europe', and 'our liabilities in vital portions of the British Empire' – Ireland, Egypt, India, the Middle East – had 'increased rather than diminished'. Having outlined the critical state of affairs throughout the empire, Wilson finally warned the Cabinet that

we must face the fact (and prepare public opinion to face the fact) that we may be called on in the near future to furnish a military effort in defence of vital British interests that is beyond the strength of the forces now available, and that it may therefore be necessary to have recourse to some form of remobilization, that is to say compulsion.

I do not consider that any form of voluntary enlistment will give us the men we want in the time events may grant us, for when the emergency arises we must have trained men, men of the right age, and men of the right qualifications for the different arms and branches and for the essential services of maintenance which are the most difficult to fill. Some form of compulsion will therefore be necessary.

I am aware of the grave objections to such a course, and I would hesitate to recommend it to the War Cabinet were I not convinced that there is a serious possibility of the emergency arising.

It is for the Cabinet to decide what course to adopt. In this paper I have . . . shown that should the contingencies arise which are considered as possible by the highest authorities in England, Ireland, Egypt and India then, in my opinion, we have not the necessary military force to ensure the safety of the Empire.[24]

But Wilson's deep concern about the inadequacy of the numbers of troops available fell on deaf ears in a Cabinet more concerned with domestic political realities than gloomy imperial hypotheses. From their point of view any further extension of compulsion was quite out of the question.

If conscription, therefore, was not to be retained permanently, the War Office would have to look seriously to the problem of gaining more voluntary recruits. On 9 January the Army Council met to discuss 'how we are to garrison India & the Ports & Ireland when we have no regular army & no conscript army'. All they could do was to reduce the age of enlistment from eighteen years to seventeen 'on the chance of getting some boys'.[25] The army, however, needed weightier recruits than 'boys', and the search for troops was eventually to encompass India, the dominions and Africa. In addition, the War Office was to seek to share its onerous military burden at times with both the Admiralty and the Air Ministry. In 1919, though, the problem was still simply one of domestic army recruitment, which Wilson claimed in May was 'hampered by the continuance of unemployment donations'.[26] In November the War Office pointed out to the Cabinet the need for both immediate and 'sustained recruitment to meet the requirements of the Army in 1921–22'.[27]

In the course of 1920 recruiting generally improved, doubtless stimulated by rising domestic unemployment (and despite the existence of the dole). Yet the shortage of skilled technical personnel, to which Wilson had alluded in his paper of May 1919, was particularly persistent. In May 1920 General Macready, recently posted to command the troops in Ireland, pointed out to a conference of ministers that the deficiency of technical troops in his command amounted to over six hundred men, including wireless operators, motor cyclists, telegraphists and drivers.[28] In October the Adjutant-General told the Cabinet that 'serious difficulty' had been found 'in obtaining artificers and mechanical transport drivers to meet the needs of the Army'. Two reasons were given for this: 'the general shortage of such personnel on the market' and, the 'increasing demand for Government requirements'. The latter reason was the more serious since the Irish Office, for instance, in its search for technical officers to serve in the Royal Irish Constabulary, was 'offering rates of pay which aggregate two or three times the rates for corresponding grades in the Army'.[29] Even when technicians could be recruited they seemed to cause trouble. In September 1920 Wilson noted in his diary that there was 'good cause for anxiety' since the army mechanics, along with those in the air force, were 'much in with the Unions', and even 'Beatty has Soviets starting in every port'.[30]

It was not just the political affiliations of the army mechanics which gave rise to concern, but also the general quality of the army as a whole. Many of the post-war recruits were of a distressingly low standard. In July 1919 Lord Chelmsford (Viceroy of India 1916–21) complained about the quality of troops which the War Office were proposing to draft to India. A proportion of the first twenty battalions were to be 'category B1, in other words, men who are only able to march at least five miles, see to shoot with the aid of glasses and hear *nil* [*sic*]. These are of no use for Field Army', he continued, 'and are not of the standard which we were accustomed to accept before the war'.[31] In March 1920 the CIGS toured the British forces in Germany. In Cologne he found a battalion of The Black Watch 'all very young, very raw, very untrained'. On his return to London he told Sir Maurice Hankey that fifty per cent of the troops had 'never even fired a rifle on the range'.[32] One point which particularly dismayed senior officers was the unfavourable comparison with the pre-war army. In July 1920 General Macready declared that 'the Army today was not the Army of 1913. You could not play with these men'. The senior commanders, he said, were 'first rate', but 'below that, many were young and untrained, and if the strain [in Ireland] were doubled you would get near the danger limit'. He concluded with the extraordinary observation that 'the young recruits did not like to use their weapons'.[33] In part the Army Council were hoist with their own petard, having lowered the age of enlistment early in 1919. The correlation between youth and quality was made clear by General Lord Rawlinson (CinC India 1920–5) in March 1921. In 1913, he wrote, only seven British soldiers of under twenty years of age had been invalided home, whereas the comparable figure for 1920 was 487.[34]

While the army was concerned with problems of quality it was increasingly being troubled by demands for economy which were strongly reinforced by the political complexion of the coalition government. Although Lloyd George's administration emerged from the 1918 general election with a working parliamentary majority of over three hundred MPs,[35] the balance of power within the coalition considerably limited the Prime Minister's freedom of action. Ultimately his government depended for survival on Unionist backbenchers, for the most part wedded to financial orthodoxy, anxious to reduce taxation and state interference in economic activity, and heartily suspicious of 'progressive' social policy. Lloyd George himself, while possessing a strong Liberal passion for social progress, also had a healthy Gladstonian respect for national economy. This was underlined both by the post-war financial crisis and as disenchantment with his apparently capricious policies and histrionic style of government grew in both parliament and the constituencies. Hoping to put the country on an economic even keel and needing to conciliate parliamentary and national support, the Prime Minister increasingly fell back on a policy of large-scale retrenchment.

In his quest for economy Lloyd George had the whole-hearted support of Austen Chamberlain, who became Chancellor of the Exchequer in January 1919. Chamberlain immediately discovered that the nation's finances had been thrown into chaos 'by the utter relaxation of Treasury control & of the Chancellor's supervision which has prevailed in recent years'.[36] But to reduce wartime levels and habits of expenditure was no easy task, especially where the War Office was concerned. The army estimates for 1919–20, presented to parliament in February 1919, provided for a total expenditure of £287 million. This compared somewhat unfavourably with the immediately pre-war figure of £28,845,000.[37] By October 1919 the cost for the current year had risen to £405 million, due to unforeseen expenditure caused by demobilisation delays, a railway strike, increases in army pay, an 'unexpected rise in the rupee' and the deferring of payments from Germany for the cost of the army of occupation and the dominions for the maintenance of troops in the field.[38] But continuing a high level of expenditure was clearly unsatisfactory. After less than a fortnight in office, Chamberlain presciently suggested to Churchill that a possible and cheap solution to the manpower problem 'in cases such as Ireland and India' would be 'to increase the mobility of our troops by providing them with large numbers of motor transport, and to increase their fighting power by giving them a high proportion of the most modern weapons'.[39]

The notion that technological advances might actually save money was certainly attractive and within two years Churchill as Colonial Secretary was to persuade his colleagues to adopt an economical 'air defence' policy in the Middle East. In the meantime, however, he devoted himself to protecting the army vote against excessive reduction. When in April 1919 during his maiden budget speech Chamberlain suggested that substantial cuts in defence expenditure would be made in the coming year, Churchill responded at once. He accepted that some reductions were necessary, but, he told Lloyd George, 'without in any way prejudging the matter, a large reduction in naval expenditure is essential to any satisfactory solution of the combined problem'. The army's responsibilities had been increased by the war. 'The whole East is unsettled by the disintegration of Turkey', he wrote, 'and we shall have large additions of territory in Palestine and Mesopotamia to maintain'. Taking wartime inflation into account, even an army of pre-war size 'would undoubtedly cost a great deal more . . . I do not see', concluded the former First Lord, 'why there should not be a great saving from the Navy, at any rate until some entirely new competition develops'.[40] But the Chancellor was not disposed to let the army off as lightly as Churchill wished. In July he emphasised to his colleagues the 'extreme gravity of the situation' and observed that the continued excess of expenditure over income was 'the road to ruin'. The army, he noted, was 'the greatest difficulty'.[41]

Chamberlain was not the only minister concerned about military expenditure. Addison, by now Minister of Health, responded to the Chancellor's worries by urging that the nation's limited resources ought to be diverted from service spending in order to provide for a peaceful and orderly social and industrial reconstruction.[42] On 5 August the Cabinet met to discuss these issues. Introducing a lengthy review of 'the whole position of the country', the Prime Minister declared that 'the outlook was full of anxieties, and not free from perils. The War had made a great change in our position. Before the War we were a creditor nation, and now we were a debtor nation'. Over and above everything else was the problem of expenditure, and in some areas the government would have to reduce spending perhaps to a level lower than might ideally be wished. Neatly adopting a military metaphor to hammer service expenditure, he argued that the government 'must be prepared to take risks just as the soldier had to take risks; and they must decide what risks they could best afford to take'. He counselled his colleagues to consider the effect on public opinion of continuing an excessive level of military spending. British arms, he said, 'had destroyed the only enemy we had in Europe', and if the country now 'maintained a larger Army and Navy and Air Force than we had before we entered on the War, people would say, either that the War had been a failure, or that we were making provision to fight an imaginary foe'. Although external threats had been eliminated, there were now dangers on the domestic front. The government, he warned, 'could not take risks with Labour. If we did, we should at once create an enemy within our own borders, and one which would be better provided with dangerous weapons than Germany'. The first priority, therefore, was to provide for 'the health and labour of the people. We had to lay at once the sure foundations of national health and industrial prosperity'.

Confronted by this uncompromising statement, Churchill assured the Cabinet that economies could be made in his departments. By 1920, he thought optimistically, 'events would no longer govern expenditure, which would then be controlled by the policy decided upon by the Cabinet', and he ventured to make a forecast, 'which was necessarily very vague', that expenditure on both the army and the air force in the coming year would not exceed £100 million. Churchill went on to discuss the size of the army, which at the beginning of the year had consisted of over two million men. By the end of the financial year he hoped that it would contain no conscripts whatever, and that 'we should not find it necessary to maintain more than about 320,000 men'. This compared with a pre-war figure of about 255,000, 'of whom 75,000 were in the Army in India, and 180,000 were in England or in our garrisons abroad'. When Lloyd George asked why so much larger a force should be required than in 1914, Churchill simply remarked 'it should be remembered that our responsibilities during the War had considerably increased, especially in regard to Ireland and the East'.[43]

Arising from this discussion came the definition of the famous 'ten year rule', which was agreed at a Cabinet meeting ten days later. The rule instructed the service ministries when framing their estimates to assume 'the British Empire will not be engaged in any great war during the next ten years, and that no Expeditionary Force is required for this purpose'. It was confirmed that the 'principal function' of the army and the air force was 'to provide garrisons for India, Egypt, the new mandated territory (other than self-governing) under British control, as well as to provide the necessary support to the civil power at home'. In order to save manpower they also urged that 'the utmost possible use' be made of 'mechanical contrivances, which should be regarded as a means of reducing Estimates'. The Cabinet finally insisted that the army and the air force should aim at a *joint* estimate not exceeding £75 million.[44] Wilson thought that the Cabinet had got hold of the wrong end of the stick in suggesting such an unrealistically low figure. What was required, he wrote in his diary, was to calculate the number of troops needed to keep 'our four storm centres' – Ireland, Egypt, Mesopotamia and India – quiet, and not to work 'from the allotment of an arbitrary sum'.[45] The CIGS, indeed, was vindicated by 'events', which continued for some time to 'govern expenditure'. The army estimates did not fall below the Cabinet's figure until 1922–3.

Despite the army's manifold post-war burdens, Churchill, continually under pressure from both Prime Minister and Chancellor, laboured to reduce military spending. By the spring of 1920 he was able to announce an army estimate for 1920–21 of £134 million, of which he told the Cabinet £48 million was due to 'temporary obligations', particularly the garrison on the Rhine and the British forces in the Middle East.[46] Yet

Chamberlain had to struggle all the way to spread the gospel of national thrift. In June 1920 he grumbled that 'departments still show the greatest reluctance to terminate minor kinds of expenditure which grew up during the War' and sardonically observed that it would be 'optimistic to expect that Army Estimates will not be exceeded'.[47]

The Chancellor did not merely confine himself to exhorting thrift upon his colleagues. Early in 1920, after the government had accepted the conclusions of the Cunliffe committee report on currency and foreign exchanges, which had sharply criticised the extent of government indebtedness, Chamberlain sought to check inflation by prohibiting all further borrowing. Thus he offered ministers a stark choice between cutting expenditure and the electorally perilous alternative of increasing taxation.[48] By the middle of 1920, moreover, the need for economy was becoming increasingly pressing since the post-war boom, which had to some extent masked the impact of high government expenditure, was beginning to collapse. In August the Cabinet finance committee proposed that a 'committee of national expenditure' composed of 'outside' experts should be set up to review all government spending and recommend possible reductions. The committee, who were evidently desperate for some viable answer to the problem, thought that this might bring the public and the House of Commons face to face with 'the real position'. But Churchill firmly objected to the idea on the grounds that questions of expenditure, particularly in the service ministries, were the prerogative of the Cabinet, and Chamberlain had to be content with sending round the traditional 'estimates circular' in October 1920.[49] In his note to ministers, however, the Chancellor warned that 'in the absence of cogent reasons to the contrary, Parliament will expect the Estimate to show a reduction upon this year's expenditure'.[50]

Chamberlain was especially anxious for further reductions in War Office spending and on 9 December he told the House of Commons that the Cabinet were 'convinced of the necessity of curtailing military expenditure to the most extent compatible with the fulfilment of our Imperial obligations and national safety'. While in itself Chamberlain's words simply reflected the anodyne manner in which British governments conventionally communicate with parliament – even Sir Henry Wilson would not necessarily have objected to the statement – the Chancellor's real message was that expenditure *would* be cut. The principal area for economy, he said, was 'the Near and Middle East'.[51] Yet the very next day Churchill informed the Cabinet that he required a supplementary army estimate of nearly £30 million due to unforeseen expenditure in the Middle East and Ireland.[52] 'Finance dominates everything', wrote Hankey at the beginning of 1921. 'At the very moment when we are threatened with so many perils in these regions [the Middle East] we find it impossible to continue the overwhelming burden of cost which our military forces entails'.[53]

The government's concern with expenditure was pointed by its increasing electoral weakness. From March 1919 to March 1921 (inclusive) the coalition lost fourteen of the thirty-eight seats it defended at by-elections, and over the whole life of the government only two seats were won from the various anti-coalition parties.[54] Opposition came from both ends of the political spectrum. In November 1919 a 'Stop-the-Waste' candidate, supported by the local Unionist association, was elected for the Isle of Thanet constituency and took his seat in parliament as an independent. In the same month the Labour party gained widespread successes in local government elections. In December Labour won the Spen Valley seat from the coalition Liberals whose candidate was beaten into a poor third place by an Asquithian Liberal. In 1920, seats were gained from coalition Liberals at The Wrekin by an independent Unionist standing on an 'anti-waste' ticket, and by Labour candidates at Dartford and Southern Norfolk. The victory of an independent Unionist over a coalition Unionist at Dover in January 1921 was followed by the formation of the Anti-Waste League which put forward successful candidates in the St. George's, Westminster, and Hertford by-elections in June 1921. These victories tapped popular dissatisfaction with the prevailing concomitant evils of excessive government spending and high levels of taxation, while at the same time they stimulated the growing opposition to Lloyd George on the coalition Unionist backbenches.[55] With economic depression, moreover, came mass unemployment, and by mid-1921 there were over two million wholly unemployed in Great Britain.[56] It seemed to the government, therefore, that political survival depended to a great extent on national economy. Expenditure, wrote Chamberlain shortly after handing over his office as Chancellor to Sir Robert Horne in April 1921, was 'the weak joint in the Government's armour'.[57] Seeking to strengthen this joint, Lloyd George, supported by Horne, returned to the proposal for a 'business committee' on national expenditure and, despite Churchill's continued opposition, gained Cabinet approval on 2 August for a committee to be chaired by Sir Eric Geddes. 'The fact is', wrote H. A. L. Fisher in his diary, 'the PM is dead tired & wants to throw a sop to Anti-Waste'.[58]

The Geddes committee went to work almost at once and towards the end of October Sir Henry Wilson got the first indications of what he described as 'fantastic proposals for reducing the Army to futility'.[59] On 14 December, Geddes circulated an interim report to the Cabinet and, as Wilson had feared, it demanded heavy cuts in all the armed services. This was a red rag to the War Office. The report maintained that the 1922–3 army estimates provided for manpower on far too lavish a scale. A reduction of fifty thousand officers and men could be made, it argued, and the estimates reduced from £75,197,800 to £55,000,000.[60] Wilson declared that the Geddes cuts were 'frankly terrifying', and noted 'our 20 million is estimated at 28 Battns, 8 Cav: Regts & other arms in proportion'. It was, he somewhat extravagantly asserted, 'in short the kiss [of death] of the Empire'.[61]

The Geddes committee, taking the 'ten year rule' at its face value, argued that one obvious area for economy was in the War Office's provision for an expeditionary force to meet possible overseas emergencies. In their formal reply to Geddes, however, the General Staff emphasised that the army was *not* maintained for intervention in Europe, but 'for the protection of our overseas territories, and for the support of the Civil Power in the maintenance of law and order throughout British territory at home and abroad'. The size of the force, therefore, was governed solely by 'our oversea commitments'. The General Staff appended a dismal (and familiar) list of these commitments, indicating that any reduction in the army would be undesirable, if not downright dangerous.[62] Sir Laming Worthington-Evans (who had succeeded Churchill as Secretary for War in February 1921) nevertheless told the Cabinet that by a reduction of 30,000 men and various other economies he felt he could lower his estimates to just over £60 million.[63] Partly, no doubt, to mollify his original opposition to the Geddes committee, Lloyd George appointed Churchill to head a committee with the task of adjudicating between the views of Geddes and the War Office. The Churchill committee criticised Geddes for comparing the 1922–3 army estimates with those for 1914–15 without making any adjustments for inflation. To take into account the decreased purchasing power of the pound, they argued that the pre-war figure of £27 million should be multiplied by a factor of two and a quarter, which produced a sum very similar to the Secretary for War's revised estimate of £60 million. Noting their opinion 'that the forces at the disposal of the Empire are now reduced to a weakness unprecedented since the South African War', they agreed with Worthington-Evans that the army could not be contracted by more than 30,000 men, but they proposed that by making administrative economies the total army estimate could be brought down to £58,600,000.[64]

Although the eventual estimate of £62 million exceeded both Worthington-Evans' figure and that of the Churchill committee, public and parliamentary pressure for economy was eased by the sweeping cuts made in Sir Robert Horne's 1922 budget. The total expenditure of £910 million showed a reduction of £326 million on the previous year, of which in fact only £64 million were directly attributable to the 'Geddes axe'.[65] The Anti-Waste campaign died down and civil servants thankfully returned to the old system of promoting economy by means of an annual Treasury circular and internal estimates committees. With that ponderous humour so beloved of many bureaucrats Sir George Barstow, controller of supply services at the Treasury, was thus moved to speculate on the comparative merits of a Geddes axe and a circular saw.[66]

The economy campaign provided a cheerless end to Sir Henry Wilson's career in the army. All he could think of for his successor, Lord Cavan, was that he had 'a horrid job ... in front of him' and 'the thankless task of carrying out the Geddes Commee [proposals]'.[67] So it was to be. Cavan himself recorded that 'the whole of my four years as C.I.G.S. was a period of retrenchment ... a struggle for existence' and, after 1922, 'the work of the Estimates Committee was heartbreaking'.[68]

The costs of continued global Great Power status which put such a strain on the national finances in the early 1920s were to provide constant difficulties for British governments over the following fifty years. But the other chief domestic concern which preoccupied the post-war leaders was a passing phenomenon, most acute in 1919–21 and, briefly, in 1926. During this period there was a very real and persistent fear among many politicians and generals that revolution might come to Britain. They had, after all, seen the collapse of the Russian empire, mutinies in the French army, revolution in Germany and unrest sweeping across central Europe. Why then could revolution not happen at home? 'Our real danger now', wrote Wilson the day before the armistice was signed, 'is not the Boches but Bolshevism'.[69] There was a general feeling in government circles that industrial unrest might easily stimulate 'revolutionary' activities, and the Cabinet were kept fully informed by the Home Office of all developments in a regular report on 'revolutionary organisations in the United Kingdom', the contents of which can have done little to ease the minds of the more timid ministers.[70]

The position was rendered all the more serious by the evident weakness of the government's own forces. The army was severely dislocated by demobilisation difficulties, while in the navy widespread dissatisfaction with pay and conditions turned into open mutiny on several occasions in 1918–19.[71] There were doubts, moreover, as to the reliability of the police who had actually gone on strike in London in August 1918. A year later almost 2,400 of the 60,000 police in England and Wales stopped work in various parts of the country. The most seriously affected centre was Liverpool where severe rioting broke out and the army was called in to restore order.[72] In the light of these uncertainties it was understandable for the government to overreact to some extent. In January 1919, for example, when a general strike in Glasgow, which it was feared might presage a nationwide stoppage, developed into street violence, both infantry and tanks were rushed to Clydeside and machine gun posts were set up in the City Chambers. The use of such Draconian measures illustrates both government panic and the immediately post-war propensity to rely on military methods. Yet they were also apparently effective. The strike folded and militant revolutionary activity in Glasgow trade unionism largely dwindled away.[73]

The post-war industrial boom did little to assuage labour discontent. In February 1919, the pre-war 'Triple Alliance' of miners, railwaymen and transport workers was re-formed, and although the Sankey Commission in June temporarily satisfied the miners, in September the railwaymen, alone, struck against a threatened reduction in wages. This 'direct action' was settled relatively quickly – 'the Government's organisation fairly knocked the strikers endways', commented Hankey[74] – but it raised problems for the army which the General Staff were not slow to perceive. In November, Churchill circulated to the Cabinet the report of the Commander of Home Forces (Lord Haig) on the use of troops during the strike. Assuming that demobilisation was to continue and the army in Great Britain reduced to eighty-two battalions, Haig concluded that 'in the event of serious industrial unrest developing, this force would be inadequate to meet all the demands likely to be made upon it'. In a covering note to the paper the CIGS pointed out that 'if all the protection duties anticipated by the various Civil Government Departments ... had been demanded, it would have been impossible for the Army in Great Britain, large as it was at the time, to have provided the necessary numbers'. It had been calculated that about two and a half times the number then available (about 100,000) would actually have been needed. Warming to a familiar post-war theme Wilson observed that following the completion of demobilisation he would be left with an army of 40,000 infantry, made up of 12,000 temporarily retained conscripts and 28,000 regulars 'mostly recruits with young and inexperienced non-commissioned officers, and weak in training and discipline'. This force, he solemnly maintained, 'will be totally inadequate numerically to carry out the abnormal protection and other duties for which, at present, the Army is responsible'. Internal security was an unwelcome and onerous burden, and the CIGS declared it to be 'of paramount importance' that the army 'should not be used, except as a last resort, in any future industrial disturbances, but be allowed to prepare itself for its legitimate duties in the defence of the Empire'.[75]

Despite his reservations as to the use of troops in aid of the civil power, Wilson recorded disappointment in his diary that the railway strike had not been fought to the finish. 'The Strike is over', he wrote on 6 October, '& I am very sorry as no one has learnt his lesson. L.G. has a genius for giving in at the wrong moment ... We shall have the whole thing over again later on'.[76] The CIGS was repeatedly to be appalled by Lloyd George's 'genius for giving in'. Wilson would have no truck with such compromise and his continual cry in Britain, in Ireland and in the empire was one of '*govern* or be kicked out', and by '*govern*' he simply meant the forceful maintenance of law and order by his political masters.

Domestic security continued to worry Wilson. On 3 January 1920 he noted 'a long talk with the QMG this morning about Strikes. He is in complete agreement with me in cursing the criminal folly of the Govt for having *no* plan and for making none & indeed for refusing to realise the situation'.[77] He put in, therefore, another strong paper on 'internal protection', arguing that it had 'become apparent to the Army Council that the Civil Departments concerned have not yet appreciated the extent of the responsibilities placed upon them and continue to look to the Army for assistance which it is quite beyond its power to afford'.[78] On 14 January he called a meeting of his senior generals to discuss strikes. 'We have no troops', was Rawlinson's succinct comment.[79] The next day Wilson attended a meeting of the Cabinet 'supply and transport' committee, which had been specially set up to make plans for coping with major industrial stoppages. 'An amazing meeting', recorded the CIGS. 'One after another got up & said that we were going to have the Triple Red Revolution strike. One after another said there was nothing to be done . . . not one of them except Walter [Long] & Winston were [*sic*] prepared to put up a fight'.[80]

That night Wilson, Churchill and Long travelled over to Paris to see Lloyd George and on 16 January reported to a conference of ministers in Claridge's Hotel the 'very grave statements' that had been made, particularly by Sir Robert Horne (Minister of Labour) at the supply and transport committee meeting. To Wilson's amazement Lord Curzon began to press for the retention of British troops in the Caucasus. The CIGS was obdurate: 'I kept talking about necessity of securing our base . . . & did good work'. Wilson and his companions 'fairly had the "wind up"', noted Hankey later in his diary, and the CIGS privately told him that even some of the Guards battalions were unreliable. No decision was made at the meeting, but Wilson felt that 'we made a good deal of impression'.[81] Next day Hankey carefully summarised the position for Lloyd George.

I was surprised [he wrote] to hear that so serious a view was taken of the outlook. Without hearing the evidence it is difficult to understand the reason for the very obvious preoccupation of the First Lord and the C.I.G.S. as to the future. So far as I have been able to judge, though there are many clouds on the horizon, on the whole, the sky seemed to be getting clearer, the output of coal is steadily increasing, trade is getting going, I understand that bankers all over the country are not dissatisfied with the outlook, labour is a good deal divided in its own house, and so far as my opportunities for observation extend, the spirit of labour as a whole is better . . . Still, I would not venture to put these more general considerations in the balance against the views of an expert like Sir Robert Horne.

Moreover, the resources at the disposal of the Government are obviously inadequate and ought in any event to be strengthened and organised in order that we may be prepared for any emergency.[82]

For the meantime Hankey had still 'too much confidence in the collective good sense of my fellow-countrymen' fully to believe in the imminence of red revolution.[83]

On 18 January there was a further meeting in Paris. During a discussion of British military commitments, the question of contributing troops for an Allied force to supervise the League of Nations plebiscites in Danzig and Silesia was brought up. Churchill formally recommended that the proposed eleven battalions should not be sent. The CIGS thought that there would be a serious loss of British prestige if the troops did not go, but he felt that there were quite simply not enough soldiers in Great Britain as it was. Lloyd George agreed and the next day he told the French that Britain was unable to send any troops 'to the Plebiscites',[84] although later in the year, when domestic tensions had eased somewhat, several British battalions were sent to Silesia. For the time being, however, it was some small relief for the War Office. So serious did Wilson consider the position that on his return to England he set the General Staff to preparing plans for 'mutiny & Revolution' in Great Britain. On 28 January Rawlinson spent the morning working out a scheme with Wilson 'in the event of Soviet Government at Liverpool'. By the beginning of February the plans were far enough advanced for the CIGS to describe 'my proposals of 18 Battns (of which 10 are Guard) to safeguard London & my general policy in regard to quartering all possible troops in the South – away from the Midlands and North – & near the salt water'.[85]

During the spring and early summer of 1920 the position at home improved and even Churchill began to share Hankey's sanguine opinions. In June he told Lord Riddell that he thought the country was quieter than it had been for years. 'No doubt there are strikes', he said, 'but there is nothing in the shape of a big political movement calculated to cause anxiety. We are through the worst'.[86] But Churchill's optimism was premature. In August 1920 concerted trade union action and the threat of a general strike effectively prevented Britain giving military assistance to Poland – strongly urged by Churchill himself – in its war with Russia. At the same time there were rising fears that the miners might strike for increased wages. In September the Home Office's weekly report, raising the spectre of both industrial action and unrest among unemployed ex-servicemen, announced bluntly that 'we are in the midst of a crisis'. Not only was it probable that the miners would stop work, and receive active support from the Triple Alliance, but 'the temper of ex-Service men' was also 'unsatisfactory, and unless something can be done to reduce unemployment it may become serious.

It must be remembered', concluded the report alarmingly, 'that in the event of rioting, for the first time in history the rioters will be better trained than the troops'.[87]

This domestic crisis could hardly have come at a worse time for the War Office. Rebellion was flaring up in Mesopotamia; in Egypt it seemed that the local reaction to Milner's recently-published scheme for self-government might very well necessitate an increase in the British garrison, and the position in Ireland (as always) looked bleak. On 6 September Wilson asked Allenby, on leave from Cairo, if he might draw on him for troops '& he was most emphatic that I could *not*'. The same day Macready told him that if he took troops from Ireland it would precipitate a complete British withdrawal. Nor was this all, for there were still doubts as to the total reliability of the armed forces at home.[88] On 15 September, nevertheless, Wilson assured Lloyd George that the army was 'sound' and outlined the steps he had taken 'as precautions'. All sailings of troopships from England had temporarily been halted and arrangements had been made to bring one battalion back from the Rhine and two from Constantinople. In order to provide rallying points for 'loyalists' in the event of a really serious emergency, Wilson had turned every infantry depot in the country 'into a small arsenal by storing 5000 rifles & sets of equipment, a number of M[achine] Guns & Lewis Guns & ammunition, also food, etc.'.[89]

The miners did not immediately strike at the beginning of September, but delayed action in the hope of gaining some positive help from their colleagues in the Triple Alliance. The railwaymen and transport workers, however, offered only moral assistance and on 16 October the miners came out alone. Five days later, nevertheless, it seemed that the railwaymen might, after all, stop work and Wilson feverishly made arrangements to move tanks, which he had concentrated at Woolwich, to 'Scotland, York, Worcester & Aldershot'.[90] This time even Hankey was rattled. 'I cannot see my way through these strikes', he wrote, 'I think that economic causes will break them in time, but there are extremists at work and serious trouble may come'.[91] But the government, who had taken national control of the mines during the war, temporarily settled the strike on the miners' terms, leaving a more permanent arrangement to be made after the date when the pits were to be handed back to their private owners – later settled as 31 March 1921. Elsewhere in the empire, except in Ireland, the crisis also passed. The Mesopotamian rebellion was put down more quickly than had been anticipated and large-scale unrest failed to materialise in Egypt. But it was in the autumn of 1920 that the empire as a whole came closest in peace-time to foundering on the rock of military weakness.

In Britain there was still one more great industrial storm for government and army to ride through. Again the emergency stemmed from a dispute in the mines. Wilson, as usual, was worried by the army's overseas commitments. In February 1921, on holiday in Madrid (but regularly receiving War Office papers), he pondered whether

we shall want troops in England. It looks as though we certainly should in Ireland, we certainly shall in C[onstantin]ople (or clear out), we certainly shall in India, *and* that fool Curzon is agreeing to send troops . . . to Vilna & to Silesia and we have *no* Reserves at all. If we send 2 White Battns to C-ople it means that 2 N[ative] I[ndian] Battns go to India & we shall never see them again, and we are committed for an indefinite period to 4 White Battns in C-ople.

There is no doubt we are losing our Empire.[92]

But troops were to be wanted in England. On his return to London Wilson learnt that a coal strike was in the offing. 'This is nice', he thought, 'seeing we have only 10 Guard & 18 Line Battns (of which 7 are Irish) in the U.K. & we are just sending 4 Battns from the Rhine to Silesia'.[93] As the date approached for the transfer of the mines back to the private owners, the likelihood of a dispute grew greater. The miners, moreover, once more prepared to invoke the Triple Alliance. Although Wilson himself believed that there would not be a 'Triple strike', he still felt that it was necessary to 'prepare for & consider the worst', and he prepared elaborate plans to reinforce the army in Great Britain.[94]

In his search for troops the military commitment which incensed Wilson most at this stage was the force theoretically supervising the Silesian plebiscite. On 1 April the mine owners, having failed to come to any agreement with the union leaders, began a lock-out. The following day Wilson went down to Chequers to see Lloyd George and pressed on him 'the necessity for bringing back the 4 Battns from Silesia'. He argued that even if the Triple Alliance did not come out 'we should still want them for Ireland'. Wilson told the Prime Minister that unless he could bring back not only the Silesian battalions, but also three from Malta, one from Egypt and, if possible, two from Constantinople and three from the Rhine command, he 'would only be able to hold England at the cost of losing Ireland . . . I asked LG if he wanted to be PM of England or of Silesia'.[95]

On 4 April the Cabinet 'notwithstanding the political objections to a withdrawal of troops from Upper Silesia, which were fully recognised', agreed that 'the risk at home from Sinn Feiners, Communists, and other dangerous elements, was sufficiently great to necessitate their return'.[96] On 7 April Wilson recorded that, in addition to these troops and the three battalions from Malta, he had been able to get three infantry battalions from Egypt, although General Harington in Constantinople could spare none.[97] Still, however, there was a shortage of manpower. The next day a conference of ministers noted that apart from withdrawing troops from Ireland, 'which was not deemed advisable beyond the three Battalions already brought in', the only way to increase the government's military forces was by recruiting additional troops. The conference therefore decided both to call up the Reserves of all three services and to raise a special paramilitary 'Defence Force'.[98] By 14 April Wilson was able to tell the Military Attaché in Paris that the Defence Force was 'going along nicely' and that he was now unlikely to have to call on the Army of the Rhine for more troops since the Admiralty was lending him sailors and marines amounting 'to about 25 battalions'.[99] Despite J. H. Thomas's sweeping claim to Lloyd George that 'Jesus Christ couldn't prevent the railwaymen coming in',[100] on 15 April – 'Black Friday' – the Triple Alliance failed to strike and the miners had to struggle on alone.[101] Conditions were no longer propitious for a general stoppage or, indeed, a 'revolutionary' outbreak. Economic depression and mass unemployment took the steam out of industrial action and union militancy ebbed. In Lord Rawlinson's view the emergency had had its advantages for Wilson. 'The crisis', he wrote, 'will have been useful to you in gaining your ends. It will, at any rate, have frightened the "frocks" into withdrawing some of their more distant commitments, and make you stronger at home in the event of any serious trouble'.[102]

The need to retain strong military forces in Great Britain was one argument the General Staff employed in their opposition to the proposed Geddes cuts and Sir Henry Wilson's forebodings about the uncertain domestic position came out very strongly in the paper which they submitted to the Cabinet:

The situation at home has changed for the worse since 1914. Before the war the question of internal security in Great Britain hardly existed as a military pre-occupation. During the last year it is true that the revolutionary forces have received a decided check, but the snake is only scotched and not killed. We have to reckon as a permanency with organised forces of disruption subsidized and abetted by our enemies abroad, whose purpose is to destroy the whole fabric of society and make all government impossible.[103]

But by the end of 1921 there was no longer any immediate threat of revolution, if, indeed, there ever had been, *pace* the occasional fears of politicians and generals. Violent conflict was avoided at home both because of Lloyd George's adroitness in dealing with labour militancy (his 'genius for giving in') and also because such revolutionaries as there were within the state failed miserably to take advantage of Britain's post-war weakness: 'confronted with the greatest revolutionary opportunity in generations, the socialist movement showed itself largely unaware of its existence'.[104] But in other parts of the empire the British government was not so fortunate. In Ireland, in India, and in the Middle East, violent conflict seemed very much to be the order of the day.

Chapter 3

Imperial problems old and new

Before the First World War the generally agreed doctrine of imperial defence in Britain assumed that the major armed service role would be taken by the Royal Navy. The function of the 'senior service' was to protect the United Kingdom from invasion and maintain the freedom of the high seas, particularly in order to secure imperial communications. The army's principal task was to provide for the defence of India and the occasional minor colonial campaign. But by 1918, with the German naval threat removed, and for the years immediately following, it was clear that the maintenance of British interests was more closely involved with the army than the navy. During these years, while the empire seemed threatened by rising internal discontent – with which apparently only the army could deal – this was to remain so. It is, therefore, to the army that we must look in any examination of imperial defence following the First World War, when the empire included larger stretches of territory held by military force than at any previous time in its history.

Britain's unusual status as a great military land power – such a position had not been enjoyed since the end of the Napoleonic Wars – was reinforced by the military effort of the empire as a whole. In December 1918, for example, there were over a quarter of a million men from the dominions serving in the various expeditionary forces.[1] Thus it superficially seemed as if the old problem of persuading the dominions to take a share in imperial defence had been solved. But the dominions themselves soon signalled that such a belief was no more than a romantic imperial illusion. Although in 1914 they had rallied swiftly to the British cause, after the armistice they withdrew their troops just as quickly. Dominion private soliders, like the British, understandably assumed that the war had ended in November 1918, but the dominion military authorities, unlike Sir Henry Wilson and his British colleagues, were able to act promptly on this supposition.

A month after the armistice the CIGS proposed that Canada and Australia should provide troops for the army of occupation in Germany. Having shared with the British army 'the vicissitudes and glories of the various campaigns now successfully concluded', Wilson hoped that 'the great Overseas Dominions' would 'equally be ready to participate in the irksome but necessary duties of garrisoning occupied territory'. But both the Canadian Prime Minister, Sir Robert Borden, and the Australian, W. M. Hughes, bluntly told the Imperial War Cabinet that public opinion in their respective countries would not permit the retention of units overseas for whatever purpose.[2] In March 1919 Hughes tackled Lloyd George about the unsatisfactorily slow repatriation of Australian soldiers. 'Now that hostilities have ceased they are naturally anxious for a speedy return', he commented. A month later the South African Premier, Louis Botha, made a similar protest.[3] The Canadians were equally unhappy, especially since there was a sizeable Canadian Expeditionary Force still on active service in Siberia. In December 1918 the General Staff in Ottawa informed the War Office that Canadian public opinion was 'strongly opposed to further participation', and the following February Borden warned Lloyd George that he had instructed his Minister of Militia to withdraw the Canadian troops from Siberia 'as soon as Spring opens, say about April'. The War Office had no choice but to acquiesce with this, although Churchill thought that a letter should be sent to Borden 'which in courteous terms brings out clearly the fact that in this respect British troops have not received the support from their Canadian comrades in this adventure which they had a right to expect'.[4]

The reluctance of the dominions to co-operate in a centralised imperial defence system was just one manifestation of a phenomenon posing increasing problems for imperial policy-makers: nationalism. In the dominions' case this was a relatively benign challenge, involving as it did more a desire for some degree of political sovereignty *within* the 'British Commonwealth' (as it was increasingly being called), rather than urgent demands for complete independence from the 'mother country'. A more serious threat, however, came from nationalism in other parts of the empire, notably Ireland, Egypt and India, none of which regarded Great Britain with quite the same daughterly affection as the dominions. In each of these countries the development of local politics and the expansion of local aspirations (to a very great extent stimulated by the war) did much to create what has been called the post-war 'crisis of empire'.[5] While none of these challenges were individually on a very great scale, collectively they seemed to pose a serious threat. This problem was amplified by the fact that the challenges were strongest where imperial strategic needs demanded the maintenance of close imperial control. Southern Ireland was believed to be vital for home defence. Egypt and the Suez Canal constituted a key link in the chain of communications with the east. India was quite simply the most important component part of the empire.

For military thinkers throughout the nineteenth and first half of the twentieth centuries the defence of India and its communications was the keystone of the imperial strategic system. 'In fighting for India', remarked a War Office colonel in 1902, 'England will be fighting for her imperial existence'.[6] Ever since the French expedition to Egypt in 1798–9 the security of communications with the east had been of concern to London. The establishment and development of 'fortress' colonies along the route between Britain and India was a symptom of this concern. The opening of the Suez Canal in 1869 and the supersession of the sea route round the Cape emphasised the strategic value of the Middle Eastern line of communications and led, directly or indirectly, to formal British involvement in Cyprus (1878), Egypt (1882) and Somaliland (1884). In the late nineteenth century a direct threat to India itself arose in the guise of Russian expansion in Central Asia. Overwhelming naval power, supported by small army units in the chain of bases from Gibraltar to the Persian Gulf, could clearly do little to defend India against invasion from Russia, and the planners in London became preoccupied with the military problem of defending the North West Frontier. The seriousness with which this question was taken is illustrated by the fantastic estimates which were made of the numbers of troops required actively to defend the sub-continent. In 1904 Kitchener, then Commander-in-Chief in India, calculated that 160,000 men would be needed immediately to reinforce the 200,000-strong Army in India, and another 300,000–400,000 troops in a second year of war.[7] Such calculations, however, had little relevance. While they may have brought theoretical 'war games' to a satisfactory conclusion for the War Office, their real effect was to startle the Cabinet into seeking a diplomatic solution to the military problem. The Anglo-Russian Alliance of 1907, thus, eased the burden of imperial defence by securing the frontiers of India and lifting Russian pressure from parts of the route east.

The problem following the First World War was in many respects similar. Although in the immediate aftermath of the conflict the threat from Russia seemed negligible, there were those, such as Curzon and Milner, who felt that a 'forward' policy of defending India could once and for all secure 'Britain's proudest possession' from any future Russian expansion. The scene, moreover, seemed well set for the implementation of such a policy. 'From the left bank of the Don to India is our interest and preserve', noted Sir Henry Wilson following the armistice with Turkey at the end of October 1918.[8] This military *imperium* was food and drink indeed to Curzon, who asserted the 'supreme importance' of the Caucasus, over which, he declared, 'it is essential, in the interest of India and our Empire, that we should exercise some measure of political control'.[9]

Curzon's plan was to create a zone of buffer states between Russia and the imperial lifelines in the Middle East – what Henry Wilson described, and rejected as impracticable, as a *cordon sanitaire* around Russia.[10] In

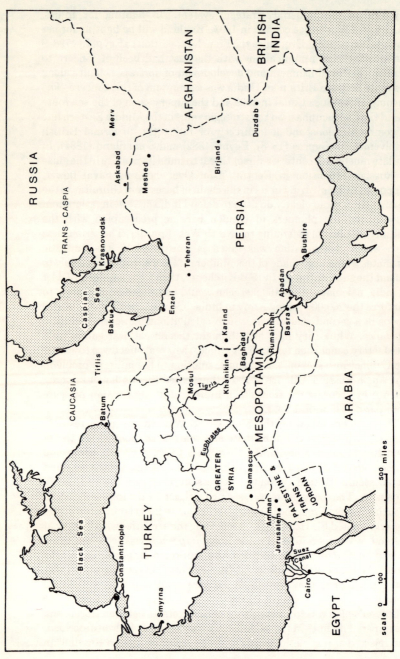

The Middle East, 1918–22

the Foreign Office, however, this objective seemed to be perfectly sensible. Following the collapse of the Russian empire, independent national republics had sprung up in the Caucasus and Transcaspia – weak new states which depended for their continued existence on the support of a British 'presence' in the region. Curzon's vision was that this area might be transformed into an enormous British sphere of influence protecting the vital arc of empire from Egypt to India.

To this grandiose scheme Curzon added his hope that Persia would be established as a loyal British client state. The Anglo-Russian Convention of 1907 had provided for British and Russian spheres of influence in the north and south of the country, with a 'neutral' zone in the centre. During the war, despite Persia's technical neutrality, a considerable number of British troops had been deployed in the country, both to counteract the effect of Turkish and German intrigues in Teheran and to safeguard the British-controlled oilfields near the Gulf. Following the war, with Russian influence apparently destroyed by the Bolshevik Revolution, the stage seemed set for a full-scale, if 'informal', British take-over. At first Curzon's policy met with success and he seemed to have gained all he wished in the Anglo–Persian Agreement of August 1919. Justifying the agreement to the Cabinet, he noted that since Great Britain was about to assume the mandate for the former Ottoman territory of Mesopotamia,

which will make us coterminous with the western frontiers of Persia, we cannot permit the existence, between our Indian Empire in Baluchistan and our new Protectorate, of a hot-bed of misrule, enemy intrigue, financial chaos, and political disorder. Further, if Persia were to be left alone, there is every reason to fear that she would be over-run by Bolshevik influence from the north. Lastly we possess in the south-western corner of Persia great assets in the shape of oilfields, which are worked for the British Navy and which give us a commanding interest in that part of the world.[11]

The strategic value of Middle Eastern oil was a small but significant consideration influencing British post-war policy.[12] Oil production in the region was not large at any time during the period in question. In Persia it was only about one per cent of world production, in Egypt it was negligible and in Mesopotamia it was as yet hardly more than a hope. The Admiralty, nevertheless, naturally concerned for supplies of fuel oil, consistently pressed upon the Cabinet the importance, actual and potential, of the Persian and Mesopotamian oil-fields. Before the war the navy secured most of its oil fuel from Mexico and the USA.[13] From a strategic point of view this was clearly unsatisfactory, and strenuous efforts were made in London to find an independent British source of supply. Persia was one possibility, and Churchill in 1913 as First Lord of the Admiralty had been instrumental in promoting the British government's patronage of the Anglo-Persian Oil Company (which later became British Petroleum). From 1915 to 1918, when the British had complete control over the oil wells, there was a systematic increase of production to over one million tons of oil in 1918, almost ten times the amount produced in 1913. After the war, in which, as Lord Curzon put it, 'the Allies floated to victory on a sea of oil',[14] interested parties urged upon the Cabinet the importance of both Persian oil and the unproven Mesopotamian reserves.

It would, however, be foolish to suggest that oil played a really major part in the formulation of British policy towards the Middle East. It was frequently cited by ministers and generals as an *additional* reason for a British 'presence' in the region, but the primacy of India and imperial communications was never challenged by petroleum. Imperial visionaries might quite plausibly argue that Britain needs must retain troops in Persia in order to secure an independent oil supply but in retrospect it seems that the clumsy British involvement in Persia had quite the opposite effect by alienating the Persians, providing an *entrée* for the Russians and admitting American oil interests who, it appeared, needed no military support at all in order to extract oil.

Curzon's great system of imperial defence in the Middle East was the child of 'war imperialism'. During the war money and effort was given without stint to any plan which might contribute towards winning the conflict. But in the hard light of the post-war world, imperial vision had to be tempered with domestic economy. Widespread opposition at home (and abroad) grew up to what Sir Henry Wilson termed Britain's wholesale 'interference' in everyone else's affairs. Another senior general alleged ominously that 'the habit of interfering with other people's business, and of making what is euphoniously called "peace" is like "buggery": once you take to it you cannot stop'.[15] Whatever the truth of this matter, the Treasury had not the money and the War Office not the men to support a massive extension of empire in the Middle East, even in the high cause of defending India.

From the very start Lloyd George was sceptical about the value of major British intervention along the frontiers of south Russia and in August 1919, when pressed to retain British troops in Armenia, he complained that 'the poor old British Empire is asked to do everything and gets not a word of thanks in return'.[16] Edwin Montagu at the India Office, although at first supporting Curzon's Persian Agreement, saw no need to retain troops in south Russia. 'So far as the defence of India is concerned', he wrote in December 1918, 'it does not seem to me necessary to us to give a thought to the Caucasus. I feel that this region is entirely outside the range of our interests . . .'.[17] But not everyone was quite so opposed to 'intervention'. Milner offered qualified backing to Curzon's policy in south Russia, urging the support of 'friendly' forces in those regions 'which most closely affected the interests of the British Empire and were most easily got at'.[18]

Some of the strongest and most consistent opposition to the 'forward' policy for the defence of India came from the Indian government itself. Absorbed as it was with internal unrest and the introduction of domestic reforms, Delhi had little enough time to spare for wider considerations of external defence. The India Office in London, however, was initially more enthusiastic and expansive. In December 1918 the Political Department of the India Office presented to the Cabinet a paper on 'Indian Desiderata for Peace Settlement'. It noted that there were important commercial and strategic interests for India in the Middle East and declared that in Mesopotamia 'a barrier must be set up . . ., whatever its precise form, that will effectually close the land line to the head of the Gulf against any potential enemy of the British Empire'. Persia, too, was important for it 'lies across the most vulnerable flank of our Indian position and the defence of India must always be the governing consideration in our Persian policy'.[19] This thinking underlay Montagu's original attitude towards the Anglo-Persian agreement. But he did not offer unconditional support. 'I am only committed to it', he told the Viceroy, Lord Chelmsford, 'as long as the recognised Persian Government wants it'.[20] Chelmsford and his advisors had no confidence at all in the agreement. It was, he wrote in February 1920,

to my mind . . . based on sand. It would stand only so long as it had the support of British bayonets . . . For ourselves in India we have little concern with what may happen in Persia . . . If His Majesty's Government wish to give military support to Persia it must be at the expense of the Imperial Exchequer. We cannot use Indian funds for bolstering up a policy which is little or no concern to us.[21]

The Government of India were markedly reluctant to fund the maintenance of Indian troops outside the sub-continent itself. This was an attitude which many in London found puzzling. Delhi's intransigence in the matter of employing either Indian troops or Indian revenues for external defence perplexed not only the active proponents of the 'forward' policy, but also less expansionist ministers. Austen Chamberlain, for example, who as a former Secretary of State for India could claim some authority in Indian affairs and who as Chancellor in 1919 had consistently pressed for the reduction of British overseas commitments, voiced his frustration with the Indian position in a letter in April 1921:

In regard to Persia and the Middle East generally I will only say that I find some difficulty in understanding the position taken up by the Government of India. They disclaim all interest and all responsibility and refuse financial help. I do not know that this represents their permanent state of mind, but Heaven knows, we have burdens enough on our shoulders here and India cannot expect us to pay the whole cost of what I may call her external frontiers. I know that the financial difficulties of the Government of India are as great as ours but I cannot understand their assumed attitude of perfect indifference to the peace of Persia and the Arab countries.[22]

In the event, the 'forward' policy of defending India was to fail in the face of Indian intransigence, War Office and Treasury opposition, and local political instability in both Persia and south Russia.

In contrast to the question of defending the landward approaches to India, securing the line of communications between Britain and the 'jewel of empire' stimulated little friction. There was never any question that the string of fortress colonies and coaling stations along the route east should not be maintained. The most pressing problem for imperial strategists concerned the future status of Egypt and the maintenance of British control over the Suez Canal. Lord Milner's Mission to Egypt in 1919–20 was charged with the task of reconciling Egyptian national aspirations with British strategic needs, and although Milner proposed in May 1920 that Egypt be granted a degree of independence, it was not imagined that there should be any accompanying derogation of British strategic or diplomatic authority over the country.

Concern for Egypt was not confined to Britain or India. At the 1921 imperial conference in London the Premiers of both Australia and New Zealand declared their peoples' deep interest in Egypt and the Canal. Anything that menaced the Canal, asserted Hughes, affected 'the whole of the Empire vitally'. For the Prime Minister of New Zealand (William Massey), the Canal was 'the British Empire highway from the very heart of the Empire, where we are to-day, to India, to Australasia, to the whole of the Far East'. Massey even went so far as to say that he did not know 'of any country so important to the Empire as Egypt, with the exception of Britain itself. Even Australia and New Zealand might be parted with and the Empire would go on, but I do not think you could run the Empire without keeping control of the main artery'.[23] The security of the Suez Canal, therefore, remained a high priority for imperial strategists following the war, and the preservation of British paramountcy in Egypt a primary aim for the rulers of the empire.

Although the Egyptian question loomed largest when the defence of imperial communications was being considered some less important problems concerning the security of the route east arose in the aftermath of the war. One such was the future of Cyprus which in 1915 had been offered to Greece as a bribe to enter the war on the Allied side. At the time this offer was declined, but since Greece finally had joined the Allies in 1917, it was feared after the war that the Greek leader, Venizelos, might renew demands for the island. Lord Curzon was opposed to any transfer of sovereignty and in January 1919 circulated a paper which stressed the important strategic position of the island 'on the flank of the Suez Canal route' and noted that 'so long as it remains in our hands, it cannot be used against us'. The Colonial Secretary, Walter Long, wrote a concurring note, and annexed to it a paper by Trenchard pointing out that the strategic importance of Cyprus had been enhanced by the development of air power. 'With the increasing range of aircraft', wrote Trenchard, 'the main lines of communication to Alexandria and through the Suez Canal will be within easy striking distance. The possession of Cyprus by hostile Power would therefore prove a serious threat to our principal sea communications with the East'.[24] These arguments were strong enough to ensure that Cyprus remained British.

A similar flurry of excitment over the future of British Somaliland prompted Lord Milner to argue its strategic importance in May 1919. It had been suggested that some of the territory be transferred to Italy as part of the 'equitable compensations' for her part in the war. Such a 'surrender', argued Milner, would involve 'a weakening of our strategic position at one of the "nodal points" of the Empire'. The expansion of Italian power in north-east Africa would, moreover, 'cut right into the heart of that great sphere of British influence extending from the centre of East Africa through the Sudan, Egypt, Arabia and the Persian Gulf to India, which is the real British "Empire", apart from the Dominions'. Milner tried to enlist the support of the CIGS for his case, but Wilson was not impressed with the strategic value of the territory. 'Milner rang me up to say that L.G. was going to give Somaliland to the Italians', wrote Wilson in his diary, 'and would I put in a protest. So long as we keep Berbera and the oil reported there the Italians can have the rest of the country!'[25] Despite Wilson's trenchant view, in the end Britain retained control of this 'most useless possession in the whole of the British Empire'.[26]

The protection of imperial communications in the Indian Ocean was one reason put forward supporting the outright British annexation of German East Africa (later Tanganyika). In October 1918 both Lord Curzon and the Colonial Office circulated papers highlighting the dangers arising from possible enemy occupation of the German East African harbours and in December the India Office declared an interest in the territory because, *inter alia*, 'in the hands of a Power hostile, or potentially hostile, to Great Britain, it might afford a base for enemy naval activity in the Indian Ocean'.[27] These arguments based on the security of sea communications did not, perhaps, carry as much weight as the romantic attraction of filling in the line of British possessions 'from the Cape to Cairo'. 'From the point of view of Imperial security', wrote L. S. Amery, 'the linking up of South Africa with Egypt and our Eastern possessions is a matter of enormous importance'.[28] In 1918, besides, the British were *de facto* in control of German East Africa and the granting of the 'Tanganyika Territory' to Great Britain as a 'B' Mandate by the League of Nations was never effectively in doubt.

A new set of problems bearing on the security of the imperial route east arose from the dissolution of the Ottoman empire. For much of the nineteenth century British policy towards the 'Eastern Question' had been concerned with maintaining the territorial integrity of that empire. To a great extent this policy aimed at limiting Russian expansion towards the eastern Mediterranean and the spheres of British strategic and commercial interests in the Middle East. The final defeat of Turkey in October 1918, principally by British forces, left the way open for a complete reassessment of British policy. It had been generally accepted since early in the war that, with the defeat of Turkey, the Ottoman Empire must be destroyed, and the problem facing the British peace-makers was the establishment of a new system which, like the old regime, would satisfy the strategic needs of the empire in the Middle East. The two most important needs, in 1918 as before the war, were the security of the imperial system itself and the route east, along with British, or at least international, control of the Dardanelles.

In meeting these two main policy objectives British freedom of action was limited by a number of treaties and agreements which had been made during the war.[29] The Treaty of London of April 1915, for example, offered Italy territorial compensations on the Mediterranean littoral of Asia Minor. The Sykes-Picot Agreement (May 1916) effectively divided the northern Arab provinces of the Ottoman Empire between Britain and France, and the Balfour Declaration (October 1917) announced that His Majesty's government viewed with favour 'the establishment in Palestine of a national home for the Jewish people'. The British Government had also during the war made various agreements with Arab protonationalists regarding the post-war establishment of an independent Arab kingdom in exchange for Arab support against Turkey. The problem of coming to a settlement in the Middle East was further complicated by the fact that for the peace conference in Paris the treaties with Germany and Austria-Hungary took first priority. Not only was the making of peace with Turkey delayed, but Lloyd George in particular also tended to use Middle Eastern settlements as bargaining counters in the negotiations for what he seems to have regarded as the more important western treaties.

British policy towards the Middle East immediately following the war was directed principally by Lord Curzon and his creature the Cabinet eastern committee. Because of his great interest in and knowledge of the region, Curzon's influence as chairman predominated on the committee. Until November 1919, moreover, while Balfour was away at the peace conference in Paris, Curzon acted as Foreign Secretary. The key to Curzon's Middle Eastern policy was his firmly-held belief that British imperial interests in the Middle East could only be provided for by the destruction of Turkey as an expansionist power and as the centre of

pan-Islamic feeling. In the eastern committee his policy towards Turkey
was generally supported by Balfour (when he attended) and Lord Robert
Cecil (Parliamentary Under Secretary of State in the Foreign Office).
Curzon, however, did not go unchallenged in the committee. Balfour,
while accepting the basic premise that the Ottoman Empire ought to be
dismembered and the Turks expelled from Constantinople, was more
reluctant than Curzon to take on direct, if only 'temporary', military
responsibilities in the Caucasus. More strident opposition came from
Edwin Montagu who was strongly against expelling the Sultan from
Constantinople for fear that this would irrevocably inflame Muslim
opinion in India. Montagu had an unlikely ally in another member of the
committee, Sir Henry Wilson, who felt that Britain had not the military
strength to impose such harsh terms on the Turks, and who believed that
in order to attain peace in the Middle East Britain ought to 'make love to
the Turk'. It was, he said, the only way ever to get any peace in Arabia, in
Egypt, in Aden, in Mesopotamia and in India'.[30]

Despite this opposition from the India and War Offices, by the end of
1918 Curzon had obtained in the eastern committee some general lines of
policy towards the Ottoman lands. There was to be no imperial Ottoman
restoration and no formal Allied annexations of territory while the Arab
provinces of the empire were to gain some measure of self-determination
under European advice and support. No agreement was reached on the
future of Constantinople. On 7 January 1919 the committee dissolved,
but it was agreed that its work should be carried on by less elaborate
inter-departmental conferences, summoned when necessary by Lord
Curzon. These conferences continued to be known popularly as the
'eastern committee'.[31]

The signing of the Treaty of Versailles with Germany in June 1919 and
the gradual revival of Cabinet government (formally re-established in
November 1919), enabled ministers and their advisers to pay closer
attention to Middle Eastern questions. It was not a moment too soon for
Curzon who had complained in March that while everyone was discussing
'the probable or possible attitude of Germany', no-one appeared to 'turn a
thought to what may happen in Turkey'. He sensibly argued, moreover,
that the longer the matter was left, the more difficult it would be to
impose on Turkey the severe treaty he desired[32] and thus threaten his
plans for a 'Moslem nexus of states' to protect the Anglo–Indian defence
system in the Middle East.[33] Yet, in the end, Curzon succeeded neither in
his aim of expelling the Turks from Constantinople nor in the more
extravagant of his plans such as the creation of an independent Armenian
republic around the internationalised port of Batum. Throughout 1919
opposition hardened towards his 'tough line' with Turkey. Churchill and
Sir Henry Wilson were both anxious to inject a note of military realism
into the discussions. In April Wilson told Churchill that he was 'in a hurry

to get out of Constantinople', and in August the Secretary of State wrote to Balfour asking him if he could give 'any indication of how long we are expected to maintain an army at Constantinople?' Churchill observed that there was an army of 40,000 men in Constantinople and on the Black Sea shores. 'The strain of this upon our melting military resources', he added, 'is becoming insupportable'.[34] The gloomy Montagu was, as always, wholeheartedly opposed to a harsh Turkish treaty. 'I feel that a peace such as is proposed will be hateful to Indian Mohammedans', he told Lloyd George, 'and cannot fail to augment the forces already strong which make for disaffection in India'. Montagu was additionally worried about the possibility of Indian soldiers being employed. 'I cannot contemplate the use of Indian troops', he wrote, 'the use of Mohammedan troops, to enforce a peace which I am perfectly certain will be regarded as unjust and unfair throughout India'.[35] Even the old imperialist Milner would not take Curzon's side and assured Montagu in August 1919 that he would 'continue to urge the preservation of the Turk in his "homelands" including Constantinople & Adrianople'.[36]

Curzon's desire for a harsh Turkish peace was shared by Lloyd George, who retained throughout his administration an extraordinary anti-Turk and pro-Greek bias. The Treaty of Sèvres with Turkey, finally signed in August 1920, contained one concession to the 'moderate' party by retaining the Sultan, although powerless, in Constantinople. This had been done, Lloyd George assured Montagu, largely out of deference to Indian views and representations.[37] The rest of the treaty was not so lenient for it established international control over the Straits, policed by an Allied garrison, and transferred territory in Asia Minor to both Greece and Italy. It was a monument to Curzon's short-sighted intransigence and the Prime Minister's overwhelming phil-Hellenism. When Lloyd George's friend and confidant, Lord Riddell, questioned him in June 1920 as to the wisdom of granting so much Turkish territory to Greece, the Prime Minister declared his views with some passion:

The Turks nearly brought about our defeat in the war. It was a near thing. You cannot trust them and they are a decadent race. The Greeks, on the other hand, are our friends, and they are a rising people. We want to be on good terms with the Greeks and Italians.

We must secure Constantinople and the Dardanelles. You cannot do that effectively without crushing the Turkish power. Of course the military are against the Greeks. They always have been. They favour the Turks. The military are confirmed Tories. It is the Tory policy to support the Turks. They hate the Greeks. That is why Henry Wilson, who is a Tory of the most crusted kind, is so much opposed to what we have done.[38]

Yet such support for the Greeks was not unreasonable at a time when Greek armies were waging successful campaigns in both Thrace and Anatolia, and there were widespread fears of a Turkish revival. Lloyd

George, moreover, had an 'invariable devotion to what he conceived to be the oppressed',[39] he nursed a Gladstonian hatred of the Turks – 'the greatest scoundrels unhung'[40] – and retained profound if misplaced confidence in the ability of the Greek leader, Venizelos. For the War Office and the Indian Office, however, Lloyd George's intemperate dislike of the Turks and love of the Greeks were seen as a major stumbling-block to the pacification of the Middle East and the easing of unrest in India.

The success of Greek arms in Asia Minor in the summer of 1920 masked the fact that Britain alone had not the military power required to enforce the Treaty of Sèvres. While for a time the Greeks proved to be able local sub-contractors for British policy, the Cabinet had little time for Henry Wilson's complaints that he 'had not enough troops to carry out . . . policy in Ireland, C—ople, Palestine, Mesopotamia'. In June 1920 he thought 'we are notably in a worse place than in 1914. Then we had France & Russia as Allies; now we have Greece!'[41] The Greek advance into Anatolia also for a time disguised the rising strength of Turkish nationalism led by Mustapha Kemal, whose forces had briefly been involved in minor engagements with British troops in June 1920, and who was utterly opposed to the Sèvres Treaty. The defeat of Venizelos in the Greek general election of November 1920 seemed to present a suitable opportunity to throw over the Greeks and come to terms with the Kemalists. 'Now is the time', urged Churchill, 'to abandon the policy of relying on the weak and fickle Greeks'.[42] Lloyd George and Curzon, however, remained largely unmoved in the face of either Churchill's proposals or, indeed, Montagu's continued pleas for a 'just' Turkish peace, and although the Cabinet approved fresh negotiations with the Turks in January 1921 at which the Kemalists could be represented, it is clear that neither the Prime Minister nor the Foreign Secretary were prepared to make great concessions.[43] In May 1921 Worthington-Evans, the Secretary for War, circulated a paper to the Cabinet in which Wilson and the General Staff declared that since it was 'out of the question' that reinforcements be sent to Constantinople, the British garrison 'should be withdrawn before they become involved in a dangerous situation owing to a Nationalist advance'. On 31 May the paper was discussed in the Cabinet. Churchill and Montagu supported Wilson, while Mond (Minister of Health) urged that large reinforcements be sent. H. A. L. Fisher heretically suggested that it was 'far more important to hold C—ople than Ireland and we ought to send troops from Ireland to C—ople'. No decision was taken. 'A truly amazing Cabinet', commented Wilson.[44]

The government's uncertain approach to Turkish policy during 1921 is illustrated by several abortive attempts to open negotiations with the Kemalists, but by the end of the year the poverty of the Prime Minister's policy had been exposed by the progressive collapse of the Greek armies following their defeat by the nationalist Turks at Sakarya in September and the gradual falling away of Allied support. In April the Italians began to withdraw from Asia Minor and in October the French secretly negotiated a separate peace with the Kemalist government. In April 1922 the Italians followed suit. Only the neutral zone protecting the Straits now remained in Allied occupation. When the Greek forces finally disintegrated in the late summer of 1922 and the victorious Turkish nationalists entered Smyrna at the beginning of September it was clear that Lloyd George's obstinate pro-Greek policy was in ruins. The way was now open for a direct confrontation between Kemal's armies and the Allied troops defending the Straits which he had vowed to expel from Turkey. Realising this, on 19 September the French and Italians withdrew their troops from Chanak on the Dardanelles and the Ismid Peninsula opposite Constantinople.

But Lloyd George, and, indeed, the whole Cabinet were prepared for war over the defence of the Straits. On 15 September the famous telegrams to the Dominions were sent asking if assistance would be forthcoming in the event of war with Turkey. Only New Zealand offered immediate and unqualified support.[45] The empire clearly did not set such high store by the imperial necessity of holding the Straits as it did, for example, by holding the Suez Canal. On 11 October, General Harington, the British commander at Constantinople, adroitly persuaded Kemal to negotiate and thus paved the way for a settlement at last to be made with the Turkish leader by Lord Curzon at Lausanne in the summer of 1923. This treaty swept away that of Sèvres, Smyrna was restored to Turkey and the Straits were merely 'demilitarised'.

The need to establish some sort of lasting settlement in Asia Minor was accentuated by the post-war revival of Russian expansionism. Although in the immediate aftermath of the Bolshevik revolution it seemed to many that aggressive Russian imperialism had been destroyed, it soon became accepted that the new Soviet leaders in Moscow posed as great a threat to the empire as the *ancien régime* at St. Petersburg had done. The principal exponent of this view in the government was Winston Churchill, whose obsession with the Bolshevik challenge and vigorous championing of counter-revolutionary 'White' Russians exasperated his military advisors and soured his relations with Lloyd George. The debate in London following the war centred on the extent to which aggressive Bolshevism should be met. Wilson, who had no truck with Bolshevism itself, objected to active intervention in Russia on purely military grounds. 'The invasion and occupation of Russia at the present time', he dryly declared in February 1919, 'is not considered to be a practical proposition'.[46] Lloyd George's attitude owed more to his general post-war policy of 'appeasement'; his anxiety to bring both Germany and Russia back into the European swim. But any hope that the Prime Minister may have had of such a policy succeeding with Russia had first to surmount the obstacle of British military intervention in the Russian civil war.

British troops had originally intervened in Russia following the revolution in order to maintain, so far as was possible, those anti-Bolshevik forces which remained committed to war against the Central Powers. After the armistice, however, there seemed to be no justification for continued intervention except on the grounds of an anti-Bolshevik crusade. This was particularly true of north Russia where there was no direct threat to British imperial interests, no need of a 'cordon sanitaire', and no new national republics, as in the south, to provide the excuse of 'self determination' for continued British military involvement. Sir Henry Wilson had been an ardent interventionist at the start of his term as CIGS, but when the subject came up for discussion after the armistice he presented a paper to the Cabinet recommending, regretfully, that since there were not the resources to take active military measures against Bolshevism, the government were obliged 'to do all we can in the way of material to give our friends a fair start, then to withdraw'. On the last day of 1918 Lloyd George persuaded his colleagues to agree in principle against intervention in Russia.[47]

Churchill, however, remained wedded to the extravagant notion that Britain could underwrite a major military campaign in Russia. In February 1919 he told Lloyd George (at the time in Paris) that he had set the General Staff to work on a 'concerted scheme for waging war against the Bolsheviks'. The reaction was immediate. Lloyd George wired back:

Am very alarmed at your . . . telegram about planning war against the Bolshevists. The Cabinet have never authorised such a proposal. They have never contemplated anything beyond supplying armies in anti-Bolshevist areas in Russia with necessary equipment to enable them to hold their own, and that only in the event of every effort at peaceable solution failing . . . An expensive war of aggression against Russia is a way to strengthen Bolshevism in Russia and create it at home. We cannot afford the burden. Chamberlain says we can hardly make both ends meet on a peace basis, even at the present crushing rate of taxation; and if we are committed to a war against a continent like Russia, it is the road to bankruptcy and Bolshevism in these islands.[48]

Reluctantly Churchill had to acquiesce in the 'limited character of our assistance' to Russia, but later in the month he was still complaining to the Prime Minister that there was no 'will to win' behind any of the British military ventures in Russia and that 'at every point we fall short of what is necessary to obtain real success'.[49]

All through 1919 Churchill continued to fight his vain battle against the Prime Minister and the majority of the Cabinet. Lloyd George, however, was becoming increasingly concerned about the high level of military expenditure generally and he regarded the intervention in north Russia as little more than a costly and futile distraction. Just a fortnight after the 'ten year rule' had been formulated, the Prime Minister made his views plain in an important memorandum on the 'North West Russian Position':

I earnestly trust the Cabinet will not consent to committing British resources to any fresh military enterprises in Russia. They have decided to withdraw from Siberia, from Archangel, from the Baltic, and after furnishing General Denikin with one more packet, to let the Russians fight out their own quarrels at their own expense. I hope nothing will induce the Ministry to deviate from this decision . . .

I am anxious for another reason to have done with these military ventures in Russia as soon as possible. I cannot help thinking that they have taken away the mind of the War Office from important administrative tasks which urgently needed attention. If the amount of intense and concentrated attention which has been devoted to the running of these Russian wars had been given to reducing our expenditure, I feel certain that scores of millions would have been saved.[50]

Churchill protested that the 'whole effort of the administrative branches of the War Office is concentrated upon the problem of demobilising the Army in all parts of the world, and reducing it down to the lowest level compatible with the safe and efficient discharge of the obligations laid upon us by State policy'.[51] He continued, however, to stress his opposition to the Russian Bolshevik régime and sent Lloyd George a letter and a memorandum on the subject on 22 September.[52] This merely served to exasperate the Prime Minister:

You know [he replied] that I have been doing my best for the last few weeks to comply with the legitimate demand which comes from all classes of the country to cut down the enormous expenditure which is devouring the resources of this country at a prodigious rate. I have repeatedly begged you to apply your mind to the problem. I made this appeal to all departments, but I urged it specially upon you for three reasons: the first is that the highest expenditure is still military; the second that the largest immediate reduction which could be effected without damage to the public welfare are foreseeable in the activities controlled by your Department. The third is that I have found your mind so obsessed by Russia that I felt I had good ground for the apprehension that your great abilities, energy and courage were not devoted to the reduction of expenditure.

I regret that all my appeals have been in vain. At each interview you promised to give your mind to this very important problem. Nevertheless the first communication I have always received from you after these interviews related to Russia. I invited you to Paris to help me reduce our commitments in the East. You there produce a lengthy and carefully prepared memorandum on Russia. I entreated you on Friday to let Russia be for at least 48 hours and to devote your weekend to preparing for the Finance Committee this afternoon. You promised faithfully to do so. Your reply is to send me a four page letter on Russia, and a closely printed memorandum of several pages – all on Russia. I am frankly in despair.[53]

It is arguable that this dislocation of policy with regard to Russia would not have occurred had not Lloyd George been in Paris attending the Peace Conference and Churchill, unsupervised, in London for most of the time. One of the great problems in the direction of policy at this time was that the British ministers and their advisors were 'scattered between London and Paris, rushed, harried and intolerably overworked'.[54] Nevertheless Lloyd George eventually got his way and Churchill had to abandon his ambitions for a great anti-Bolshevik crusade. Even before the acrimonious exchange of letters in September the British evacuation from north Russia had begun and, with some delays, continued on until the early autumn. In September 1919 the last British troops embarked at Archangel.[55] The army was not displeased since the White Russians were at the best uncertain allies. 'These Russians are a curious crew to deal with', wrote Rawlinson, who had been sent out to supervise the evacuation. 'Of course they are in a tight place here and I am sorry for them but they seem to be quite helpless and want us to do everything for them'. 'One cannot help getting tired of constantly nursing children who resolutely refuse to grow up', thought Wilson.[56]

British intervention in south Russia was more intractable than that in the north for it was more closely linked to the vital strategic interests of the empire. Lord Curzon's strong defence of a British 'presence' in the region effectively delayed the withdrawal of British troops from the Caucasus but War Office pressure, the need for economy and Lloyd George's growing desire for an accommodation with Soviet Russia and the normalisation of Anglo Soviet relations prompted the Cabinet to agree in June 1920 to the final evacuation of all British troops from Batum.[57] By this time, too, direct trade negotiations with the Bolsheviks had begun in London. The Cabinet had 'grasped the hairy paw of the baboon'.[58] In south Russia itself Soviet military advances throughout 1920 and in the spring of 1921 gradually but inexorably reincorporated the short-lived anti-Bolshevik republics into Russia proper. The stage was now set for a renewal of the *status quo ante* and the revival of Anglo-Russian rivalry as the principal basis for strategy and diplomacy in the Middle East. Although Soviet and British troops briefly came into contact in May 1920, the chief threat which Britain had to meet was not military but from Russian propaganda. 'I don't believe that India is in any danger', Lloyd George told Lord Riddell in January 1920. 'When Russia was well equipped the Russians could not cross the mountains'. When Riddell suggested that the chief danger was Bolshevik propaganda Lloyd George agreed, 'but you can't keep ideas out of a country by a military cordon'.[59] A diplomatic cordon, perhaps, was possible. This was Curzon's aim with his Persian policy, the Indian government's with their negotiations in Afghanistan, and even, mistakenly, the Prime Minister's pro-Greek policy. The threat of Russian infiltration, moreover, hung over Churchill's attempt to secure British imperial interests by the establishment of friendly and pliant regimes in Britain's Arab mandates.

From the Russian side there is evidence to suggest that the Soviet leaders were well aware 'of just how thinly stretched were the military resources of the British Empire in the aftermath of the World War',[60] and that for them England's extremity might be Russia's opportunity. At the 'First Congress of the Peoples of the East' in Baku during September 1920 Zinoviev called for a 'holy war, to be directed first of all, against British Imperialism'.[61] In February and March 1921 the Soviet government concluded treaties with Turkey, Persia and Afghanistan, confirming, no doubt, Curzon's opinion that 'the Russian menace in the East is incomparably greater than anything else that has happened in my lifetime to the British Empire'.[62] This menace was taken into account during the trade talks. The British side announced that they would only sign on conditions including 'that the Soviet Government will refrain from any attempt by military action or propaganda to encourage any of the peoples of Asia in any form of hostile action against British interests or the British Empire'.[63] Although there was prolonged opposition in the Cabinet from Curzon, Milner and Churchill to the Anglo-Soviet Trade Agreement,[64] the agreement was finally signed in March 1921. In economic terms it had little significance, but it marked a step in the re-establishment of normal relations between the United Kingdom and Russia. It was also a personal triumph for the Prime Minister who carried most of his Conservative colleagues with him in his conciliatory policy.

Despite the understandable British nervousness and delicacy of approach towards the Bolsheviks, in part explained by domestic considerations, the Russian threat to the British imperial system was not as great as it might at first have seemed to be. The Soviet administration in Moscow had their own domestic fish to fry and there was no possibility that the revolutionary trumpet-call at the Baku congress would be backed up with any real military force. The Russian treaties of 1921 with the nationalist governments of Turkey, Persia and Afghanistan, moreover, actually posed no great threat because those governments quickly emerged as more nationalist than Bolshevik and, paradoxically, throughout the inter-war years they served as a sort of buffer between Russia and the empire in India and the Middle East. With supreme irony (and at negligible cost to Britain), Turkey, Persia and Afghanistan themselves in the end provided as effective a 'cordon sanitaire' around Soviet Russia as even Curzon could have wished.

The apparent Soviet challenge which Zinoviev threw down at Baku was only one of a plethora of problems facing Britain's post-war imperial rulers. In the aftermath of the war the initial response to any difficulty was almost invariably military and this put peculiar pressures on the army. Sir Henry Wilson's abiding concern throughout his time as CIGS, from February 1918 to February 1922, was that Britain did not have enough troops to garrison the empire. Time and time again in his private and official writings he recorded his anxiety that government policies outran military capability. The simple and straightforward answer to the problems of military manpower which soon became apparent after November 1918 would have been to raise more troops. Indeed, every conceivable source of manpower, domestic, dominion, Indian and colonial, was investigated. But accompanying the search for troops was a sustained effort on the part of the War Office to bring Britain's military commitments into line with the available resources. After the immediately post-war enthusiasm for taking on increased responsibilities, retrenchment soon became the watchword of the day. Sir Henry Wilson, therefore, strove to reduce the crippling burdens which his political masters imposed upon the army. Equally, however, he also fought against any suggestion that the army itself should retrench. In this, no doubt, he was simply playing the proper part of the CIGS in protecting the interests of the army, but his arguments in support of his case dove-tailed marvellously together. On the one hand we must reduce our responsibilities overseas since we do not have sufficient troops to maintain our positions, whereas on the other hand we must maintain the size of the army *because* of the magnitude of these immense overseas commitments.

Towards the end of April 1919 Wilson wrote a paper for the War Cabinet entitled 'The military situation throughout the British empire, with special reference to the inadequacy of the numbers of troops available'[65] and this may be taken to be the maxim which the CIGS was unwillingly obliged to adopt in his continuous review of imperial defence. In a minute covering a very long and disquieting memorandum by the General Staff on 'British military liabilities' in June 1920, Wilson wrote: 'I would respectfully urge that the earnest attention of His Majesty's Government may be given to this question with a view to our policy being brought into some relation with the military forces available to support it'. In the same paper the Adjutant-General pointed out: that 'if the Army is to be converted into an efficient fighting force', it was urgently necessary to incease its size, 'to recruit large numbers of men for the Army Reserve, and to devise some means of attracting tradesmen to the Colours'.[66] Winston Churchill had already drawn attention to the need for continued recruitment to meet 'the dangers and responsibilities of the immediate future' when he had introduced the 1920–21 army estimates to the Cabinet in February 1920.[67] When he came to deal with a supplementary estimate at the end of the year he pointed out that 'owing to the Irish situation and other dangers in other parts of the Empire, I have found it necessary to continue recruiting'. Even so, 'the Supplementary Estimate of £29,750,000 still, however, does not take into account any margin for unforeseen contingencies'.[68] It was this parlous state of affairs which Wilson described to Lloyd George as 'the dangerously weak & narrow margin of troops on which we are running the Empire'.[69]

The converse to the manpower difficulty was the overextension of the army. In August 1920 Wilson wrote about the necessity of reducing British commitments in the Middle East.

> Ever since January, 1920, [he claimed] the General Staff has consistently and repeatedly advocated the urgent necessity of concentrating our forces in those areas which are vital to us.
>
> Once again, I cannot too strongly press on the Government the danger, the extreme danger, of His Majesty's Army being spread all over the world, strong nowhere, weak everywhere, and with no reserve to save a dangerous situation or avert a coming danger.[70]

The following March he warmed to his subject in a letter to Arnold Robertson, the British representative on the Inter-Allied Rhineland High Commission:

> Owing to the "Frocks" having flung the British Army out of the window the day after the Armistice, the British Empire at the present moment has no army worth the name, and in addition such semblance of troops as we have are scattered in the most scandalous manner – the great bulk of them in Ireland; very few in England; three battalions on the Rhine; four battalions in Silesia; one battalion at Gibraltar; two battalions at Malta; two battalions at Constantinople; two battalions in Palestine; seven battalions in Egypt; and two battalions on the sea coming back from the East.[71] Was ever such distribution of troops made in the face of any enemy? . . .
>
> I keep on saying to the Cabinet, or to anybody else who is good enough to listen to me in a bus or tube, that the policy for England is quite simple and consists in this, get out of those places which do not belong to you and cling on like hell to those which do.[72]

With the army stretched as it was, Wilson was compelled to rank the problems of imperial defence in order of priority. At the top of his list were the 'main bases' of the empire: Great Britain and Ireland in the west and India in the east – 'on their stability depends the whole political, economic and military structure of the Empire'. Next in importance was placed Egypt, 'the "Clapham Junction" of Imperial communications, and the chief connecting link between the two main bases'.[73] On several occasions in his diary and correspondence Wilson recorded 'our threatres in order of importance'.[74] In each case the United Kingdom, India and Egypt head the list. Mesopotamia, which Wilson thought valuable as a source of oil, comes next, although by the end of December 1921 it had been reduced merely to 'the lower part of Mesopotamia'. In July 1920 Wilson described only these as 'the theatres vital to us'. Constantinople, Batum, Palestine, Persia and the Plebiscite Areas were all classed as of only secondary importance. If this was Wilson's order of priorities, we find his general policy of imperial strategy in a letter written to General Haldane in December 1920. The only chance of saving the empire, he wrote, was to withdraw 'from anything which costs us money and is not absolutely vital to the safety of the Empire'.[75] Therefore, with these factors in mind – the general problems besetting Britain and her overseas interests, the scarcity of military resources, the CIGS's sensible order of imperial priorites, and his realistic overall strategy – we may examine the military defence of the British empire in the years immediately following the First World War.

Chapter 4

Searching for imperial manpower

The principal difficulty facing the Secretary for War and his military advisers in the post-war period was that of reconciling the maintenance of increased imperial responsibilities with the demands of Treasury, Parliament and public for economy. In November 1920 Sir Maurice Hankey summarised the dilemma in a letter to A. J. Balfour:

> The present times [he wrote] are not easy for our Military Authorities. They have a very young army on which heavy, indeed too heavy, demands are constantly being made. They are conducting difficult military operations in Persia and in Mesopotamia; they have to supply garrisons of the Rhine, Constantinople, Egypt and Palestine; and the Irish affair is an immense strain on them. All this has to be done with an army of pre-war size.[1]

But the post-war demands on the army were not of pre-war scale, especially in terms of internal security throughout the empire. Indeed, they far outstripped anything with which the pre-war army had had to cope, not so much in terms of depth – nothing in the post-war years matched the magnitude of the South African War – as in breadth. Never before in peacetime had the British army been stretched so thinly across so many world-wide commitments, or 'storm centres' as the CIGS put it. In the face of these apparently intractable problems it was natural, therefore, for the War Office to seek aid in shouldering its manifold obligations. Since it had proved politically impossible to continue conscription for any substantial period, it was hoped that the empire might provide alternative sources of manpower and it was to the traditional imperial reserve, India, that they turned first.

India's greatest contribution to the imperial war effort had been made in the Middle East and following the armistice London unquestioningly assumed that India would continue to play a major role in the supply of both men and material for the region. The Indian government, however, did not share London's happy confidence and soon began moving to reduce their commitments there. Early in December 1918 the Army Department in Delhi told the India Office in London that, 'in view of the extreme difficulty of our financial position and our own urgent needs', the 'drain both in money and material on the resources of India cannot any longer be met without the gravest embarrassment'.[2] But on the question of manpower the Indian administration was at first prepared to offer some assistance. Although noting that the Indian Army had before the war been 'maintained primarily for the defence of the Indian frontiers and for the preservation of internal security', Delhi saw no difficulty at this stage in continuing to maintain depots in India for 'those Indian formations retained overseas'.[3] Happy days indeed for the War Office! Chelmsford, nevertheless, was anxious to prevent any extension to India's existing overseas commitments. Telegraphing Montagu at the very end of 1918, he declared that intervention in south Russia would make India 'morally responsible for maintenance of law and order throughout Trans-Caspia and would thus impose on us financial and military commitments considerably in excess of those we now find such difficulty in meeting'.[4]

Throughout 1919 the Indian attitude hardened. The principal stumbling-block to any substantial Indian participation in imperial defence – as was to be the case throughout the inter-war years – was the question of who should foot the bill. It soon became abundantly clear to the policy-makers in London that the Indian government was not in any hurry to pay for what they believed were 'imperial' responsibilities. In September 1919 Austen Chamberlain complained to Lord Curzon that at a recent meeting about military expenditure in Mesopotamia, the India Office's contribution had been 'limited to a warm support of whatever the military desired, coupled with the condition that no part of the expense was to fall on Indian funds!'[5] Montagu naturally saw the matter rather differently. 'I cannot rid my mind of the obsession', he told Chelmsford, 'that a good many people here are trying to establish a routine of running up a heavy bill of costs over whatever item of Imperial policy happens to suit them at the moment, and sending in the account to India as an afterthought'.[6] From India the Viceroy moved to the offensive. 'One of our great difficulties', he wrote in December 1919, was maintaining some 180,000 Indian troops throughout the Middle East. Chelmsford did not mince words: 'I must point out also that India in this way is being exploited by the War Office because they find that they can maintain Indian troops abroad without those extremely objectionable questions in Parliament which would be asked if they were British and not Indian forces'.[7] He was, of course, quite right. Much of the pressure put on India to assume imperial defence obligations in the post-war period stemmed directly from the increasing calls in Britain to reduce military expenditure.

Delhi's unwillingness to meet what London saw as justifiable military responsibilities in the Middle East was also confirmed by unrest, both internal and on the frontiers. Until early 1922 domestic security posed serious problems in India. The largely bi-communal Congress agitation, the Muslim Khilafat movement and the Moplah rising in August 1921 all served to limit both troop reductions within India and any extensive overseas employment of the Indian Army. In February 1922 the Government of India told London that the reduction in the British garrison which they had hoped to make (a proposal viewed with alarm in London) would temporarily have to be postponed because of 'pernicious agitation'.[8] By August 1922, however, the crisis seemed to have passed and Lord Lytton, writing to Montagu (now no longer Secretary of State) from Government House, Dacca, remarked that 'matters have now improved to such an extent that it is difficult to believe how short a time ago the whole country was disorganised by political agitation'.[9] For the time being, therefore, the domestic military burden was eased in India.

In the immediate post-war years the problems of securing the Indian periphery were just as pressing for the government in Delhi. The Kuki-Chin rebellion in Burma, which had broken out in 1917, was not finally stamped out until the spring of 1919,[10] while across the sub-continent the situation on the North West Frontier was far from satisfactory. The 'Third Afghan War' from May to August 1919 came at a bad time for the Indian Army whose resources had been 'depleted by a long war' and when internal disturbances had necessitated 'the temporary redistribution of troops'.[11] In October 1919 the Indian government were reluctantly forced to consider active operations on the Waziristan frontier against hostile local tribesmen. Despite Delhi's wish to keep the action as limited as possible, they found it necessary to undertake 'extended operations' and the area was not pacified until the beginning of September 1920.[12] The frontier was still sufficiently unsettled in January 1921 for Rawlinson to use it as an argument against demands in the Viceroy's Council for the reduction of military expenditure. Not only was the news from Kabul bad, where Sir Henry Dobbs (Foreign Secretary to the Indian government) was attempting to secure a treaty with the Amir, but internal security, especially in the Punjab, was 'far from satisfactory', and, finally, the Bolsheviks in India were 'more active than ever'.[13]

It was against this background of internal and peripheral disorder that London seemed incessantly to call for Indian troops to serve in imperial garrisons. These demands reached a peak in the summer of 1920 when the Mesopotamian rebellion broke out. Although there were already some 50,000 Indian troops in Mesopotamia, following the outbreak of violence in August the War Office arranged for an additional nineteen battalions to be sent as reinforcements from India.[14] In view of the emergency these troops were not begrudged by Delhi. London, indeed, had been assured on 7 July that 'in the event of a Mesopotamian crisis arising, and the despatch of reinforcements becoming absolutely necessary, you may rely on us to do our utmost to render such military assistance as we are able from the resources at our disposal'.[15] The demands made by the imperial government in respect of the Mesopotamian crisis, however, were of such magnitude that they seem, for the first time, sharply to have brought home to the Indian government the full extent of the imperial military burden which London expected them to share. From this point on the Indian government began to protest strongly about the supply of overseas garrisons from the Indian Army and to argue forcefully that their military and financial responsibilities extended little further than the frontiers of India itself.

Early in September 1920 Montagu circulated to the Cabinet an important telegram from the Viceroy which observed that 'recent demands received by us for reinforcements for Mesopotamia on a large scale have forced us to consider the whole question regarding supply of overseas garrisons from Indian Army'. Although no direct requests for Indian troops had been received, it appeared in Delhi that the British government was assuming that India would provide a proportion of the permanent garrisons – numbering over 40,000 men – in both the new Middle Eastern mandates and various colonies. 'We invite attention', wrote Chelmsford, 'to the fact that we have not been consulted as to probable political effects in India of accepting an engagement of this magnitude'. He informed London that public opinion in India was generally opposed to the widespread employment of Indian troops overseas and went out of his way 'definitely to emphasise' that the Indian government 'could not accept an obligation to supply permanent overseas garrisons to mandatory territories', nor even provide any other 'large overseas forces'.[16] As had been the case before the war, although now with even greater resolution, the Indian government displayed a marked reluctance to slip easily in with London's plans for the imperial disposition of the Indian Army. This prudence was particularly understandable in the immediate post-war period, preoccupied as Delhi was with introducing political reforms. Domestic constraints mattered in India as well as the United Kingdom, and increasingly so. The Government of India Act (1919), which embodied the 'Montagu-Chelmsford' reforms, provided for the establishment of a legislative assembly which many in British India feared might well develop into a forum for nationalist views, criticisms of imperial policy, and, no doubt, 'extremely objectionable questions' about the employment of Indian troops overseas.

Chelmsford's telegram, however, was no more than a forceful restatement of India's pre-war position, arguing as it did that the Indian Army had no obligation to supply troops for permanent and extensive external garrisons. The principle, moreover, that India should not pay for such garrisons had, in Indian eyes, long been established. In January 1919 Montagu told Chelmsford: 'I have pointed out by law and practice Indian revenues are not called upon to maintain an army in excess of Indian requirements on a reasonable estimate of same, and as present advised I am strongly opposed to any alteration of this principle'.[17] The principle was applied frequently. In April 1920 Chelmsford noted that 'in order to meet the overseas requirements of His Majesty's Government', especially in the Army of the Black Sea, extra units might need to be maintained in India. 'We assume', he added, 'in that case the cost of additional units . . . will be charged to His Majesty's Government'.[18] In December 1920, the Indian government announced that it would cease contributing towards the cost of the South Persian Rifles (an irregular force with British officers) at the end of the year since 'we have consistently protested against payments being made from Indian revenues on account of South Persian Rifles, and have maintained that this expenditure cannot in fact legally be met from Indian revenues'.[19] When in February 1921 the question arose of sharing the costs of General Malleson's intelligence mission in east Persia, the Viceroy objected to India taking any share in the expenditure on the grounds that the Mission 'had a definite military objective of a purely Imperial character'.[20]

Despite the strong general views expressed by Chelmsford in the September telegram, the Indian government continued to accept that the Indian Army would supply, at imperial expense, small colonial garrisons for such places as Aden, Colombo, the Malay States, Hong Kong and North China. In order to meet these demands more conveniently the interesting proposal was made by India early in November 1920 that trans-frontier Pathans might be enlisted into a 'Colonial Garrison Regiment (India)'. These wild Afridi tribesmen from the North West Frontier were currently precluded from enlistment in the regular army 'owing to their unreliability as demonstrated by their conduct during the late war'.[21] In March 1915, a number of Afridi Pathans from the 5th Battalion, 13th Frontier Force Rifles, deserted to the German lines on the western front. The remaining Afridis in the battalion had been immediately drafted to East Africa and a 'faint question mark' hung over them for the rest of the war.[22] In 1920, however, Chelmsford told Montagu that 'as they cannot subsist in their own territories, it is essential to find employment for them'. The proposed regiment was to include five overseas battalions and a combined depot in India, the battalions comprising half Pathans and half Hindus, 'the former increasing gradually at the expense of the latter'. Among the advantages of this scheme would be the consequent reduction of the Indian Army's liability for overseas duties, a restriction in training costs through the maintenance of only one depot and the fact that the Pathans themselves would be kept busy and quiet.[23] Presumably also the creation of a specialised unit for supplying colonial garrisons would make it easier to calculate the charges liable to the imperial account.

But the scheme came to nothing. Not surprisingly the Foreign Office regarded the proposals 'with misgivings' and asked for 'assurances from competant military authorities' that the troops would be sufficiently reliable for the protection of the British communities in China. The Army Council refused to agree 'to try dangerous experiments in overseas defended ports', but were prepared to accept battalions with only one company of Pathans as a start. The Colonial Office, who were the most alarmed of all, refused to countenance the proposal 'even on the restricted scale' suggested by the Army Council, and they earnestly hoped that none but 'thoroughly loyal Indian troops' would be selected for garrison duty in the Far Eastern colonies.[24]

A more reasonable scheme was suggested in January 1921 for the creation of a distinct force for service in the Middle East to consist of eight thousand Indian soldiers organised in ten battalions of eight hundred each. These battalions would be raised and initially grouped in India, but future recruits would be trained in Mesopotamia – a plan which the Indian authorities pronounced to be 'feasible'.[25] But this proposal was also abandoned, for when the Colonial Office, having adopted an 'air defence' scheme for Mesopotamia, stated their 'complete requirements of Indian troops and personnel . . . . from October 1st 1922', they amounted to only two infantry battalions and one pack battery of artillery. As a reward for Indian persistence, however, the Colonial Office agreed, without question, to bear the full cost of both these units themselves and also their training battalions in India.[26]

By mid-1921 the Indian government had laid down definite terms for the use of the Indian Army outside India and, having become acutely sensitive to local political opinion, it based those terms on a resolution passed by the new Legislative Assembly in March 1921. The Assembly, after a debate on the employment of Indian troops beyond the frontier, declared

That the Army in India should not, as a rule, be employed for service outside the external frontiers of India except for purely defensive purposes, or with the previous consent of the Governor-General in Council in very grave emergencies, provided that this resolution does not preclude the employment on garrison duties overseas of Indian troops at the expense of His Majesty's Government and with the consent of the Government of India.[27]

The Viceroy was agreeably surprised by the moderate tone of this resolution and deduced from the Assembly debate (in contrast to his views of the previous September) that 'there is strong feeling in country in favour of employment of Indian troops on garrison duty over-sea with Government of India's permission', but subject always to the condition 'that no additional expense is caused thereby to Indian revenues'. He also told Montagu that he had 'ample evidence that opinion amongst Indian ranks of Indian Army is strongly in favour of their being given opportunities of serving overseas'. Delhi therefore proposed that, apart from the troops required for the mandated territories in the Middle East, India would provide a total of eight battalions for the Far Eastern garrisons, Colombo, Aden and the Persian Gulf.[28] London seemed incapable of making a quick decision on these firm Indian proposals and in June 1921, having further considered the question in the Viceroy's Council, the Indian government stated their position at its plainest. They announced that India was 'ready to accept as a permanent liability the obligation, which we undertook before the war' to provide units for garrison duties in China, the Malay States, Colombo and Aden. They were also prepared to supply troops for the Middle Eastern mandates, but 'on the clear understanding that all charges connected with the extra active battalions' would be borne by the British government. 'Public opinion in India', they asserted, 'will not tolerate any longer a system under which our troops are retained or sent back to suit the fluctuating requirements of His Majesty's Government'.[29] Rawlinson, who had pressed strongly for the continued large-scale supply of overseas garrisons, told Wilson that this was 'the best we can do in this direction', especially since there had been 'a good deal of opposition in council from the three black Mohammedan members . . . partly because they did not approve of their co-religionists being ordered abroad in order to police mandated areas and possibly fight against people of their own religion'.[30]

The irony of this Indian decision to supply garrisons on a permanent basis for the Middle Eastern mandates (however conditionally) was that it came too late. The imperial government's greatest manpower crisis had been in the late summer of 1920 when such was the shortage that the War Office, if not the Cabinet, were prepared even to pay for troops, from whatever imperial source.[31] The Indian government, on the other hand, were so alarmed by the extent of their liabilities as revealed by the Mesopotamian rebellion that they began to back pedal furiously on the whole question of supplying overseas garrisons from the Indian Army. In the spring of 1921, with calmer counsels prevailing in Delhi (prompted by the unanticipated moderation of the Legislative Assembly), they agreed to take up at least some imperial military responsibilities, but added the one condition that the home government was now not so readily prepared to meet – the condition that for imperial defence the imperial exchequer should pay. The British government had been as alarmed as the Indian by events in Mesopotamia and the crisis acted as a powerful catalyst towards retrenchment. British troops were expensive and London henceforth sought with greater vigour to find suitable and cheaper substitutes. Early in 1922 Rawlinson told Wilson that he had heard from 'Squibbie' (Sir Walter) Congreve (GOCinC Egyptian Command 1921–3) that the Colonial Office apparently wished to garrison Palestine and

Mesopotamia with Indian troops instead of British 'because they are less expensive'. Everybody, observed Rawlinson dryly, 'is trying to get rid of British troops and stuff them on to somebody else, because they cannot afford to pay for them'. How right he was. 'The fact of the matter is', he continued, 'that the cost of the British soldier has gone up so inordinately since the war that no country can afford to maintain him. As a result, it is difficult to see how we can keep this Empire together'.[32] The supply of *Indian* troops, moreover, was becoming both less guaranteed and also more expensive because of the Indian government's insistence on strict imperial book-keeping. But before imperial manpower resources might be said to be completely exhausted the War Office was assiduously to explore further avenues of imperial military potential. Would it be possible, for example, for Britain to switch some of the defence load to the dominions?

Although at the end of the war the dominions had refused to participate in the armies of occupation, the War Office continued to bear them in mind as a possible source of troops. They were spurred into direct action by the manpower crisis of 1920. On 9 September – shortly after the Cabinet had learned of India's doubts regarding the long-term supply of troops – the General Staff forwarded a memorandum on 'reinforcements for Mesopotamia'. In it they described how India was currently providing large reinforcements, but only at 'considerable risks to herself'. There were, continued the paper, no available troops in the British army. In these circumstances, therefore, it had become necessary 'to consider other possible sources from which white troops could be obtained, and the suggestion has been made that the Dominions of Canada, Australia and New Zealand could afford some measure of military assistance during the present period of strain'. South Africa was not included. The assistance which the General Staff foresaw the dominions providing could either be in the form of sending troops directly to Mesopotamia or in the indirect form 'of relieving British troops in India or elsewhere so as to free the latter for service in Mesopotamia'. Canada, for example, might be asked to relieve the British battalion in the West Indies, and New Zealand to relieve that at Singapore.[33] Clearly, the General Staff had not only the temporary needs of Mesopotamia in mind when they put forward this memorandum. Some permanent sharing of the burdens of imperial defence might reasonably be expected to arise from the scheme if it were accepted by the dominions. The real problem, moreover, was not one of expense but of manpower as the Staff were at pains to point out that all expenses should be met by the British government unless the dominion in question particularly wished to make a contribution.

On 15 September when the Cabinet discussed the War Office paper they were also reminded of the Viceroy's telegram 'calling attention to the difficulties and danger anticipated from the continued employment of

Indian troops outside India'. The CIGS declared that the War Office would be glad to receive 'reinforcements of a brigade or even of a battalion'. There was some criticism by ministers that the offer to maintain dominion troops at imperial expense was 'a departure from the general principle adopted during the war that the Dominions should pay for such co-operation as they could give'. The Cabinet decided, however, that the Colonial Secretary should telegraph the Governors-General of the dominions concerned to ascertain how the proposal would be received, 'but that in doing so he should make it clear that the Cabinet was not committed to the proposal'.[34] By 26 September a reply had been received from each dominion.[35] New Zealand, typically, was the only one of the three which offered assistance, the Premier considering 'that without difficulty volunteers sufficient for a battalion would be forthcoming'. On 30 September the Cabinet agreed 'that it would be undesirable to accept the New Zealand offer if the other Dominions took a different line'. Next day the Colonial Secretary telegraphed New Zealand thanking them for their offer but adding, not without some degree of truth, that 'in last ten days situation has so much improved that we may now not have to avail ourselves of the proffered assistance'.[36] Two years later a better known call for dominion assistance was made at the height of the Chanak crisis. Then the pattern was to be the same as it had been in September 1920.[37]

The General Staff, evincing a marked propensity to flog dead horses, refused entirely to be discouraged by the disappointing reaction of the dominions to their scheme for reinforcing Mesopotamia. On 23 February 1921, with an imperial conference pending, they prepared a paper suggesting military subjects 'for inclusion in the agenda for the Imperial Cabinet'. In it the old ground of co-ordinating military thought throughout the empire and standardising establishments and equipment was covered, but when the Staff went on to consider 'the more immediate military problems with which we are faced' the chimera of active military co-operation was chased once more. It was noted 'that the enforcement of the terms of the Peace Treaty is being carried out entirely by Imperial and Indian troops', that the military commitments of the empire were larger than ever before, and, that in the case of a serious emergency 'the strain thrown on the forces at the disposal of the Imperial Government might prove beyond their strength'. This being so, 'if the Dominions (and India) were prepared to bear even a small portion of the load, the burden would be distributed, and thereby lightened'. The Staff did not envisage begging any immediate assistance from the dominions but, rather, suggested the creation of some permanent machinery to render such assistance more readily available. One clear advantage of this arrangement would be 'the maintenance of the present strong feelings of comradeship throughout the Imperial and Dominion Forces, which can best be kept alive by fighting alongside each other in wars however small'.[38] Thus the General Staff envisaged a happy imperial future of constant military co-operation and a dominion partnership with Great Britain in regular active service throughout the empire.

In a shorter paper prepared in June 1921, the War Office summarised the possible emergencies which might beset the empire in the near future. These included unrest in Egypt, disturbances in Palestine, widespread trouble in Mesopotamia, a general rebellion in India and 'anti-foreign risings in China'. Since in the present circumstances Great Britain would be 'hard put to it' to deal with these emergencies, the conference were particularly urged to consider the possibility of dominion participation in imperial defence 'so that, should in the future, any Dominion wish to take military action in conjunction with other forces of the Empire, the necessary machinery will not be found wanting'.[39] This rather begged the question whether or not the dominions actually desired to participate in any joint military adventures. In the event they did not and formal military co-operation for most of the inter-war years involved little more than the occasional secondment of dominion officers to British establishments.[40]

Another possible source of manpower lay in the colonial empire. The war of 1914–18 revealed to British defence planners effectively for the first time the potential value of African possessions as a reservoir of military manpower. British observers were particularly impressed both by the extensive recruitment of native troops by the French in north and west Africa and the long drawn out resistance of von Lettow-Vorbeck's native army in German East Africa. A specific suggestion to use African instead of Indian troops in an imperial garrison was first made in April 1919, when it was proposed that the King's African Rifles might be employed in Mesopotamia.[41] But it was not until January 1920 that Churchill initiated a detailed War Office investigation of African military potential. 'I am strongly in favour', he wrote to Sir Henry Wilson, 'of our beginning to employ African troops from West and East Africa, as well as from the Soudan [*sic*], for Imperial purposes outside the African continent'. Among the advantages of using African soldiers was 'safety in variety' and, added Churchill, 'having regard to the possibility of solidarity between the Hindoos and Mohamedans of India, we ought carefully to consider in what way a new element may be introduced into our garrisons of the Middle East'.[42]

The War Office opened the batting on 14 January by asking the Colonial Office for their agreement to the temporary exchange of one battalion of the King's African Rifles with the Yemen Infantry battalion based at Aden. 'Much valuable knowledge', they argued, could be gained 'as to the possibility of using African troops in substitution for a proportion of Indian troops in other theatres such as Palestine and

Mesopotamia'. This would be especially useful 'in view of the possible future shortage in Indian troops for overseas garrisons which may follow the measure of self-government now being granted in India'. On 4 February the War Office followed up this first approach with a 'note on the possibility of employing African native troops overseas' which they circulated to both the Colonial and Foreign Offices. Three suitable sources of manpower were considered: the King's African Rifles in east Africa, the West African Frontier Force and 'the Soudanese'.[43]

Immediate reactions were not favourable. Early in February Sir Herbert Read (assistant Under-Secretary to the Colonial Office) replied with a number of objections. As the Army Council were aware, he wrote, 'the King's African Rifles are raised, administered and maintained by the Protectorate Governments in Eastern Africa as their garrisons, or rather, police forces, at the strength required for this purpose'. This, therefore, precluded 'the possibility of their being employed elsewhere, save as an exceptional measure in time of grave emergency'. An Arab battalion, he added, 'would not be a satisfactory substitute for a King's African Rifles battalion in East Africa, and the suggestion that a battalion of Yemen Infantry should be sent there is considered impracticable'.[44] The Foreign Office, who were responsible for Sudanese affairs, told the War Office that the Sudanese troops in question formed part of the Egyptian army, paid for by the Egyptian government and under the orders of the Egyptian War Office. Thus their use for imperial purposes 'could only take place with the consent of the Egyptian Government, and this consideration would appear in itself sufficient to preclude the idea of employing them for garrison duty overseas'. They promised, however, to ask the Governor-General of the Sudan if there was any possibility of recruiting Sudanese directly for an imperial force.[45] But Sir Lee Stack thought that the suggestion to recruit Sudanese was completely unviable. 'Very considerable difficulty', he wrote, 'is being experienced at the present time in obtaining sufficient men to maintain the existing establishment of Sudanese units'. 'This settles the matter', was the Foreign Office view.[46]

In the case of east African troops, however, the War Office were not so easily put off. Reflecting on Read's discouraging reply to the original proposal, Colonel Kirke (deputy Director of Military Operations) noted that 'the difficulties now raised by the Colonial Office as regards African troops are not very different from those which were originally met when sending Indian troops overseas'. The Colonial Office attitude, he suggested, was 'since it never has been done in the past, therefore it cannot be done in the future' – undeniably a persuasive argument and one which the War Office themselves employed from time to time – but, 'so far', he wrote on 30 March, 'they have not produced any arguments which tend to show that the scheme is unworkable'.[47]

A second War Office memorandum was sent to the Colonial Office early in April 1920, along with a plea for the reconsideration of the scheme. This paper covered much the same ground as that of 4 February. It was mooted, moreover, that the employment of selected African units in the Middle East might be 'the first step towards a truly Imperial East African Force to which the present Colonial Forces are bound to come in the end by a process of evolution similar to that which has obtained in India during the last century'. The War Office also proposed to send a General Staff officer 'with experience of the African fighting races' to east Africa to discuss the question with the local Governors and senior officers of the King's African Rifles.[48] Taking advantage of the happy chance that the Governors of both Uganda and East Africa (Kenya) were in England, the Colonial Office responded to this fresh approach by arranging an inter-departmental conference on 14 April. At the meeting Sir Herbert Read re-stated the Colonial Office objections. The African, he said, would not serve overseas 'unless he had his woman with him', Africans 'could not be recruited to serve overseas since they strongly object to serve in another part of Africa', 'the labour situation was already very difficult, and ... enlistments would make matters worse'. Colonel Kirke felt afterwards that the Colonial Office were 'very anxious that no new ideas should be introduced into the country. They say that the African native is at present ignorant, and therefore very amenable, and they fear that if he served in more enlightened countries he may be a source of danger when he returns'. Both colonial Governors had taken a similar line, which Kirke felt was 'really the basis of the Colonial Office opposition'.[49]

By now the Colonial Office might not unreasonably have imagined that the War Office would drop their proposal to investigate east African military potential, but they failed to appreciate the deep-rooted alarm with which the General Staff viewed current political developments in India. 'There is no doubt that we shall have to face increasing opposition to the use of Indian troops outside India', warned the DMO, 'and it is imperative that we should prepare to organise substitutes'. He therefore suggested that Churchill should intervene personally and ask Lord Milner, the Colonial Secretary, to permit someone to investigate the matter on the spot.[50] Churchill, who has been behind the scheme from the beginning, wrote to Milner who overrode the specific objections of his departmental advisors and agreed to let a staff officer go out to east Africa. After some further delaying tactics by the Colonial Office, the War Office nominated Colonel H. F. L. Grant of the General Staff, and arrangements were made for him to visit Kenya, Uganda, Tanganyika and Nyasaland between March and June 1921.[51]

The inclusion of Tanganyika in Grant's itinerary is noteworthy. The fighting qualities of African troops employed by the Germans in the territory during the war had particularly impressed many British officers.

When the draft terms of the new League of Nations' mandates were published late in 1920, the General Staff objected to the article prohibiting the 'military training of the natives for other than police purposes and the defence of territory' in so-called 'B-class' mandates such as the former German colony. In a closely-argued Cabinet memorandum, which nevertheless begged a whole host of questions, they noted that the acceptance of League mandates had greatly increased British responsibilities in the 'East' and had tended 'to make our military liabilities of an indefinite and far-reaching nature'. It was, moreover, 'only just that some distribution of the military burden should be contemplated', so as to avoid exceptional strain falling on the United Kingdom or India. Since the Government of India had indicated an unwillingness 'to provide troops for service outside India, on the same scale as hitherto', there was now a need to find additional native troops from other parts of the empire. The most feasible source was Africa where Britain now controlled 'a comparatively large native population containing a considerable proportion of first-class fighting material . . . greatly superior to any at our disposal elsewhere in the East'. It is, they asserted, 'therefore to Africa that we must look in the first place for any considerable relief of that portion of the military burden imposed by acceptance of the various Eastern mandates, which India may not be able to bear'. The French, they added, had 'refused to be bound in their mandates by conditions limiting the external use of troops raised in mandatory territories'. If British military authorities were not allowed to enlist men in Tanganyika, this would

cripple at the outset any serious endeavour to utilise the native man-power resources of Eastern Africa either for the defence of any of our possessions in the African Continent, or for the defence of any mandatory area elsewhere, or for relieving the general military burden of the United Kingdom or India.[52]

But it was all to no avail. When the Cabinet came to discuss the question in April 1921, they decided not to challenge the League's limiting provision on the employment of native troops.[53]

Early in 1921 the possibility of recruiting an imperial force in Africa was raised once more in the War Office. One of Churchill's last acts as Secretary for War was to appoint a committee to examine the whole question of garrisoning Mesopotamia. He set it the task of examining the possibilities both of establishing a white 'Imperial Mesopotamian Police' and also of framing a scheme whereby native troops might be enlisted 'for special permanent service in Mesopotamia'. Although he wished the committee to look first at the provision of Indian native soldiers, Churchill thought it 'essential' for them to examine as an alternative the possibility of using African troops, instead of or as well as Indian. 'Both West African and East African sources must be explored', he instructed, 'Look what the French are doing with their African troops'.[54]

On considering the recruitment of Indian troops, the committee rejected an idea to organise them into a military police force, arguing, *inter alia*, that if the force were permanently to be stationed in Mesopotamia, it would probably decline rapidly 'owing to the proclivities of the Indian for money-lending and for inter-marrying with the local women'. The India Office, moreover, having consulted Delhi, declared that the only way to create a special 'Colonial Force' for service 'wherever native troops are required outside India' would be 'by recruiting in India *ab initio*', a solution which the committee thought would be both slow and expensive. Turning to Africa, the committee took evidence from the Chief of the Air Staff, Sir Hugh Trenchard, who had served in the West African Frontier Force before the war. Trenchard assured them that there would be no difficulty in raising eight battalions from the fighting tribes of west Africa, 'especially from the Yorubas'. Colonel Meinertzhagen, the Chief Political Officer in Palestine and who had had experience with the King's African Rifles, similarly assured the committee that 8,000 men could easily be raised in east Africa. From the Colonial Office, however, Sir Herbert Read again rehearsed his department's adamantine opposition to the raising of African troops for imperial service. The climate of Mesopotamia would not suit, such a scheme would disrupt local labour markets, when the men returned they might refuse to work for their chiefs under the patriarchal system and the Arabs would certainly resent a garrison of African troops. The majority of the committee, nevertheless, were inclined to favour the recruitment of Africans and were strongly of the opinion that they would be preferable to Indians, 'as they have no caste system, are easily disciplined, and have been remote from Bolshevik propaganda'.[55] They noted, however, that the potential of east Africa would be clearer after Colonel Grant had completed his forthcoming enquiry into 'local conditions'. In an appendix to the report Colonel Kirke, for whom Sir Herbert Read had become something of a *bête noire*, found some comfort in the fact that with the imminent reorganisation of departments, the Colonial Office would become responsible for the security of Mesopotamia. 'If the Colonial Office find themselves faced with the necessity of providing troops for Mesopotamia', he remarked smugly, 'they will modify their attitude of continued obstruction which has hitherto hampered our efforts to explore this question'.[56]

As it happened Kirke was not to have the satisfaction of seeing his counterparts in the Colonial Office climb down, for when Winston Churchill himself as Colonial Secretary (from February 1921) became responsible for military expenditure in Mesopotamia, it was not Africa but the air force to which he turned. The factor which carried most weight with him was that of finance. Despite their enthusiasm for raising troops in Africa, the War Office Mesopotamian committee had come firmly to the conclusion that 'the cost of an African battalion in Mesopotamia would be considerably more than that of an Indian battalion'.[57] Since one of Churchill's principal policy objectives with the new Middle Eastern department in the Colonial Office was to save the British government 'millions',[58] it was understandable that he eventually chose the cheaper and more immediately available alternative of an 'air defence' scheme.

In the meantime Colonel Grant proceeded on his mission to east Africa. Ironically his report came out strongly in favour of employing African troops overseas. On 9 June he told the War Office that there were no serious local objections and that even the Governor of Kenya had changed his mind and now supported the scheme.[59] In his final report he estimated that within five years up to 9,000 men could be recruited and available for service overseas.[60] But by this time the issue was a dead letter and the War Office climbed down with as good a grace as possible. Forwarding Grant's report to the Colonial Office, Sir Herbert Creedy (permanent secretary to the War Office) noted that since the enquiry into African military potential had been set in motion 'the situation had somewhat altered, in that considerable reductions of our overseas garrisons in the East have been found possible while India has consented still to furnish a certain number of troops for oversea service'. The War Office furthermore had been relieved of direct responsibility for much of the Middle East. In these circumstances, therefore, 'the Army Council feel that they are not themselves in an immediate position to proceed further with plans for the use of African troops'. Creedy concluded, however, by asserting that Churchill's original views were 'based on conditions which still exist, although possibly for the moment not in such acute form; and . . . the time may come when the necessity for a strong force of African troops will be clearly demonstrated'.[61] Twenty-five years later, indeed, British defence planners once again investigated African military potential. Faced with the unequivocal loss of the Indian Army and burdened with extensive post-war military responsibilities, there was a 'search for manpower' during the aftermath of the Second World War, in many ways reflecting that which followed the First. Yet although there was some limited employment of East African troops in the Far East in the early 1950s, the briefly-revived romantic notion of an 'Imperial African Army' was soon, and finally, laid to rest.[62]

The debate over how to meet the problems of post-war imperial defence in part echoed some of the tactical arguments which had existed during the First World War itself. Like the commanders on the western front, the post-war General Staff at times seemed simply to respond to military difficulties by calling for more cannon fodder. But like those who during the war had supported the use of tanks, many post-war decision-makers were increasingly attracted to the idea that the sharp cutting edge of technology might satisfactorily cut the Gordian Knot of imperial defence needs. To a great extent, although not generally in the War Office, the aeroplane was seen as a panacea for the army's problems of imperial security. Needless to say the Air Staff, acutely conscious of just how vulnerable in a period of post-war retrenchment their fledgling force was *vis-à-vis* the army and the navy, were the most enthusiastic in promoting air force capabilities. In December 1918 Sir Frederick Sykes (Chief of the Air Staff 1918–19) forwarded a memorandum on 'the air power requirements of the Empire' to the Secretary for War. 'Highly specialised forces', wrote Sykes, 'are now essential components of all fighting efficiency', and he set out a number of recommendations for the organisation of the post-war air force, including the creation of a 'striking force' to be utilised, when possible, 'for Imperial police work'. 'In air power', he continued, 'we possess a rapid and economical instrument by which to ensure peace and good government in our outer Empire, and more particularly upon its Asian and African frontiers'. He regarded the Middle East as an especially fruitful field of aerial operations. The group of countries comprising Egypt, the Sudan, Palestine and Mesopotamia, he declared, was 'one of very great political, strategic and commercial importance to the Empire'. It included 'many strategic points d'appui' and contained 'great reservoirs of oil fuel, upon which commodity', he noted prophetically, 'both our air power and sea power will depend'. Sykes concluded by arguing that the Middle East offered 'considerable scope for Air Force police work'.[63]

Aerial police work was favoured in other quarters as well. In the spring of 1918, faced with an acute shortage of troops and widespread unrest in Ireland, Lord French, the Viceroy designate, had proposed to establish a number of strongly-entrenched 'Air Camps', and with 55 aeroplanes police the entire country. It would, he thought, 'put the fear of God into these playful young Sinn Feiners'.[64] Although this scheme came to nothing, the aeroplane was not entirely forgotten as a possible weapon against the Irish extremists. In March 1921 the Cabinet home affairs committee recommended that General Macready should be given discretion to use 'armed aeroplanes for operations in Ireland', but the Cabinet, fearing the likelihood of an 'untoward incident', imposed such strict conditions on their employment that they were only really to be useful for transporting senior officers and running an airmail service. 'They gave Macready permission to do a little aeroplane bombing', noted Wilson in his diary. 'I don't think he ought to do more than just show the natives that it can be done, at present they don't care a button for aeroplanes because they know they are not allowed to shoot or bomb'.[65] In farther flung parts of the empire, however, the operational freedom of the air force was not so carefully circumscribed. Perhaps also the natives were more impressionable than the Irish. In March 1919 'aeroplanes performed very useful service' in quelling civil unrest in Egypt.[66] During the Afghan War of 1919 the Indian General Staff declared air raids to have been 'most effective' and the Commander-in-Chief of the Indian Army reported that the bombing of Kabul had been an important factor 'in producing a desire for peace at the headquarters of the Afghan Government'.[67] In 1920 it was alleged that the successful use of air power had enabled the authorities in British Somaliland to put down unrest inspired by the 'mad Mullah' in only twenty-three days.[68]

After assuming ministerial responsibility for air as well as war in January 1919, Winston Churchill seems quickly to have been persuaded that the use of the RAF for imperial policing might both promote strategic efficiency and provide much needed relief on his departmental estimates. On 31 January, in reply to a plea for economy from the Chancellor of the Exchequer, he bluntly asserted that he was going to consider the broad problem of military spending in India 'so as to make the air play its true part in relieving the expensive men we shall have in the future to keep across the seas'.[69] At the beginning of May he wrote to Lloyd George envisaging an even grander role for the air force. It could, he argued, take on a part of 'the work hitherto done by the Army in the garrisoning of our Eastern possessions. It must also be made to take the place of naval expenditure on cruisers built or maintained in commission and on the arrangements for watching and patrolling the coasts'.[70]

But Churchill's lavish, if somewhat vague, plans for the service, although vigorously encouraged by his new Chief of the Air Staff, Sir Hugh Trenchard (appointed in February 1919), were just as strongly resisted by both the army and the navy. Specific proposals for 'air defence' served only to stimulate professional jealousies and emphasise departmental inertia. In April 1919 the acting civil commissioner in Baghdad, Lieutenant-Colonel A. T. Wilson, circulated a paper which argued that air power might effectively be applied in Mesopotamia. If just three squadrons were stationed in the country, he suggested, 'it should be possible to reduce the existing garrison materially'.[71] The initial War Office reaction was not entirely favourable. Although accepting that aeroplanes might be useful for 'policing', one staff officer noted that the army of occupation in Mesopotamia should be above all a 'field army'. Mesopotamia, 'no matter what its ultimate size may be, will have open frontiers, vulnerable to attack', although he did not say from whom. Thus it was necessary to retain a large garrison of conventional land forces. 'However valuable the air service may be now and in the future', he announced with striking military confidence, 'this arm will not progress beyond the position of being an auxiliary (though a very necessary one) to an army in the field'.[72] The DMO for his part agreed 'that Aircraft may eventually enable us to reduce a portion of our military force which is required for Internal Defence, but not to any great extent'. Yet he cleverly argued that 'considerable military force' would be required to secure the airfields, petrol dumps and repair facilities without which aeroplanes were 'helpless'.[73] Churchill was not impressed by these arguments and criticised the DMO for not taking into account recent advances in the size, power and range of aircraft which provided increasing possibilities of supplying air bases directly from the air. 'It is', he minuted reprovingly, 'just because these possibilities are not studied in the light of the present and future developments that a limited view is taken'.[74]

The idea of employing air power to police Mesopotamia remained a lively topic of debate. In March 1920 Churchill circulated a paper prepared by the Air Staff containing 'a preliminary scheme for the military control of Mesopotamia by the Royal Air Force' which seemed to him 'to be the only way of saving the province from being hopelessly crushed by military expenditure'. Churchill's statesmanlike concern for *Mesopotamian* finances was a particularly deft touch since it was the War Office which was currently footing the bill. He rejected the idea of 'marching a large army into Mesopotamia' and holding it 'with posts and garrisons . . . We must adopt that sort of quasi-military control which we have used with so much success in the Sudan and Nigeria'.[75] In May Churchill gave Trenchard a further opportunity to expound the air defence scheme in a collection of memoranda by both the War Office and the Air Ministry on the general position in Mesopotamia. The air force, wrote Trenchard, could not only maintain internal order but could also promote 'the gradual pacification of areas now in a chronic stage of unrest'. All that would be left for the army to do would be 'the safeguarding of aerial bases against likely local concentrations'.[76] A. T. Wilson in Baghdad, although he had lost some of his earlier enthusiasm for air power, thought that the plan, 'stripped of the nonsense which has been written about it in the Air Ministry', had 'some good points'.[77] Others were not so sure. Lord Curzon told the inter-departmental conference on Middle Eastern affairs in April 1920 that he was 'rather nervous' about the scheme. 'An aviator must necessarily be a young man', he said, 'and it did not follow that he would necessarily be the best person to conciliate tribesmen'.[78] The War Office were characteristically cool. The committee on Mesopotamia, which Churchill appointed in January 1921, so summarily dismissed the proposal to police the country with aeroplanes supported by a small mobile force of armoured cars that the Air Ministry member refused to sign the final report. 'In my opinion', he wrote bitterly, 'the Committee have been influenced by the preconceived ideas of the General Staff which are adverse to the substitution of regular by irregular forces'.[79]

The Mesopotamian rebellion of 1920, however, so quickened the government's desire for economy that Churchill was able at last to press forward successfully with the air defence plan. His move to the Colonial Office in February 1921, moreover, released him from the clutches of the military sceptics. In April 1921 the Middle East conference at Cairo approved the RAF defence scheme in principle and in August the Cabinet added their approval. In its final form the scheme provided for an air force garrison of eight squadrons (in 1922), supported by armoured car companies and locally-raised Arab levies.[80]

Sir Henry Wilson had little confidence in this policy of 'Hot Air, Aeroplanes & Arabs', and he greeted the replacement of the army by the air force as the chief 'peacekeeping' force in Mesopotamia with the greatest ill grace. 'Nor can Winston call on me any longer to pull him out of a mess', he wrote rancorously to Rawlinson in India, 'nor can he call on you, and so having got into a mess, whenever that day comes, he can only hop into an aeroplane and fly away, shouting Ta-ta to any poor bloody native who is stupid enough to back us'.[81] Wilson's mordant comment was typical of the attitude with which the army regarded the RAF's assumption of responsibility for Mesopotamia. Far from being grateful for this relief in their world-wide military burden, the General Staff both resented being superseded in a traditional imperial function and feared that the air force might thus gain a larger slice of the shrinking service estimates. 'I am afraid the War Office are taking it badly', wrote Trenchard's secretary with commendable understatement after the Cabinet decision of August 1921. 'They are very bitter about it and will do everything in their power to render impossible any sort of co-operation with them. It seems a great pity, but I suppose we are up against vested interests and shall have to fight accordingly'.[82]

While the RAF were encroaching on army vested interests, the War Office in turn were threatening those of the navy. Confronted with the increasing difficulty of finding enough troops to garrison Ireland the General Staff looked covetously towards the Royal Marines as a useful source of available manpower. The Sinn Fein policy of attacking and destroying coast guard stations, which began in the spring of 1920,[83] was sufficient excuse for the army to ask the navy for assistance. On 26 May Sir Henry Wilson pressed Lord Beatty to supply one thousand marines to defend the 140 threatened coast guard stations. Beatty said he would do what he could to help, but he did not think he had any men to spare.[84] Evidently his staff at the Admiralty thought differently, and they sharply put a stop to Beatty's unreasonably co-operative attitude. Next day the First Sea Lord circulated a Cabinet memorandum noting that the army were primarily responsible for any assistance to the civil power. It was 'a considerable departure, therefore, from policy' for the navy to provide any forces 'for dealing with a situation requiring armed intervention on shore', even to protect naval installations. 'The Admiralty', he declared, 'are of the opinion that the Navy should not be called upon to do so unless it is absolutely unavoidable'.[85]

Over and above any issue of principle the navy, not unnaturally, were loath to become directly involved in the Irish imbroglio, but on 28 May at a conference of ministers in Downing Street the Admiralty were obliged to agree to send a force of eight hundred marines to Ireland.[86] This was the thin end of the wedge, for by June the Chief Secretary was asking if marines could be made available for general service in Belfast. Walter Long, the First Lord, was appalled. 'The Marines', he complained to Lloyd George, 'were sent over on the clear understanding that they should be used for protecting such posts of Coast Guard Stations etc., and it would be quite contrary to all precedent to use them as a military force in aid of the Civil power'.[87] Long had his way but a year later when the government were reinforcing Ireland with all available troops in anticipation of a major military effort over the summer of 1921, the Cabinet decided 'that the Admiralty should be asked to make available, if possible, one or more Battalions of Marines to be placed at the disposal of the War Office for use in Ireland'. Two marine battalions were organised and trained for this purpose, but, following the truce of July 1921, they were never utilised.[88]

One further method by which it was sought to relieve the army of some of its responsibilities was the reversion to, and in some cases an extension of, the nineteenth-century policy of creating special quasi-military forces and gendarmeries to police the empire. In July 1920, when the formation of a British gendarmerie in Palestine was under discussion, Sir Herbert Creedy summarised for the Foreign Office the general principles underlying such forces:

I am to point out that His Majesty's Government has had considerable experience with . . . local forces on the Frontier of India, Burma, etc., and that nomenclature varies, such as Khyber Rifles, Waziristan Militia, Chitral Scouts, Mekram Levy Corps, Burma Military Police, but they all carry out the same duties irrespective of whether they are classed as Gendarmerie, Levies, or Military Police, and their advantages are as follows:-

(a) They carry out small operations and so avoid the necessity of moving Regular troops, consequently the latter can be kept concentrated in conditions conducive to health and training.

(b) Being localised they are usually cheaper as they do not require the same standard of comfort as Regular troops.

Invariably these local forces are placed under the control of the Civil Authorities, otherwise the above advantages would be largely decreased, but, in the event of any combined operations they are usually placed at the disposal of, and under the orders of, the Military Commander.[89]

An additional advantage, which Creedy inexplicably failed to mention, was that such forces were generally no burden at all on the War Office budget. The army, moreover, was always rather reluctant to take on the role of policemen. Sir Nevil Macready, who had more experience than most in this field,[90] took the proper constitutional view 'that the soldier stands by to assist civil authority (unless and until Martial Law is proclaimed) but is not a substitute for it'.[91] Such was the overextension of Britain's military commitments (and the consequent shortage of troops) following the war, that early in 1920 it was proposed to bolster up the police in Great Britain itself with a special civil volunteer force. In January a scheme prepared in the Home Office to create a temporary force of at least 10,000 men was put to the Cabinet. Since the army was 'so reduced that it cannot give the support which it has given in every big strike since 1911', this force would be necessary until troop numbers had been made up by voluntary enlistment.[92] Although the government decided that circumstances were not sufficiently grave to adopt this proposal,[93] at the height of the industrial crisis in the following spring they decided to enlist a special 'Defence Force', subject to the Army Act, 'to protect loyal citizens who are volunteering to carry on essential services'. Nearly 30,000 men joined up. 'It was recognised', recorded the Cabinet minutes, 'that the raising of additional troops was the only method by which a material increase in the forces available could be effected'.[94]

That the Cabinet were driven to the extreme of recruiting a quasi-military force in Great Britain itself illustrates both their sharp anxiety that serious industrial unrest might turn into revolution and also the lengths to which they were driven by the chronic shortage of military manpower. The simple strengthening of forces which would act immediately 'in aid of the civil power', moreover, reduced the possibility of the government having to consider the ultimate resort of martial law. This was the case in Ireland. When the task of restoring law and order went beyond the capabilities of the Royal Irish Constabulary (already an armed police force run on military lines), the Auxiliary Division of the RIC – popularly known as the 'Black and Tans'[95] – was formed to provide a 'half-way house' between conventional police methods and full-scale martial law. The Black and Tans, however, failed satisfactorily to fulfil this requirement and the army perforce had to retain their irksome semi-military, semi-police, role in Ireland. This state of affairs, Wilson told Churchill in November 1920, 'was not fair on the soldiers & if the present regime was continued much longer the P.M. would have the Army against him or else have a mob instead of an Army'. Wilson, with dubious political insight, 'asked Winston to remember that in the end the authority of the Cabinet rested on the bayonets of the soldiers'.[96] Wilson's answer to the problem was the thorough-going imposition of martial law, but the Cabinet, their martial *via media* having failed, chose the arguably more effective solution of a complete military withdrawal from southern Ireland. The establishment of a Special Constabulary in the newly-created Northern Ireland, however, was to relieve the army of many of its duties there in 1921–22.

In other parts of the empire gendarmerie schemes reflected more directly traditional imperial policy. In areas where the conditions required for a completely civilian police force did not obtain, the creation of a semi-military police force was an attractive alternative to military rule. Mesopotamia is a case in point. Churchill's committee on Mesopotamia of January 1921 was asked, *inter alia*, 'to form a scheme for raising as soon as possible an Imperial Mesopotamian Police similar in quality and organisation to the Cape Mounted Rifles or Canadian Mounted Police, and somewhat similar to the Auxiliary Division of the Royal Irish Constabulary'. The committee, noting that 'conditions in Mesopotamia are very different from those prevailing in the Cape and in Canada', decided against the idea of a white police force. It would cost rather more than regular troops and it was considered that it would be difficult to maintain the discipline and efficiency of such a force. The unfortunate example of the Black and Tans was perhaps in the committee's mind when they concluded that 'in a tropical country the type of man it is proposed to recruit is likely to deteriorate rapidly through drink and there are many temptations to peculation'. This would, they added somewhat unnecessarily, though with a shrewd appreciation of the nature of imperial power, tend to undermine 'the general prestige of the white man, and the loss of such prestige would have consequences of the gravest nature'.[97] Although this scheme was still-born, Churchill later set up a British-officered Palestine Gendarmerie. Ironically the force gained most of its recruits from the disbanding Auxiliary Division of the RIC. The Black and Tans, moreover, provided many of the personnel for the RAF's armoured car companies in Mesopotamia.[98]

In many ways the Black and Tans epitomise the poverty and incoherence of imperial defence policy in the aftermath of the war. They represented one response to the apparent shortage of manpower – a response, indeed, which assumed that security problems could be met simply by the expedient of recruiting additional forces. They were formed to counter violent nationalism, and the fact that they could be transplanted to Palestine and Mesopotamia to some extent indicated the similar techniques employed by British decision-makers to counter apparently similar empire-wide unrest. Hastily mustered, inadequately commanded, part-military and part-civilian, they reflected the hand-to-mouth strategies of a British government desperate to discover any solution to the plethora of post-war challenges. Above all, the Black and Tans, comprising for the most part unemployed (and perhaps otherwise unemployable) recently-demobilised junior officers and NCOs, embodied the sometimes frighteningly difficult problems – not just 'military' – which accompanied the transition from war to peace throughout the British empire.

Chapter 5

The Irish ulcer

In his speech at the opening session of the Northern Ireland parliament on 22 June 1921, King George V declared that 'everything which touches Ireland finds an echo in the remotest parts of the Empire'.[1] This assertion reflected a common British tendency to place the Irish question in an imperial context. Without, perhaps, going so far as to agree with Engels' contention that Ireland was 'the first British colony', both proponents and opponents of home rule tended to perceive the Irish problem through imperial spectacles. Gladstone, for example, during the preparation of the first Irish Land Act in 1870, asserted that 'the end of our measure is to give peace and security to Ireland, and through Ireland to the Empire'. In the 1880s the opponents of home rule couched their beliefs in equally imperial terms. Lord Salisbury wrote that 'the highest interests of the Empire, as well as the most sacred obligations of honour, forbid us to solve this question by conceding any species of independence to Ireland', and Lord Randolph Churchill, at the height of the 1886 home rule controversy, declared dramatically, 'Like Macbeth before the murder of Duncan, Mr Gladstone asks for time. Before he plunges the knife into the heart of the British Empire he reflects, he hesitates ...'.[2] The fundamental difference between the Unionists and the Liberal home rulers was that whereas the Liberals wanted to grant home rule to Ireland in order to pacify the country, and thus strengthen the United Kingdom, the Unionists believed that any such measure would not only mean the break up of the United Kingdom but also, inevitably, presage the disintegration of the empire. In political terms, 'goodbye Tipperary' was tantamount to saying 'farewell Leicester Square'.

In the years immediately preceding the First World War, unionist opinion became galvanised as never before by the increasing probability of home rule legislation being passed at Westminster. There was, moreover, the possibility that Asquith's Liberal government might try to coerce Ulster into accepting home rule. 'I *cannot* bring myself to believe that Asquith will be so mad as to employ force', wrote Sir Henry Wilson in November 1913; 'it will split the Army and the Colonies as well as this country and the Empire'.[3] In March 1914, nevertheless, the army *was* split when a number of cavalry officers at the Curragh Camp near Dublin resigned rather than accept orders which, as they thought, were aimed at coercing Ulster. There is also evidence to suggest that feeling ran as high in the navy and that similar incidents would have occurred had the 'senior service' been required to take offensive action against the Ulster unionists.[4] Following the Curragh 'mutiny' a letter was published in the *Pall Mall Gazette* from a young subaltern in Ireland who had resolved to 'carry on'. 'At a time like this', he wrote, 'the Army must stick together. If once we start to disintegrate the Service, then goodbye to the Empire and anything else that matters'.[5]

Ulster, of course, was the fulcrum of the Irish question. In 1914 Milner thought that Henry Wilson had 'saved the Empire' by supporting the Ulster unionists, and six years later Wilson extravagantly told the Prime Minister that only 'loyal Ulster stood between England & the loss of her Empire'.[6] In September 1920, James Craig, who later became the first Prime Minister of Northern Ireland, warned Lloyd George that 'civil war on a very large scale' in Ireland, which he regarded as a distinct possibility, would have serious results 'in shaking the foundations of the Empire'.[7] Some Liberals saw the problem differently, but took just as imperial a view of the matter. In June 1920, Smuts wrote to Lloyd George: 'I need not enlarge to you on the importance of the Irish question for the Empire as a whole'. His thesis was that change was required in both Ireland *and* the empire to ensure survival and thus he was to welcome the eventual settlement with the more moderate Irish nationalists which granted 'dominion status' to southern Ireland in 1921.[8]

It was a point of view with which Sir Henry Wilson could never agree. Following the Anglo-Irish treaty of December 1921, he regarded the empire, quite simply, as 'doomed'.[9] As an Anglo-Irish protestant of Ulster stock Wilson's sympathies naturally lay with unionism, but his deep concern for the Union stemmed also from his belief that Ireland itself occupied a vital position within the empire. He regarded the island not so much as an imperial influence or example, but as a strategic necessity for the United Kingdom. Indeed the Union had been founded on strategic requirements. One of the principal factors behind Pitt's creation of a 'United Kingdom' in 1800 was the threat of invasion from and rebellion within Ireland during the wars with France. By 1918, however, Ireland's importance lay more in naval defence. The German U-boat campaign in the Atlantic during the Great War served to emphasise the importance of naval bases in Ireland for the defence of the sea approaches to the British Isles and underlying every attempt to find a political and constitutional solution to the Irish problem following the war was a basic British belief in the vital importance of Ireland and the essential strategic unity of the British Isles.

In the aftermath of the First World War Irish problems, in common with many others, took second place to the peace-making in Paris and a policy of 'drift' throughout 1919 merely exacerbated the problems of 'John Bull's other island'. Irish nationalism, like that in India and Egypt, emerged from the war strengthened and intensified. In September 1914 John Redmond's moderate nationalist party had at last, as they thought, realised their ambitions when the Home Rule Bill received the Royal Assent even though a suspensory act postponing the operation of home rule for the duration of the war was passed simultaneously. Asquith, moreover, recognising the strenuous and potentially violent objections of Irish unionists (particularly in Ulster) to an all-Ireland parliament in Dublin, pledged that the home rule legislation would not come into effect until its provisions had been reviewed and, perhaps, modified 'in such a way as to secure at any rate the general consent both of Ireland and the United Kingdom'.[10] In August 1914 most of both unionist and nationalist Ireland rallied to the British war effort and throughout the conflict an estimated 500,000 Irishmen volunteered for service in the British forces.[11] But by the end of the war, the events of the Easter Rising and its aftermath in 1916, the 'conscription crisis' of 1918, and continued British procrastination over home rule had produced such a change in Irish nationalist opinion that in the 1918 general election the Redmondite home rule party was soundly defeated by the more extreme candidates of Sinn Fein standing on a republican and abstentionist ticket and the country itself had been reduced to a state of 'suppressed rebellion'.[12]

This, then, was the critical state of affairs which faced the ramshackle Irish administration in 1918. The government of Ireland was entrusted primarily to three officials: the Lord Lieutenant (also known as the Viceroy) who resided in Ireland; the Chief Secretary, who was generally a member of the Cabinet; and the permanent Under-Secretary, who had his office in Dublin Castle. Although the Lord Lieutenant, as Governor-General, was technically at the head of the British forces in Ireland, the day-to-day running of the army was left to the General Officer Commanding-in-Chief of the Irish Command which, as one of the eight home commands of the British army, came directly under the orders of the War Office in London. The Royal Irish Constabulary, which being an armed force with its own peculiar regulations and not governed by the Army Act was unique in the empire, came under the Chief Secretary's remit and was directed by the Irish Office. The Chief Secretary himself was largely an absentee from Ireland because of his Cabinet duties and the fact that he had no parliamentary Under-Secretary to represent him at Westminster. By convention the offices of Lord Lieutenant and Chief Secretary were never conferred on Irishmen. This Byzantine structure came under the critical eye of the Royal Commission appointed to enquire into the causes of the Easter Rising and it reported in June 1916 that 'if the Irish system of government be regarded as a whole, it is anomalous in quiet times and almost unworkable in times of crisis'.[13] Viscount French, who was appointed Lord Lieutenant in May 1918, soon came to realise the inadequacy of the Irish administration and in his first report following the armistice he called for 'a careful enquiry into the practical efficiency of the "Castle Rule" which obtains at present'.[14] Despite these strictures no immediate move was made, although when Lloyd George re-established formal Cabinet government late in 1919, he included for the first, and only, time both Viceroy and Chief Secretary in the Cabinet. In October 1919 a Cabinet committee on Ireland was set up, but its brief extended to little more than a consideration of the adjustments required to the Home Rule Act before it could be brought into operation.[15] Lord French and the Chief Secretary, Macpherson, had, in the meantime, to battle on as best they could with the restoration of order in Ireland.

Throughout 1919 there was a gradual intensification of the Irish nationalist guerrilla campaign. At first this was directed principally towards the RIC, but by the end of the year increasing numbers of attacks were being made on the army. To meet this terrorism the Chief Secretary had at his disposal in early 1919, 9,000 policemen[16] and General Shaw, the army commander in Ireland, had nearly 20,000 men 'capable of field operations', which he regarded as quite insufficient for his needs. The first few attacks seem to have induced near panic among Shaw and his staff officers. In May 1919 Sir Henry Wilson reported to the Cabinet the Irish Command's estimate that 'the Sinn Fein organisation controls some 100,000 well-organised, though indifferently armed, men'. It was therefore necessary, argued Dublin, 'to contemplate no mere police measures, but active military operations of a serious nature'. In the face of as yet only sporadic Irish terrorism this was nonsense. It could be argued that the generals were displaying unusual foresight about the development of violence in Ireland. But their analysis is more probably explained by a number of mutually-supporting factors. The army's own *amour-propre* prompted an assumption that military action would be both necessary and effective. Perceptions of militant Irish nationalism, moreover, were strongly coloured by memories of the 1916 Rising, which had certainly involved specifically 'military' conflict with a disciplined, organised and uniformed opponent. There was also the legacy of experience during the Great War when it had been assumed that most if not all problems were susceptible to a military solution. Shaw had asked for immediate reinforcements of eight infantry and two machine-gun battalions in all. Even this was against the sharp objections of Haig, who feared 'grave unrest' in Great Britain itself. 'It is hoped that this danger may have subsided for the time being,' Wilson told the Cabinet, 'but it must be remembered that such a situation may recur at any time, very possibly when the crisis is most acute in Ireland and elsewhere'.[17]

While the CIGS was proposing intensified military operations in Ireland, and warning (as always) of an empire-wide manpower shortage, his political masters hesitated to commit themselves to an unequivocally military policy. Indeed, throughout the British campaign in Ireland – more so than in any other post-war theatre of operations – there was a continuing and frequently acrimonious debate between the proponents of a 'military' solution and those who hankered after a less forcibly stringent strategy, perceiving more fully both the political and the military difficulties accompanying *any* Irish policy.

Shaw's problems were compounded by the fact that since Ireland was a 'home' command the Adjutant-General's department in the War Office regarded it as a convenient source of manpower for supplying drafts for units overseas. In May he complained to the Viceroy that, as far as he could make out, it was the case in the War Office of the left hand not knowing what the right hand was doing. He was receiving at least some of the reinforcements he had requested, but at the same time his units were being 'constantly depleted by large drafts for overseas' and he was finding it most difficult to maintain 'the necessary garrisons' throughout the country.[18] This confusion in the War Office was merely a reflection of the fact that, as Sir Henry Wilson maintained, there were not enough troops to garrison the empire and also that Ireland was still an area of only relatively minor concern in which many British decision-makers hoped order could be restored under the existing regime by the local police force assisted with occasional military action. By the beginning of 1920, however, this possibility was rapidly receding and it became increasingly clear that more radical action would have to be taken in Ireland.

At first, with the authorities still clinging to their hope that a 'civil' solution would obtain in Ireland, it seemed that action need be no more radical than a few changes in personnel such as Sir Joseph Byrne, the Inspector-General of the RIC. Early in December 1919, Walter Long, chairman of the Cabinet Irish committee, after a visit to Dublin where he had consulted both the Chief Secretary and the Viceroy, told the Cabinet that the Irish administration was convinced Byrne was 'not the man for the work'. At the end of the month Lord French wrote to the Prime Minister in much the same vein and suggested that perhaps Byrne could be found a colonial governorship.[19] Lloyd George agreed that Byrne should go. 'He is an able and intelligent man', he told French, 'but has always given me the impression of an official who is overwhelmed with the hopelessness of his task'.[20] He was rather more revealing to Bonar Law:

Byrne clearly has lost his nerve . . . It may of course very well be that the task in Ireland is a hopeless one and that Byrne has simply the intelligence to recognise it. However, until we are through with Home Rule a man of less intelligence and more stolidity would be a more useful instrument to administer the interregnum.[21]

Byrne was replaced by Long and French's nominee, T. J. Smith, the Deputy Inspector-General, an Ulster protestant from Belfast whose unionist sympathies reflected closely those of Walter Long.

A second change of personnel that came up for consideration towards the end of 1919 was that of General Officer Commanding-in-Chief. Shaw's appointment to the Irish Command in 1918 had been a temporary one for only two years, instead of the more normal four. He was, moreover, only a Lieutenant-General and the Irish Command was conventionally the prerogative of at least a full General. Indeed, in the happy days before the war it had frequently been used as a convenient final resting-place for distinguished senior generals coming up to retirement. This was exactly what Churchill planned to do in the summer of 1919. In July he offered the job to Sir William Robertson, the former CIGS who was then commanding the occupation forces in Germany.[22] Sir Henry Wilson had no objection in principle to Churchill's plan, but he told him that in view of the special circumstances in Ireland he thought the Prime Minister ought to be consulted before the appointment was finally confirmed.[23] Lloyd George, who had once described Robertson as having the brains of a 'superior clerk',[24] was not at all enamoured with the proposal. He wanted instead to send Sir Nevil Macready to Dublin.[25]

Macready was in many respects the ideal candidate. He had considerable experience of commanding troops 'in aid of the Civil Power' both in south Wales at the time of the Tonypandy dispute in 1910 and also in Belfast during the 'Ulster crisis' in 1914. As Commissioner of the Metropolitan Police he had dealt successfully with the police strike of 1919. He was, in Asquith's words, a man of 'cool head' and 'good judgment',[26] and Lloyd George was clearly attracted by Macready's Liberal sympathies and his constant support for Irish home rule, which had flown in the face of established army opinion in the years before the war. The only fly in the ointment was that Macready himself was most reluctant to go to Ireland. When Macpherson had been appointed Chief Secretary in January 1919, Macready had written to him in startlingly acerbic terms: 'I cannot say I envy you for I loathe the country you are going to and its people with a depth deeper than the sea and more violent than that which I feel against the Boche'.[27] While Macready vacillated, Robertson, who actually wanted the job, pestered Wilson for confirmation of the appointment.[28] Churchill, in his turn, pressed the Prime Minister for a decision. 'Now that the Rhine [Command] is coming to an end', he wrote in October 1919, 'I cannot leave Robertson without any appointment, and Ireland is the only one open . . . In my opinion he is unquestionably the best man'. In February 1920, he told Lloyd George that 'the matter has now become urgent, as General Shaw's temporary appointment will come to an end in the next few weeks'.[29] Despite Churchill's pressure and Macready's reluctance, Lloyd George determined to have Macready and in the end it seems that Lord French finally persuaded the general to take up the appointment, which was formally made on 25 March 1920.[30] Churchill, who told Wilson that the appointment had been made 'virtually over my head', proposed to promote Robertson to Field Marshal 'as a consolation prize' and explained to him that 'owing to the repeated murderous outrages in Ireland, the Government decided that it was necessary to appoint an officer with special police experience'.[31] 'The Baton goes to Robertson', commented Wilson, who had no love for his dour Scottish predecessor, 'because there is no job for him i.e. because he is unfit for Ireland therefore make him a Marshal. All very disgusting'.[32]

Churchill's championing of Robertson illustrates the haphazard and generally ill-considered British approach to Ireland during 1919–21. Robertson was undoubtedly an able soldier, but hardly 'unquestionably the best man' for a job which required subtlety, flexibility and political nous. Robertson's chief claim to the Irish Command simply lay in the time-honoured War Office tradition of Buggins' turn. Perhaps Churchill was actually reflecting Lloyd George's view that 'stolidity' rather than intelligence was required in Ireland. Yet in this case, with characteristic inconsistency, the Prime Minister plumped for agility rather than phlegm. The truth of the matter was that the government had no very clear idea at all as to how they might successfully cope with the admittedly complex Irish problem. In the absence of any fixed policy, and following Lloyd George's habitual procedure in such circumstances, they merely oscillated from one stratagem to another, hoping no doubt to light upon some 'solution'. It was, possibly, a less than satisfactory decision-making technique.

Sir Nevil Macready's appointment to the Irish Command in the spring of 1920, however, marked the beginning of a reassessment of Irish policy. At the start of April, Macpherson, worn down by the pressures of the Irish Office, relinquished the Chief Secretaryship at his own request. He was replaced by Sir Hamar Greenwood, a bluff Canadian who brought fresh vigour and determination to the Irish administration. The appearance of these two new men on the Irish scene, moreover, marked the end of Lord French's effective influence on policy. French, like Macpherson, had been feeling the strain of office. In January 1920, his private secretary, Sanderson, had told Wilson that French was 'as brave as a lion, but so erratic & unbalanced' and by the summer H. A. L. Fisher considered him to be 'a shadow of his former self and quite useless'.[33] Although French made the proposal in April 1920 that the 'Castle' administration be examined by a special committee, from this time on the direction of Irish affairs was largely left to Macready and Greenwood.

Macready soon found fault in Dublin. 'Before I had been here three hours' he wrote to Long, 'I was honestly flabbergasted at the administrative chaos that seems to reign here'. He was also unhappy about the condition of the police and told Long on 1 May that the recently-appointed Inspector-General ought to be replaced. 'I am sure he is worn out', he wrote, 'and apart from that, I do not think he is, in any case, a big enough man for a post which, at the present moment, is one of the most difficult in the Empire to fill successfully'.[34] Macready's candidate for the job was General Sir Edward Bulfin who had recent experience of action against civil disorder in Egypt during the spring of 1919. But Bulfin, an Irish Catholic, flatly refused to go to Ireland on the noteworthy grounds that 'it would be most distasteful to him to do any work . . . which was not of a purely military character'.[35] An alternative was eventually found in General Tudor, an ambitious artillery officer with no 'police' experience and an old acquaintance of Churchill. He was initially appointed Police Advisor to the Irish government in May 1920, and became 'Chief of Police' in November when Smith finally retired.[36]

On the administrative side Greenwood was just as critical as Macready. 'Things are desperate but not hopeless', he wrote on 8 May with a fine sense of distinction. 'There is a sloppiness in administration and a lack of cohesion in the protective forces that is amazing'.[37] Already, however, Sir Warren Fisher, permanent secretary to the Treasury, was conducting an enquiry in Dublin. On 12 May he presented his findings to the Chancellor of the Exchequer, who found them 'worse than anything that I had anticipated'. Fisher declared bluntly that 'the Castle administration does not administer'. The Under-Secretary, MacMahon, was doing the work of 'a routine clerk', and, although 'not devoid of brains', lacked 'initiative, force and driving power'. Fisher argued, however, that MacMahon should not be replaced for he was one of the few Roman Catholics in the administration and personally quite popular, but that a Joint Under-Secretary of high ability should be seconded from London to serve alongside him. He suggested that the brilliant young Chairman of the Board of Inland Revenue, Sir John Anderson, could adequately fill this position. Fisher also put his finger on the real problem bedevilling the operation of the security forces in Ireland: the confusion between the civil and military authorities and the particular 'tendency of the Castle as a whole . . . to lean on G.H.Q. and avoid responsibility'. With 'a really able and powerful Civil Servant in control', he thought that a suitable *modus operandi* could be worked out and the continuing principle of a civil solution in Ireland maintained.[38] Fisher's proposals were accepted by a grateful Cabinet. By the end of May 1920 Anderson and a small group of able English civil servants had been transferred to Dublin Castle.

Although Macready himself felt 'the futility of relying on the civil power to quell a rebellion', he was reluctant at first to advocate the introduction of martial law 'for the reasons that the troops available were not sufficiently numerous to ensure its effective application', and he remained unconvinced that the British government would be able to impose it 'until such time as they had the country behind them in the matter'.[39] On taking up his appointment in March 1920, he had found himself faced with a chronic shortage of manpower. The demobilisation of the last of the conscript battalions the same month reduced the number of effective troops at his disposal to only 19,000, the lowest total since the war, and Lord French told members of the government in April that 'adequate military protection' could only be given to Ireland with three times this number.[40]

On 11 May, Macready presented to the Cabinet a blunt statement of 'military and police requirements' prepared by the Irish executive. His principal request was for immediate reinforcement by eight battalions of infantry, a large number of technical personnel and 234 motor vehicles. Hankey recorded later in his diary that Macready's apparent plan was 'to render the troops so mobile that by moving about the country they may from time to time surprise the Sinn Fein bands' – a neat military variant on the Prime Minister's broad political strategy. The Cabinet agreed to meet the demands for mechanical transport at once and, so far as was possible, those for technical personnel, but since Wilson argued strongly that 'if 8 Batt^{ns} were sent to Ireland we should have very little for our own internal troubles & *nothing* for India, Egypt, C[onstantin]ople, etc.', they decided simply to hold the battalions Macready requested 'in readiness' should they be required in a serious emergency. In order to ease the army's manpower problem, the Secretary for War suggested that a 'Special Emergency Gendarmerie' of 8,000 'old soldiers' be raised at once to reinforce the RIC.[41] A committee was set up to examine the proposal and on 19 May it reported against 'a gendarmerie' and in favour of the creation of eight garrison battalions, under the Army Act but limited to service only in the United Kingdom. The Cabinet, however, found such an overtly 'military' measure unpalatable and it was eventually decided to enlist ex-servicemen into an Auxiliary Division of the RIC. This was little more than an extension of previous policy, for since November 1919 non-Irish ex-soldiers had been recruited into the Irish police force.[42]

From the military point of view, however, the reinforcement of the Irish police did little to alleviate the general shortage of manpower. At a Cabinet meeting on 7 June 1920 reference was made to 'popular dissatisfaction' with British expenditure in the Black Sea region 'and on small military adventures in various centres in the Caucasus, at a time when economy was urgently necessary and when we were very much in need of troops for Ireland'.[43] The same month Churchill circulated to the Cabinet a sobering summary of British military liabilities throughout the world. In Ireland there were thirty infantry battalions and one machine-gun battalion 'with a total effective strength of about 23,000 of which, however, 3,000 have not fired a musketry course'. In addition to these troops there were seven cavalry regiments and an armoured car company. This garrison was 'clearly insufficient' and 'an additional eight battalions have had to be warned to be ready to move at short notice, and two of these have now actually sailed'.[44] On 18 June Wilson told ministers that he 'had not enough troops to carry out the Cabinet policy in Ireland, C-ople, Palestine, Mesopotamia'. In July he wrote bitterly to Churchill about the government's indeterminate policy, which provoked apparently insatiable demands for troops in Ireland. Macready, he complained, 'has never yet been able to tell me the policy of the Government beyond calling on me for troops and transport without limit to either'. Wilson reminded the Secretary of State that Ireland could not be considered in isolation. It was his duty, he wrote, to point out 'that these urgent and repeated demands from Ireland, demands which go on increasing, leave us with far too few troops in this country to meet a civil disturbance and with no troops at all to answer the call of other theatres'.[45]

In Ireland, Macready was at pains to point out the weakness of his forces. The men, he maintained, were on the whole young and untrained and beginning to show signs of strain under the peculiar difficulties of service in Ireland. 'Don't lean too hard on the Army', he warned the Cabinet on 23 July.[46] Wilson's difficulties were aggravated by the rebellion which flared up in Mesopotamia in July 1920, necessitating the reinforcement of the garrison there by two divisions, and in September by fears of a major coal strike in Britain. Fortunately India provided the bulk of the reinforcements needed in Mesopotamia, but to meet the domestic industrial crisis the CIGS had to seek troops closer to home. On 6 September he told Macready that he proposed to withdraw ten battalions from Ireland. Macready was appalled and brusquely replied that if this were done 'the whole RIC would go & he would have to "put up his shutters"'.[47] A week later Wilson explained his position to the Cabinet. He said that in anticipation of possible serious trouble at home arrangements had been made to increase the forces in Great Britain by fourteen battalions, ten from Ireland and four from the Rhine.

> It is important, however, [he continued darkly] that the Cabinet should realize the consequences of withdrawing these battalions from Ireland and on this subject the General Officer Commanding-in-Chief, Ireland, has stated that if the troops under his command are thus reduced, it will be impossible to maintain even the present semblance of Government control, and a large proportion of the country must be abandoned to the undisputed possession of the revolutionaries.
>
> It is not only the net loss of ten battalions that has to be faced, but also the possible defection and resignation of a great proportion of the Royal Irish

Constabulary and the moral encouragement which will be given to the extremists
of the Sinn Fein movement, which will also result in a considerable acquisition to
their material forces. The reduced garrison will, under such circumstances be
practically impotent as an instrument for the maintenance of law and order, unless
it can be employed for operations of a more military nature, which would only be
possible if the Sinn Fein movement were proclaimed as a rebellion.

The situation of the troops themselves also deserves consideration. The service
on which they are engaged, already most difficult and unwelcome, will become still
less tolerable if the garrison is reduced, and there is a danger of approaching the
limit beyond which cheerful and willing service is no longer to be obtained.

To sum up, the threatened strike, if it materializes, will make a demand on our
military resources which we are unable to meet without cancelling our obligations
in some other theatre; and this memorandum is submitted in order to lay the
military situation clearly before the Cabinet, and to give them time to consider and
decide which of our existing commitments is to be abandoned in order to provide
the force necessary to cope with the threatening conditions at home.[48]

Here was Wilson at his most foreboding. Against all expectations,
however, the miners' strike turned out to be something of a damp squib
and the Irish battalions were not needed. Trenchantly the CIGS had
clearly indicated the likely cost of keeping order at home, implied
(probably unintentionally) the poverty of purely military 'solutions', and
confirmed how delicate indeed was the balance of imperial security in the
summer of 1920.

In the meantime recruitment for the Auxiliary Division of the RIC
continued, and the unit reached a peak of 1,500 men in July 1921.[49] This
influx of British ex-servicemen did much to strengthen the Irish police in
numerical terms but little to improve either policeing or co-operation
with the military forces. General Tudor seems to have regarded his
reinforced RIC as a suitable tool by which alone he could defeat the Sinn
Fein extremists with a species of counter-terror, and he supported (or at
least turned a blind eye to) the notorious policy of reprisals which became
an increasingly contentious topic of debate. In June 1920 the Prime
Minister, still casting about for an effective Irish policy, privately assured
Tudor of his full support and this seems to have included his tacit
approval of police reprisals.[50] At the beginning of July Wilson noted in his
diary: 'L.G. is under the ridiculous belief that Tudor has organised a
counter-murder society'. He found this hard to accept but became more
alarmed a week later when Lloyd George

reverted to his amazing theory that Tudor, or someone, was murdering 2 S[inn]
F[einer]s to every loyalist the S.F.s murdered. I told him that this was absolutely
not so but he seemed to be satisfied that a counter-murder Association was the best
answer to the S.F.'s murders.

His suspicions were further confirmed when the Prime Minister, pressed for more information by Lord Derby, meaningfully told him 'you must not ask me any questions but the thing is in operation already'.[51]

In order to placate British public opinion, which was becoming increasingly critical of the government's Irish policy,[52] and retain at least some chance of a peaceful constitutional settlement in Ireland, Lloyd George was prepared to go to almost any lengths to avoid a total militarisation of the Irish campaign. In April 1920 he declared firmly that 'you do not declare war against rebels',[53] and he resisted the more overtly Draconian proposals of his advisors and colleagues. Wilson, for example, wanted lists of known Sinn Feiners in each district of Ireland to be posted 'on the church doors all over the country; and, whenever a policeman is murdered, pick five by lot and shoot them!'[54] Lord Curzon, who regarded Ireland as being in 'a state of open civil war', suggested at a Cabinet conference in May 1920 that 'Indian' measures could be applied in Ireland: troublesome towns and villages could be punished with progressive fines and even whole districts blockaded by the British forces.[55] The Indian parallel, however, was already strongly in the minds of those who resisted such severe measures, for the maladministration of martial law by the British General Dyer in the Punjab during April 1919 had resulted in the death of over 370 people in the 'Amritsar massacre', inflamed racial tension, intensified nationalist agitation in India, and caused a political storm at home. In July 1920, when both Churchill and Greenwood were proposing a policy of increased coercion in Ireland, 'trusting to force the Sinn Feiners into a frame of mind favourable to settlement', ministers' enthusiasm for sterner measures was tempered by the acrimonious debates on the Amritsar incident then proceeding in parliament. As Balfour put it: 'The Dyer debate has not helped us to govern by soldiers'.[56]

Such considerations seem not to have affected Sir Henry Wilson since his recommendation to the Cabinet in September 1920 for 'operations of a more military nature' in Ireland essentially meant a declaration of martial law. If this were done the control of security policy would be concentrated in the hands of the military and, as Wilson believed, this would enable really effective action be taken against the Irish Republican Army. Churchill, too, was anxious for more severe measures, although he was not yet convinced of the need to go so far as martial law. On 10 November he proposed to a secret Cabinet conference 'the substitution of regular, authorised and legalised reprisals for the unauthorised reprisals by the police and soldiers which are winked at and really encouraged by the Government'. The conference, however, turned down his suggestion, considering that 'the moment was not opportune'.[57] But in the second half of November the government was persuaded otherwise by events in Ireland. On 21 November – 'Bloody Sunday' – a dozen British officers were shot dead by men under Michael Collins' command. The following day Wilson 'urged Winston "for the hundredth time" that the Government should govern, proclaim their fidelity to the Union and declare Martial Law'.[58] One week later a police patrol was ambushed at Kilmichael, near Macroom in County Cork, and sixteen Black and Tans were killed, an event which finally led the British government to impose martial law in part of Ireland.

On 30 November, Churchill, Greenwood, Anderson and Wilson met to discuss the question. 'Greenwood inferred that he had always been in favour of it & so did Winston, their only doubt being whether we had enough troops! What amazing liars', commented Wilson. Churchill and Greenwood wanted to restrict the operation of martial law to the Cork area, but Wilson thought that it would be of no use unless it covered the whole of Ireland, excluding, perhaps, Ulster.[59] The next day the question came before the Cabinet. Lloyd George had been particularly affected by the Macroom killings. This attack, he declared, 'seemed to partake of a different character from the preceding operations'. While the others had been 'assassinations', this last 'was a military operation and there was a good deal to be said for declaring a state of siege or promulgating martial law in that corner of Ireland'. So, a purely civil security effort having failed, and both covert and overt use of counter-terror having apparently paid no dividends, the Prime Minister now turned to the army. But he stopped short of giving them an entirely free rein and the Cabinet agreed only to an 'experiment' of martial law limited to the south-west of the country.[60]

On 10 December 1920 martial law was proclaimed in four Irish counties: Cork, Tipperary, Kerry and Limerick. During the same month the Government of Ireland Act became law. It provided for separate parliaments in Dublin and Belfast, to be elected at some time between January 1921 and March 1922, and it was hoped that a special effort would be made to restore order so that the elections could be held as soon as possible. At the end of December an important conference of ministers and officials met to consider this point. Among those present were Anderson, Wilson, Tudor and three generals from the Irish Command: Macready, Strickland (GOC, 6th Division in Cork) and Boyd (GOC, Dublin District). The Prime Minister, in the chair, asked if a truce would be feasible over the election period, but Macready, Tudor and Anderson were unanimously opposed to this. Lloyd George then asked 'how long they thought it would be before the extremist gang of the Sinn Feiners was entirely broken?' Macready thought that 'the terror' could only be broken if martial law was 'spread all over the country'. Tudor, Strickland and Boyd, however, asserted that even without extending martial law the country could be controlled in four months. Sir Henry Wilson thought that 'perhaps in six months' time, if military law [*sic*] was applied to the whole of Ireland, 80 or 90 per cent of the people would be on the side of the

Government'.[61] This was welcome (although as it turned out over-optimistic) news for the Cabinet and they decided to set the Irish elections for May 1921.

On the day following the conference, as a concession to Wilson and Macready's views, it was decided to extend martial law to four further counties: Clare, Kilkenny, Waterford and Wexford.[62] Although the Cabinet had been prepared to go some way towards meeting the demands of their military advisors, they had not wholly abandoned all thought of a 'civil' solution and hesitated to impose martial law over the entire island. Henry Wilson entertained hopes that the 'logic of events' – always a dangerous logic to follow – would force the Cabinet to extend martial law, but in the meantime Macready's ability to crack down on the rebels was 'crippled' by the fact that some counties were under martial law and others not. Indeed, when Sir Warren Fisher made a second report on the Irish administration in February 1921, he curtly remarked that 'Martial Law everywhere is an intelligible policy, or Martial Law nowhere'.[63]

The extension of martial law in Ireland required also the reinforcement of the Irish garrison and this presupposed that there were troops available so to do. This was not the case in the Spring of 1921, when, once again, an industrial crisis and the possibility of civil disorder in Great Britain obliged the Cabinet to discuss reinforcing the forces at home. Although the Secretary for War told his colleagues on 4 April that 'it was not considered desirable' to withdraw any of Macready's fifty-one infantry battalions, it was subsequently decided that first three battalions, and then a fourth, could safely be removed. At the height of the crisis, nevertheless, Wilson began working out 'a scheme by which if this Triple Strike blows over – I can reinforce Macready by 30 Battns . . . This with a little more Cav[alry] & Tanks & Armoured Cars & Aeroplanes might constitute a "knock out" this summer'. On 19 April, three days after 'Black Friday', when the Triple Alliance collapsed, a War Office meeting, presumably at Wilson's prompting, agreed 'that our dangerous spot was Ireland & that once we are safe in this country we ought to concentrate on Ireland'.[64]

A month later the elections for the southern Irish parliament were held and, despite the British government's gesture of appointing, for the first time, a Roman Catholic Viceroy (Lord Fitzalan), they were a complete victory for Sinn Fein whose abstentionist candidates were elected unopposed for 128 of the 132 seats in the lower house of the new legislature.[65] Since there was no possibility that this parliament would operate in anything except a technical sense, the Cabinet were faced with the unpalatable alternatives of either offering the more moderate Irish nationalists some sort of 'dominion' home rule, or imposing crown colony government and full martial law on the twenty-six counties of southern Ireland.

At first more belligerent counsels prevailed. On 24 May the new Secretary for War, Worthington-Evans, presumably having been button-holed by Wilson as soon as he entered the Office, circulated a paper to the Cabinet on 'Ireland and the general military situation'. Worthington-Evans argued that the continuation of virtual stalemate throughout the summer and autumn would give a decisive advantage to the rebels in the coming winter. He was anxious, therefore, 'to reinforce the troops in Ireland with everything not actually required elsewhere, so that an endeavour should be made to break the back of the rebellion during the three months, July, August and September'.[66]

In an accompanying paper, Wilson and Macready outlined the action which would be taken 'were it decided by the Cabinet to make a supreme effort in Ireland this summer to re-establish law and order'. In contrast to their optimism of the preceding December, neither soldier was prepared to 'promise any definite result'. All they had to offer was a heavily-qualified conjecture that a full-blooded military approach *might* work.

If it is made clear to England and Ireland [wrote Wilson] that the Government is determined to settle this matter this summer, if all Ireland (except the six Ulster counties) is placed under Martial Law and thereby not only all the soldiers but all the Police and Auxiliaries come under one command, if the Navy give all the assistance they possibly can in watching and guarding the coasts, and if active and intense propaganda on our side be undertaken both in England and Ireland, if all these things are done, we shall run a much better chance of reaching success than we now have under our present plans.

Macready again struck a note of warning about the morale of his troops. Although the present health and discipline of the men was satisfactory, he felt that the cumulative effect of service in Ireland, which put strains on both officers and men 'incomparably greater than . . . in time of actual war', would eventually prejudice their military usefulness.

Unless I am entirely mistaken, [he concluded] the present state of affairs in Ireland, so far as regards the troops serving there, must be brought to a conclusion by October, or steps must be taken to relieve practically the whole of the troops together with the great majority of the commanders and their staffs. I am quite aware that troops do not exist to do this, but this does not alter in any way the opinion that I have formed in regard to the officers and men for whom I am responsible.[67]

Faced with these gloomy prognostications, and Macready's effective ultimatum, the Cabinet, by now perhaps willing to clutch at any straw, agreed that all possible reinforcements should be sent to Ireland and that the Irish administration should prepare for the imposition of martial law after 12 July, 'in the event of a refusal on the part of Southern Ireland to put into operation the Government of Ireland Act'.[68]

Four days later a jubilant Wilson wrote to General Sackville-West in Paris: 'The "Frocks" are, I verily believe, going to allow me to send over all the troops I have got in England to Ireland, my proposal being that every single battalion we have got except the Guard and five Irish battalions will be shipped over to Ireland this coming month'.[69] Between 14 June and 7 July the Irish command was reinforced by seventeen infantry battalions – making a total increase in troops of about one third – but the Cabinet, in the end, drew back from the brink. It seems that both the British government and the Irish republicans were materially influenced by the terrible prospect of a final military 'push', and that it acted as a catalyst towards a truce pending talks between the British and Sinn Fein.[70] By the middle of June, both Macready and Anderson had become convinced that the policy of coercion would not succeed. On 24 June, following the widespread public welcome to the King's conciliatory speech at the opening of the Belfast parliament, the Cabinet decided to invite both de Valera and Craig to take part in negotiations and to declare a truce in Ireland.[71] Following some preliminary talks, the truce came into effect on 11 July 1921.

Even after the truce, which Wilson thought the product of 'rank, filthy cowardice',[72] the possibility remained of a return to military action in the event of the Anglo-Irish negotiations breaking down. In August de Valera was demanding so large a measure of independence that even Macready thought 'we should go straight back to operations' and Wilson discussed with his Director of Organisation the practicability of enlisting twenty to thirty thousand men to help bring up to strength the battalions he was holding in reserve for Ireland. On 18 August, Worthington-Evans told Wilson that, if de Valera refused Lloyd George's terms, the House of Commons would be recalled from its summer recess and a call for recruits 'up to 80,000 to 100,000 would be made'.[73] Lloyd George himself was not averse to using this bellicosity as a negotiating weapon. In July, shortly after the truce had come into force, he reported to the Cabinet the sombre warning he had given to de Valera

that, if disorder broke out again, the struggle would bear an entirely different character. British military commitments in different parts of the world were gradually being reduced, which had enabled the Government to concentrate their forces at home. As it was immaterial whether they were quartered in Great Britain or Ireland they would be sent to the latter country, where a great military concentration would take place with a view to the suppression of the rebellion and the restoration of order.[74]

Early in August, the Prime Minister went so far as to propose 'a monstrous plan of withdrawal & blockade if hostilities were renewed'. The essence of this 'Sicilian' plan, wrote H. A. L. Fisher in his diary, was to 'hold the fat bits on the coast while abandoning the interior'. On 17 and

18 August the Cabinet Irish committee agreed that in the event of resumed hostilities there should be press censorship, close regulation of shipping in Irish waters, massive reinforcements for army units in Ireland, and the possible large scale recruitment of 'special forces'. They also asked the War Office to examine the practicability of dividing the twenty-six counties 'into sections by means of blockhouses and barbed wire', the introduction of identity cards and the imposition of food rationing. Towards the end of the month the Cabinet decided to hold back troops destined for India for possible employment in Ireland and 'considered the possibility of sending no more drafts to Mesopotamia and Constantinople respectively'.[75]

Thus Ireland still found 'an echo in the remotest parts of the Empire'. Despite, and perhaps because of, this sabre-rattling, in September the Cabinet agreed to open formal negotiations with the Irish nationalists, and by October a full-scale conference in London had been arranged. The threat of renewed hostilities hung over the conference to the end, and, whether bluffing or not, it was this threat Lloyd George finally used to bring the Irish delegates to sign a treaty on 6 December 1921.[76] Ironically in the end it could be claimed that there was a military 'solution' to the Irish problem, not so much in the actual employment of force, as in the threat of so doing, and a confirmation of Bismarck's dictum that 'diplomacy without arms is like music without instruments'.

In the Anglo-Irish treaty the British government sought to secure two main requirements. The first of these was that some constitutional link should remain between Great Britain and southern Ireland. This was provided for by the grant of 'dominion home rule' to what became the Irish Free State. Under the terms of the treaty this new state was to have theoretically the same relationship to the Crown and the imperial parliament as the existing imperial dominions. The second principal requirement, arguably the more important, was the maintenance of the United Kingdom's strategic security and the naval defence of the British Isles. In December 1919, the Cabinet had concluded that 'the experience of the recent War showed that the bases on the coast of Ireland were essential to the protection of our trade and that their occupation or use by an enemy Power might be disastrous'.[77] Time alone was to tell how important 'the Heligoland of the Atlantic'[78] was to be in a future war, but during the period 1918–22 there is no question that the policymakers in London regarded Ireland as occupying a vital strategic position. In July 1920, Lloyd George told a parliamentary deputation that it was 'essential to the interests and almost to the existence of this country that we should have complete control over the Irish coasts, and that Ireland should not under any conditions be a possible base for hostile operations against this country'. The British empire, he declared, would be 'committing suicide' if it surrendered control over Ireland. The following month in discussion with a group of southern Irish businessmen, he stressed that at all costs 'we can give up nothing that would imperil the existence of the United Kingdom', and since Ireland's position was critical for submarine defence, the control of Irish harbours was vital for Great Britain.[79] When the Cabinet came to decide the British attitude towards a possible settlement in May 1921, they agreed that 'from the point of view of the Naval and Military security of these islands, there must be no separate Irish Navy, Army or Air Force, and the Irish harbours and creeks must remain under British control'.[80]

During the negotiations which led up to the treaty the naval security question was dealt with at a special conference. The British case was put by Churchill and Beatty (First Sea Lord); the Irish by Michael Collins and Erskine Childers, the austere republican secretary to the Irish delegation. Lord Beatty said that the naval requirements had been demonstrated in the war. 'We could not', he said, 'fight a naval war unless we controlled the Irish coast. Numerous vessels could recoup in its numerous inlets'. Childers suggested that Ireland might be neutral in a future war, and if it failed to deal with the replenishment of enemy submarines, then it might be treated as a belligerent, but Beatty maintained that Ireland alone could not prevent the use of 'these inlets'. When Childers raised the question of Irish neutrality again, Churchill replied sharply 'that it was no use talking on the basis of neutrality. England would not accept it. Ireland could not be neutral. She may be inactive, but England must have the right to defend Ireland as well as herself'. In the end, Beatty put the conclusive Admiralty view from which the British would not move:

It is a strategic necessity that we should have stations in Ireland for offensive and defensive purposes. Berehaven and the south-west of Ireland are absolutely essential to us. To sacrifice it we should have to sacrifice something of infinite value which might be vital and would have been vital in the late war.[81]

Although the British conceded a limited military establishment to the Irish, the stated requirements of the Admiralty were not open to negotiation, and 'the defence by sea of Great Britain and Ireland' was provided for in the final settlement:

The Government of the Irish Free State shall afford to His Majesty's Imperial Forces:
  (a) In time of peace such harbour and other facilities as are indicated in the Annex hereto [the "Treaty Ports"], or such other facilities as may from time to time be agreed . . .
  (b) In time of war or of strained relations with a Foreign Power such harbour and other facilities as the British Government may require for the purposes of such defence as aforesaid.[82]

The Irish treaty was regarded by many as a great triumph for the

British government. Lord Rawlinson thought 'to have come to any settlement is certainly a great feather in Lloyd George's cap'. In the Cabinet there was a lot of mutual back-slapping. 'The settlement of the Irish difficulty', intoned Curzon in a typically portentous fashion, 'was one of the most remarkable events in the history of the British Empire and it represented an astonishing victory for the Empire'. A week after the treaty had been signed, Lloyd George told the House of Commons that 'the freedom of Ireland increases the strength of the Empire by ending the conflict which has been carried on for centuries with varying success, but with unvarying discredit'.[83] Some did not agree. 'What a shameful & cowardly surrender to the pistol', wrote Sir Henry Wilson – how he must have felt that his friend in India was out of touch! Lloyd George's 'cowardice' lay in not applying firm, rigorous and British rule in Ireland. 'We must either clear out, or *govern*', Wilson had written in March 1921.[84] In December, since the Cabinet had manifestly failed to 'govern', they were clearing out of Ireland and would soon clear out of the empire.

But Wilson let his obsession with Ireland cloud his professional judgment. In July 1921, Lloyd George had told him that de Valera was coming over to London and that Wilson would have a chance of 'talking with him'. The Field Marshal was incensed by this suggestion, replied that he 'did not speak to murderers' and bluntly announced that he would hand de Valera over to the police if he met him.[85] Relations between the Prime Minister and the CIGS had become increasingly strained since the war, not only over the question of Ireland, and this incident seems to have been the final break between the two men for they did not meet again until 10 February 1922. Up till that time, when army information or advice was required at a Cabinet meeting, Wilson himself refused to attend and sent another member of the Army Council to act on his behalf. Naturally this made life very difficult for Worthington-Evans, who taxed Wilson with the matter in November 1921. The Field Marshal told him that he was 'sorry to put him personally to inconvenience', but that he had no intention of changing his 'opinion about the meetings with the murder gangs'.[86] In late December 1921 Lord Derby noted that Wilson had been 'quite mad on the subject of Ireland' and had allowed this 'to taint all his work'. 'I cannot help feeling', he observed towards the end of Wilson's term as CIGS, 'that as long as he was a soldier he ought not to have allowed his political feelings to get the better of military discipline'.[87] Ireland, like Turkey, Egypt, Palestine and India, between 1918 and 1922, was an area of concern where prejudice and sentiment tended to influence attitudes and policy to a disproportionate degree. Wilson himself was a victim of such ill-considered thought. His public statements on British policy towards Ireland, both as CIGS and afterwards as Unionist Member of Parliament for North Down and chief security advisor to the Northern Ireland government, led many nationalist extremists unjustly to regard him as the man principally responsible for British repression in Ireland. Three months after he had handed over office as CIGS to Lord Cavan in February 1922, he was assassinated by two Irishmen on the steps of his house in Eaton Square, London. Ironically he was shot with service revolvers and service ammunition.[88]

The Anglo–Irish agreement of December 1921 did not mark the end of violence in Ireland. Early in January 1922 the treaty was ratified by a narrow majority in the southern Irish parliament, the *Dáil Éireann*, and shortly afterwards a bitter civil war broke out between the 'Free Staters' and the more intransigent republicans, led by de Valera. So shaky was the position of the new government that in the spring of 1922 it seemed as if the Free State might be overthrown and a republic declared in its place. Although by this time all British troops had been evacuated from southern Ireland apart from a 'controlled area' around Dublin, the War Office, once more, prepared plans for the renewal of hostilities.[89] In May, nevertheless, the new CIGS, Lord Cavan, told Austen Chamberlain that he had 'received such reports about the unpopularity of Irish service from some colonels that he . . . [was] . . . afraid to order troops to reinforce from this country'.[90]

On 22 June, the Cabinet, provoked by Wilson's assassination, summoned Macready to London and asked him if the Four Courts in Dublin, which had been occupied by republican forces since 13 April, could be captured at once by British troops. Macready thought that from a military point of view the operation was comparatively simple, but that the renewal of open hostilities by the British in Dublin would have the most serious political repercussions and would undoubtedly drive a large proportion of the Free Staters into the republican camp. Despite the general's reservations, soon after his return to Dublin on 24 June he received instructions from London to commence the reduction of the Four Courts on the following day. Unprepared for such precipitate action, Macready postponed the attack until he could be sure that all his officers and men were safely within the 'controlled area'. On 25 June, much to his own relief, he learned that the government had changed their minds and that no action was to be taken after all. Three days later, Free State forces, supplied with British arms and ammunition, began an assault on the insurgents and by 30 June the republicans had surrendered and the Four Courts reduced to ruins.[91] By the beginning of August the policy of assisting the Free State government with large quantities of munitions had begun to pay off and the likelihood of the British army resuming active operations in southern Ireland finally receded. On 22 November a conference of ministers of Bonar Law's new administration decided that the last British troops remaining in the Irish Free State should commence withdrawal on 6 December 1922.[92]

The Irish settlement was regarded as a somewhat mixed blessing by the committee appointed to examine the Geddes Report on the defence departments. They acknowledged that 'if there had been no Irish settlement, not only no reduction of the Army would have been possible, but, on the contrary, a very large increase would have been necessary to bring the rebellion to an end'. Yet, 'on the other hand, compared with the pre-war situation, the evacuation of Ireland affords no relief'. They observed that before the war Ireland had been a military asset and not a liability. Thirty thousand soldiers had been maintained there 'more cheaply than in Great Britain'. These troops, moreover, 'were always considered available as a reserve for Great Britain and as part of the general reserve for the British Empire'.[93] Some British troops, of course, remained in Ireland after the withdrawal from the south. Apart from the cadres left at the treaty ports, army units were stationed in Northern Ireland. But the maintenance of law and order in the six counties which remained part of the United Kingdom was largely sub-contracted to the new administration in Belfast, who combined economy with political security by reinforcing the police with an exclusively Protestant part-time Ulster Special Constabulary. For fifty years, comparatively speaking, Northern Ireland constituted a military asset.

The sorts of problems which the British government encountered in Ireland during the aftermath of the First World War also occurred in other parts of the world. At Britain's back door Ireland encapsulated the manifold imperial embarrassments of the period. The challenge of violent indigenous nationalism had to be met with some combination of force and favour. The difficulties of finding the right balance between coercion and conciliation were all too sharply emphasised by the near-desperate search for a settled Irish policy. For the army the manpower shortage of 1919–21 was as severe in Ireland as anywhere, and the effects of the intermittent but imperative need to secure the home base in Britain were perhaps most strongly felt by the Irish Command. Ireland also illustrated the dilemma of finding a satisfactory balance between strategic requirements and political and military realities. Above all Ireland was a continual source of weakness close to home. After the perceived threat of domestic revolution it was the most acute postwar security problem and the apparent near-impossibility of finding any satisfactory solution steadily sapped military strength and political will. Within the British policy-making community during these years Ireland was repeatedly put forward as a dreadful example of what could conceivably happen in more far-flung British territories. So it was that the suppurating Irish ulcer poisoned – although perhaps not quite fatally – the imperial body politic.

Chapter 6

India

As befitted the other 'main base' of the empire, to a very great extent the problems facing the military authorities in Delhi following the war were similar to those of the War Office in London. Lord Rawlinson, who succeeded Sir Charles Monro as Commander-in-Chief of the Army in India in the late autumn of 1920, found that like Sir Henry Wilson much of his time was taken up in resisting demands for retrenchment and the wholesale reduction of military expenditure. 'As we both foresaw before I left', Rawlinson wrote to Wilson in November 1920,

there is bound to be a pretty severe fight over finance. Certain of my honourable colleagues [on the Viceroy's Council] are endeavouring to bring pressure on me as they did upon Monro, to reduce the strength of the army and thus avoid the necessity of imposing further taxation.[1]

On the military side, however, the reduction of military spending was circumscribed by the perennial problem of security on the North-West Frontier, the post-war over-extension of the Indian Army, especially throughout the Near and Middle East, and an alarmingly high level of domestic unrest. Of these factors only the first (*because* it was 'perennial') could be solved within the framework of traditional Anglo–Indian policy-making.

Indian concern with the protection of her frontiers is illustrated by the case of Afghanistan. Traditionally regarded as 'the weak spot of Imperial defence',[2] the country had been recognised as falling within the British sphere of influence under the 1907 Anglo–Russian Agreement. The Bolshevik Revolution, however, temporarily lifted the fear of Russian infiltration from the Afghans and at the beginning of May 1919 the new nationalist and anti-British Amir Ammanulla launched an attack on the Indian frontier. Although the Afghans were soundly defeated – the Amir asked for an armistice within a month – the 'Third Afghan War' placed a considerable strain on Indian military resources.[3] There was never any question of imposing a military occupation on Afghanistan, and after hostilities had ceased Delhi's policy amounted to little more than a restoration of the *status quo ante*. The Indian Foreign Secretary, Henry

Dobbs, was given the unenviable task of negotiating a satisfactory settlement which would secure the maintenance of British access to Afghanistan and at least the relative neutrality of the Amir's government.[4] Chelmsford and Montagu were at one in this limited aim, strongly objecting, as Montagu put it, 'to diplomacy which strives to accomplish something which we have not got the force to accomplish'.[5] But it was slow work. Dobbs held inconclusive talks with the Afghan foreign minister during April–July 1920, and continued negotiations in Kabul itself for most of the following year. By May 1920 he had already become exasperated with the indecisive attitude of the Afghans. 'The only possible solution', he asserted, 'seems to be to make friends with the Bolshevists over their heads'. But he thought (rightly) that Curzon would never accept such a policy.[6]

During 1920–21 the Afghans tried to play the Indian government and the Bolsheviks off against each other. In March 1920 they initialled an alliance with Moscow which provided for Soviet subsidies to the Amir.[7] London promptly objected to any subsidies from the British side unless Dobbs could secure an Indo–Afghan treaty which would exclude the Bolsheviks from Afghanistan together. Yet it was apparent that India had not the resources to 'buy the Bolsheviks out of Afghanistan', and the Viceroy had long been of the opinion that the choice was either 'aloofness' or 'participation with the Bolsheviks in financing Afghan Government and developing country'.[8]

Despite the home government's reluctance, Indian policy prevailed. Afghanistan was not sufficiently important a concern for the policy-makers in London to take serious issue with the Government of India. A *pis aller* settlement was better than none at all. As Rawlinson recognised, 'with Persia and Anatolia in the state that they are, with the Nationalist Turk practically gone Bolo [Bolshevik], and with the Persian Government changing every month', an alliance with a Muslim power like Afghanistan would be 'of the greatest value'.[9] In November 1921, after almost eleven months' negotiation, Dobbs concluded a 'neighbourly' treaty at Kabul which did not provide for either economic or military assistance from India. Rawlinson regarded it as satisfactory, for it formed, in his opinion, 'a basis on which to build a structure that will bring Afghanistan and ourselves into close agreement and, I hope, continued friendship'.[10] In effect Delhi had reverted to the frontier policy which had largely held good since the 1850s: that of gaining as much political advantage as possible in Afghanistan while retaining the country integral as a buffer against Russian expansionist ambitions in Central Asia.[11]

The problem of Indian Army service 'ex-India' was progressively accentuated by domestic political pressures. So reluctant was India to contribute towards the maintenance of troops in east Persia in 1921 that the War Office assumed that the 'standing arbitration agreement' of 1902 was no longer in force 'owing to political changes in India, and that the determining factor in any . . . dispute under present conditions must be the state of native opinion and feeling in that country'.[12] Although Montagu denied it, this was a very important constraint hindering the accommodation of India within any *imperial* scheme of affairs. Indeed, the implicit assumption that 'native opinion and feeling' – however partially and imperfectly it may have been interpreted – was a 'determining factor' in policy-making marked a significant step in the direction of Indian self-rule. A more overtly formal move towards political autonomy was the inauguration of the 'Montagu–Chelmsford' reforms in February 1921. They gave Indian politicians a new opportunity to influence the government of their country. In addition to creating a legislative assembly, three-quarters of which was elected, the reforms established a convention that three of the eight-member Viceroy's Council should be Indians, who were thus admitted to the highest echelon of the administration.[13]

But although a measure of representation had been introduced into the central government, the Viceroy and his council remained responsible to the British Cabinet and constitutionally London retained the final say in major matters of policy. Despite this Sir Henry Wilson was not reassured by the changes. Montagu and Chelmsford, he felt, had 'lost control' and they 'now *dare* not impose the extra taxation necessary' to maintain the size of the British garrison in India. 'The . . . Council will, before long', he continued, 'refuse to allow Indian Native troops to serve outside India! And then!'[14] He was not altogether wrong. Although military expenditure was excluded from legislative vote under the 1919 Act, the levying of taxation was not. The legislature could therefore exercise an indirect influence on military affairs. In addition to reforms at the centre, the 1919 Act devolved considerable powers – including budgetary ones – to new provincial assemblies. But Delhi had to fund these additional power-centres, and fund them generously if Indian politicians were to be kept sweet. This meant retrenchment in central expenditure. To the civil administrators of the Raj, military spending – 'rather more than 32 per cent of the whole revenue of the Country'[15] – was an obvious area for economy. Either the size of the army had to be cut or an imperial subsidy gained for ex-Indian commitments. Neither alternative appealed to London. India's strategic value to the empire depended to a very great extent on its being a military milch cow. The Indian Army was only a genuine imperial asset so long as it was cheap. This then was the dilemma facing Delhi. Political control in India could only, it seemed, be bought at the cost of the imperial fire brigade. But this was a price which London was reluctant to pay.

The third important factor in India during the post-war period was the scale of internal opposition to the established government. It has been suggested, indeed, that this time 'was probably the worst moment for Britain's imperial rulers in India in the ninety years between the Mutiny and 1942'.[16] The problem was amplified by the fact that opposition to imperial rule came from both sides of the Indian religious divide. For a time, Muslims and Hindus worked closely together in the non-co-operation movement. It was Muslim agitation, however, which first erupted into open violence. Along with their Hindu compatriots, educated Muslims before the war had channelled their political aspirations largely along constitutional lines through both the bi-communal Indian National Congress and the more exclusive Muslim League, but within both communities extreme nationalists increasingly came to regard violence as a legitimate tool for political change. On the Muslim side these views tended to be concentrated in the more traditionally-minded sections of the community whose leaders came from among the *ulama*, the Islamic religious scholars and teachers. This divergence in Muslim opinion was illustrated by the attitudes which had been taken towards war with Turkey. On the outbreak of hostilities in 1914 the council of the Muslim League passed a resolution of loyalty to the government, but some among the *ulama*, taking the Kalifa's side, worked actively throughout the war against the British. Indeed, the more extreme leaders of Muslim opinion, most prominent among whom were the Ali brothers, were interned for the duration.[17]

By and large, however, the Muslims of India remained loyal throughout World War I. 136,000 men enlisted from the Muslim community in the Punjab alone, although this figure was undoubtedly enhanced by the recruiting methods employed. As Montagu delicately put it afterwards: 'Indian soldiers ... were persuaded, and, to face the matter quite frankly, persuaded with great vigour, in certain places, particularly in the Punjab, to join His Majesty's forces during the war'.[18] But it was not until after the armistice that the government in Delhi were given any great cause for concern. Peace-making, not war-making, was the stimulus for serious unrest in Muslim India. Both 'westernised' and traditional sections of the community were outraged by Allied plans to dismember the Ottoman empire and dethrone the Sultan. Both wings found expression for their fears in the Khilafat movement. Rallying to the defence of their religious leader, moreover, had more of an immediate attraction for Muslim peasants than any sort of campaign in support of far-away and largely irrelevant political advancement. Thus it seemed that, for once, all of Muslim India was united in the 'emotional and religious upheaval' of Khilafat.[19]

Muslim unrest – concentrated principally in the Punjab – raised problems of control for the British authorities. The immediate reaction was one of repression. Early in 1919, under the 'Rowlatt Acts', Delhi extended emergency wartime legislation which allowed the courts to try political cases without juries and gave the Indian provincial governments the power of internment without trial.[20] Even though this legislation was never actually invoked, its heavy-handed and insensitive nature could not fail but to inflame Indian political opinion – both Muslim and Hindu. Domestic feelings were further exacerbated by the drastic actions of General Dyer in the Punjab city of Amritsar where mob violence claimed the lives of four Europeans on 10 April 1919. Three days later Dyer broke up a prohibited meeting at an estimated cost of 379 Indians killed. He followed this up with a rigorous, if less outstandingly lethal, enforcement of martial law which effectively suppressed the disorder in the province. Since the British general's Cromwellian methods *did* succeed in 'pacifying' the Punjab[21] the full implications of the Amritsar massacre did not immediately become apparent either in Delhi or London.

On 18 April the Viceroy telegraphed that the 'internal situation' had necessitated a 'review of our military strength in the event of disorders spreading'. He assured London that with India's existing resources 'we can deal with even the worst contingency (internal disorder *plus* tribal-cum-Afghanistan complications) so long as the loyalty of Indian troops remains undoubted'. This was the crux of the matter and although the Indian troops were believed to be 'staunch' at the moment, the military authorities in Delhi thought it 'prudent to estimate our resources in worst contingency'. In these circumstances India reckoned that they would need British reinforcements of four infantry divisions and four cavalry brigades (about 70,000 troops). 'There is no present cause for alarm', concluded the Viceroy, 'but a situation which though at this moment improving, yet contains elements of grave uncertainty as to the future, has been disclosed by recent events in India'.[22] While Chelmsford in Delhi was apparently not alarmed by the prospects, Sir Henry Wilson in London certainly was. At once he began to prepare plans for reinforcing India, although he told the Military Secretary at the India Office (Sir H. V. Cox) that the most troops he could provide were nine cavalry regiments and twenty battalions of infantry – rather less than half the number that Delhi had suggested might be required. Nevertheless, with (as ever) an eye to dominion manpower, he noted in his diary that the War Office should 'look into the question of Australians & New Zealanders'. But Wilson's proposals were somewhat premature and at an Army Council meeting on 23 April Churchill insisted that no arrangements should be made to send large reinforcements to India until there was a definite request from Delhi. 'The whole thing is unsatisfactory', wrote Wilson, 'as I really have not enough troops to cope with one's possible difficulties'.[23]

A chronic shortage of manpower, however, was one problem which Sir Charles Monro did not wholly share with his counterpart in London. On

the outbreak of hostilities with Afghanistan in May 1919 Monro assured
the Viceroy that he had sufficient troops at his disposal to deal with the
emergency.[24] Even so, he requested the return of all British officers of the
Indian Army who 'are fit for service and who are now on leave or doing
duty in other threatres' and urged that wartime rates of pay and
concessions be retained in order to keep the Indian soldiers contented.[25]
Monro, indeed, had almost an *embarras de richesse* of troops in the
aftermath of the war. There were not the same great pressures put upon
the Indian General Staff as the British for rapid demobilisation, and in
mid-1919 the need to reduce numbers on the grounds of economy in India
had not yet become insistent. The Army in India, moreover, was
specifically organised in order to meet the needs of a war on the
North-West Frontier. The pre-war dispositions of the army set aside
nearly two thirds of the entire force to act as a 'Field Army', the remainder
being earmarked for internal security. Out of a total of 234,000 men in
1914, 152,000 served in the Field Army.[26]

In the summer of 1919 Munro had at his disposal in India a total of
nearly 491,000 men, but over the previous five years the proportion
between British and Indian troops had changed sharply in favour of the
Indians. From being almost one to two (British to Indian) in 1914, by
November 1918 there were more than six Indian soldiers to each British.[27]
'The Ratio' was a central tenet of the Indian military administration and
a crude index of mistrust. Before the Mutiny the proportion of British to
Indian had been almost one to nine, but following it no-one had been
prepared to risk continuing such a low figure. For fifty years it remained
high and unchallenged. Although by 1914 it had become well-nigh
immutable, such was the demand for British troops during the war that
the ratio was tacitly dropped and white units were drafted out at will.
There is little evidence to suggest that this constituted much of a security
risk. Monro, therefore, was well able to spare the 340,000 men who
participated in the Afghan war of 1919, although one reason given for the
employment of so large a force – and here his problems paralleled those of
Sir Henry Wilson – was an acute shortage of experienced officers.
Wartime 'wastage' had affected the Indian Army as well as the British.
'The solid officer varying from 5 to 15 years' service', wrote Monro grimly
in December 1919, 'is non-existent after five years of war'.[28]

Meanwhile the delayed time-bomb of Amritsar ticked away. Dyer's
action in itself had been severe enough but the real impact of the affair lay
in its aftermath. Not only was Dyer widely applauded in (British) India
and England for his 'strong' measures, but when the Hunter committee of
enquiry which Montagu had set up reported in the spring of 1920 it
emerged that the committee had divided on racial lines. Only the three
minority Indian members unhesitatingly condemned both Dyer and the
general application of martial law in the Punjab. As if this were not

enough to enrage Indian opinion, there was widespread sympathy for Dyer in the British parliament – an actual majority in the House of Lords – and the general, who had not been dismissed, merely obliged to resign from the army, benefited from a large public subscription raised in appreciation of his services. The effect in India of these British attitudes was dramatic. Both Gandhi and Congress moved away from a position of qualified approval for the constitutional reforms to one of non-co-operation. In addition, Gandhi, who had already espoused the Khilafat cause, sought to co-ordinate more closely the actions of Hindu and Muslim nationalists.[29]

For Montagu in London the Khilafat movement represented the greatest threat to Indian stability. It was one of his most abiding fears that a hard and 'unjust' treatment of Turkey by the Allies would stimulate uncontrollable unrest in India. His concern amounted almost to an obsession and his continually despondant complaints to Lloyd George on the subject probably did more harm than good. In February 1920 when the Treaty of Sèvres was being concluded with Turkey, Hankey vented exasperation with Montagu in his diary:

All this time he is staying in a nursing home, from which he bombards me with 3 or 4 or 5 letters every day, mostly protesting against something or other in the Treaty. I don't answer half of them, and they make Lloyd George and Lord Curzon (our two plenipotentiaries) very indignant, when I show them.

Hankey's somewhat uncharitable conclusion was that 'Montagu writes these letters, not in the expectation of affecting the Treaty, but to show to the Indians who make complaints about the Treaty'.[30] Whether or not Montagu was correct in his assessment of the Khilafat, and it seems that he over-estimated the power of pan-Islamism, his disquiet with the possible effects of the movement in India illustrates the increasing extent to which imperial policy-makers had to consider Indian opinion in matters which affected Britain's greatest imperial possession. There was, moreover, a pervading sense of uneasiness in many British minds, both at home and in India, regarding the whole future of British rule and the degree to which imperial control was still possible in India. This was the point, certainly, around which many of the post-war discussions about the future functions, status and composition of the Indian Army turned.

The Indian Army, on the whole, had come out well from the First World War. The disasters of the Mesopotamian campaign, however, left doubts as to the efficiency of its organisation and in 1919 a committee was appointed under the chairmanship of Lord Esher with a wide-ranging brief to examine the whole *post bellum* position of the Indian Army. In June 1920 the committee concluded that the military resources of India should be developed in a manner specifically suited to imperial necessities. That being so, along with a number of much-needed internal administrative reforms, Esher recommended that the running of the Indian Army should be placed directly under the authority of the CIGS in London.[31] This idea was an anathema to Delhi. However successful War Office control had been in Mesopotamia during the war, by 1920 the concept was already archaic and had been overtaken by events in India. No Indian government, let alone the new Legislative Assembly, would (or *could*) accept such an outright subordination of Indian to imperial interests. So far as both Chelmsford and Montagu were concerned the issue was settled by the question of finance. Early in 1919, when a War Office scheme for the incorporation of the Indian Army into a more 'imperial' force had been mooted, Chelmsford had insisted that 'so long as India pays, – and I do not suppose the War Office are going to propose to the English Treasury to take over the charges of the Indian Army, – India must control its own Army'.[32] There was, after all, a long tradition of 'no taxation without representation' in the British empire.

This was precisely the demand which the government of India expected Indian politicians to make in the Legislative Assembly when it began operating during the spring of 1921. Towards the end of 1920, therefore, they began a close examination of the 1921–22 budget with a view to reducing expenditure wherever possible. Military spending was an obvious area for economy and Lord Rawlinson, on his arrival in India in November 1920, was immediately plunged into 'the old problems of military efficiency and financial stringency'.[33] Rawlinson, however, was determined, as he told Henry Wilson, not to take

the responsibility for making sweeping reductions in the fighting forces in India . . . All the members of the Viceroy's council that I have seen so far are terrified at the idea of imposing further taxation. They say that the matter will have to be brought before the new Legislative Assembly when it meets and that to start with a demand for raising further monies for the army would be a fatal political step, for it will put in opposition not only the present extremists in this country but also a large proportion of the moderates.[34]

In January 1921 the Indian government set out their view of Indian military requirements. The Army in India, they argued, needed to maintain sufficient force to provide for three principal contingencies: the protection of the North-West Frontier against tribal or Afghan agression; the possibility of taking *offensive* action against Afghanistan 'in the event of that country forcing war on us'; and the preservation of internal security 'both in times of peace and in the event of a field force being required for active operations on the Frontier'. Although Lord Rawlinson considered that 'the provision for internal defence is already dangerously small', he had reluctantly suggested a reduction in the British establishment of 6,000 troops to 59,000 in all, but this would not be possible before 1922. As it was the British contingent was under-strength and required an actual increase of 7,000 men even to reach the proposed reduced total.[35] His proposal provoked an immediate response from London demonstrating clearly that imperial considerations still took priority over Indian. 'Recruitment and organisation of British Army', wired Montagu, 'takes account of fact that India has for many years maintained certain minimum strength of British troops'. The question of reducing the British garrison, he added, raised a vast number of difficult and complex problems and would take years to sort out.[36]

So the government went to the Assembly with little to offer other than an assurance that they had been pressing London for the early return of Indian troops serving overseas. But their anxieties were not realised. When the Assembly came to debate military affairs during its inaugural session in March 1921, although there was some general criticism of the high level of military spending, by and large their opinion coincided with that of the administration. The underlying assumption of the Esher report that a unified imperial command be established was repudiated and the Assembly affirmed that 'the purpose of the Army in India must be held to be the defence of India against external aggression and the maintenance of internal peace and tranquility'.[37] Rawlinson thought the Assembly's attitude one of 'pleasing moderation' and the budget, including some extra taxation to fund army spending, passed through 'without much serious difficulty'.[38]

One of the factors regarding internal security which the British rulers of India never fully considered was that whatever 'war games' the general staffs in Delhi or London might play, to plan for a major rebellion in India was quite unrealistic. This is not at all to suggest that such an occurrence was either unlikely or unanticipated – Rawlinson regarded it as 'a practical certainty' that there would be a war 'either within or without our frontiers during my term of office'[39] – but simply to note that the British had not the power to defeat a serious all-India rising. Two hundred and thirty thousand troops and one hundred and ninety thousand police – more than three quarters of whom were Indians themselves – would not go far into a country of 319 million people. Lord Salisbury had been of the opinion that British rule in India rested not on force but on consent[40] and this was just as true in 1921 as it had been in 1874. When considering the possibility of internal unrest Montagu – drawing an Irish parallel – warned the Cabinet in October 1920 that

if any of my colleagues think of the isolation of Europeans in India, of the smallness of the British force in India, and realise that a campaign comparable to the Sinn Fein campaign in Ireland would be almost impossible to deal with except by punishment and revenge, certainly not by prevention, they will understand the danger of the situation which has been caused [in the Punjab] by the assertion of a force we do not in reality possess in preference to the doctrine of goodwill.[41]

It is to his credit that Lord Reading, who became Viceroy in April 1921, recognised the futility of unambiguous repression and that throughout his first year in office, the 'peak year' of Hindu–Muslim agitational unity, he displayed such admirable restraint towards the nationalists, flying frequently in the face of advice from London, army headquarters and the majority of the provincial governors. The mistakes of the Punjab in 1919 were not repeated, Delhi courted the moderate Indian politicians who were prepared to work the new constitution and the non-co-operation campaign was left to run out of steam on its own, unprovoked by any official over-reaction. In February 1922, when the national protest threatened to descend into violence, Gandhi called off the campaign and mass political action in India ceased for half a decade.[42]

Despite the Legislative Assembly's compliant attitude, the Viceroy believed that Indian military policy ought to be reassessed in view of the changed political circumstances. In May 1921 he appointed a committee under Rawlinson to examine 'Indian military requirements'.[43] One of the questions which the committee considered was the provision of troops for internal security, especially the proportion of British to Indian units on such duties. Before the war what were called 'Cis-Indus Internal Security' troops had included 21 British infantry battalions and 27 Indian. During 1919 – 'a time when we fortunately had large numbers of troops in India' – the units earmarked for internal security totalled 36 British battalions and 44 Indian. It was a matter of deliberate policy that a particularly high ratio of British to Indian units was maintained in formations detailed to 'policing' duties. Yet in the early summer of 1921 this ratio was higher than it had been since the aftermath of the Mutiny, and there were actually more British units (28 battalions) than Indian (21 battalions) committed to 'internal defence'. This was bluntly defended by the Indian General Staff on the grounds that there was widespread disorder and that British soldiers were 'not influenced by religious or racial bias'. 'Until the internal situation in this country is in a much more satisfactory condition than it is at present . . .' they remarked, 'it is difficult to see how any reduction at all can safely be made in the numbers of British units told off to Internal Security'.[44]

The balance between British and Indian troops, however, was sharply – and understandably – criticised by the four Indian members of Rawlinson's review committee. They demanded a substantial cut in the number of British battalions. Rawlinson reluctantly acquiesced. 'I was unable to resist the pressure when it came to weighing the fact that we had 28 Brit. Battns and only 21 Indian in Internal security', he noted in his journal. 'It was impossible to defend these proportions'. He thought that there was no need for it, 'nor can you defend such a basis of arrangements in present Indian conditions'. Departing from the purely military perceptions of his General Staff, Rawlinson, who possessed considerable political acumen, observed that since 'we have decided to trust the Indians to lead them to self governt . . . we cannot therefore justify an Army of occupation'.[45] The final recommendation of the committee was for three British cavalry regiments and five battalions of infantry, more than Rawlinson would ideally have wished,[46] to be replaced by three Indian cavalry regiments and four infantry battalions, but subject to the proviso that any 'deterioration in the internal or external situation' might necessitate a modification of this proposal. The committee also favoured the 'adoption and publication . . . of a definite policy of Indianisation of Indian Army'.[47] In the consideration of money-saving techniques, the creation of a British-officered gendarmerie was (inevitably) suggested to Lord Rawlinson, but he thought that such a force would be more expensive and less reliable than Indian troops. He also rejected it 'because we *must* keep as many British battalions as possible in India in order to save the Expeditionary force from annihilation'[48] – that is to say, in order to protect as far as was possible the imperial functions of the forces in India.

The Rawlinson committee's proposals for troop reductions were modest enough, but within a fortnight of their first being sent to London, disturbances among the Muslims of the Madras Presidency – the 'Moplah rebellion' – obliged Delhi to postpone consideration of the committee's report.[49] Although mopping-up operations continued until the second half of 1922, the back of the rebellion had been broken by November 1921[50] and the military authorities could once more concentrate their attention on the problem of economy. This gave Rawlinson no pleasure because demands for retrenchment had escalated since the summer and it seemed likely in November that the Legislative Assembly would be satisfied with nothing less than a reduction' of twenty or twenty-five British battalions. 'We cannot possibly accept any decision of this kind', wrote Rawlinson to Wilson, 'for the Viceroy and I fully realise that it would endanger the safety of the country'.[51] Yet some concession was necessary, if only as a gesture towards Indian opinion in order to ease the passage of the budget in the spring. 'It is true that Army expenditure is non-votable,' observed Delhi, 'but, if our unvoted Budget contains expenditure of a type which we are not prepared to justify to the Legislature . . . and which, if challenged, we cannot honestly defend, our position becomes most insecure'.[52]

In February 1922, therefore, the Indian government informed London that they hoped not only to effect the reductions in British units recommended by the Rawlinson committee, but also to buy off Indian politicians through adopting its Indianisation scheme. They justified their proposed action by stressing the political and financial difficulties which faced them. 'We are confronted', they telegraphed gloomily, 'with necessity of imposing, for the second year in succession, very heavy additional taxation. That taxation will inevitably be challenged as being due to heavy expenditure connected with maintenance of our Army'. They thought it absolutely imperative that the two announcements, of reductions and Indianisation, should be made at once. 'Unless we receive your permission to do so', they cautioned, 'consequence must be, we consider, grave, involving serious risks of complete breakdown of the Reform Scheme, and rendering administration of this country most difficult'.[53]

There was not much sympathy in London for the Indian position. Since November 1921 a Committee of Imperial Defence sub-committee had been examining the Rawlinson proposals in a somewhat leisurely fashion.[54] But when Delhi forced the issue the committee quickly met on 10 February and came out very strongly against any reduction in the British garrison, although they were less unanimous on the question of Indianisation. Lloyd George declared that he thought all the Englishmen in India had got 'cold feet and that they must be cured of their feeling of discouragement'.[55] Montagu had little to offer when he sent the Cabinet's reply to Delhi. No 'further reduction' of the British troops in India could be sanctioned. The general feeling in London was that taking into consideration 'the frontier of India, its size, the importance of its communications and the political conditions', the Indian government had 'no troops to spare'. The Rawlinson committee's Indianisation proposal could not be accepted and, finally, the Cabinet absolutely forbade the publication of any part of the committee's report for 'it could not fail to reveal differences of opinion between your Government and His Majesty's Government which at all costs must be avoided'.[56]

On the same day, Montagu sent Reading a second telegram on 'the fundamental principles of Indian Government':

Reports are constantly reaching England of a widely held belief, not only among Indians but among Englishmen, that we regard our mission in India as drawing to a close and that we are preparing for a retreat. If such an idea exists, it is a complete fallacy, and its continued existence can only in itself lead to a decline in morale among the services and to intensified challenges to our authority . . . The security of the country from dangers without and within upon which depends the capacity of its Government to fulfil its primary duties can only ultimately be guaranteed by the Army in India. With regard to it we cannot take any steps which would compromise our position. If therefore we find it impossible to reduce the size of the Army or to accept a programme of Indianisation which we are compelled to believe would be prejudicial to its efficiency, it is because we believe that an acceptance of such proposals would not only lend colour to the dangerous belief in a policy of retreat, but must directly hamper us in the exercise of the functions with which we are entrusted.[57]

The Cabinet, of course, were in a good position to demand a thoroughgoing application of 'empire' in India since they could safely leave its primary application to their agents in Delhi and perhaps not necessarily be implicated in the possible failure of such a policy. Besides, to take an imperial 'hard line' with Delhi could scarcely do any harm to Lloyd George's flagging reputation on the Unionist backbenches.

Lord Rawlinson was not displeased with London's refusal to allow any reduction in the British garrison. In July 1922 he told the Viceroy that there was 'the strongest argument of all for not reducing the British garrisons in India, and nothing will induce me to agree to it even with bankruptcy staring us in the face. But', he added, 'we must both reduce expenditure and increase taxation if there is to be any hope of balancing our next budget'.[58] The army vote, moreover, still offered the richest field for economy. 'We cannot get away from it', wrote Reading to Peel, Montagu's successor at the India Office, 'that no substantial reduction can be made in expenditure unless military expenditure is tackled'.[59] In order to cut Indian spending generally, in 1922 the British government sent out a 'retrenchment committee' under the Earl of Inchcape to do for India what Geddes was supposed to have done for Britain.[60] Inchcape recommended sweeping economies, but to cut military expenditure meant either reducing the total number of troops (preferably British from Delhi's point of view) or securing some sort of subsidy from the home government. Both options were broadly unacceptable in London. When Worthington-Evans was considering both the Geddes and the Rawlinson committee recommendations in the summer of 1921, he noted that a reduction in British units would throw those units

> on to the Imperial Budget, or, as the only alternative, force us to disband them and so to weaken the armed strength of the Empire as a whole without any relief to the British taxpayer . . . It is in my opinion a question for special consideration whether the Indian taxpayer is to be endowed with this priority of right to the savings to be made by weakening the empire as a whole.[61]

Clearly the Secretary for War still regarded the Army in India as a subordinate imperial military organisation, free to be ordered about the world at will by London – as had been the case during the war. But this was no longer so. Political and constitutional developments in India had ineluctably and irreversibly begun to limit the *imperial* disposability of the Army in India.

Despite Lloyd George's attempt to 'stop the rot', there was in effect very little either he or the Cabinet could do. Between the wars there was a continuing and cumulative confirmation that the pass was already sold. In July 1921 Rawlinson had come to the conclusion that Indianisation must eventually happen 'whether we like it or not', and in March 1923 a limited, 'eight-unit' scheme was introduced.[62] Backed by the findings of the Inchcape committee the Commander-in-Chief also pushed through reductions in both the British and the Indian components of the army. 'It is', he argued, 'more important for the internal peace of India that we should balance our budget, than that we should keep the extra troops'.[63] By 1925 the Army in India had been reduced to an establishment of 197,000: 57,000 British soldiers and 140,000 Indian – respectively 24,000 and 12,000 fewer than in 1914. When the Committee of Imperial Defence sub-committee on 'Indian military requirements' finally presented their conclusions in June 1922, they 'recognised that the Indian Army cannot be treated as it if were absolutely at the disposal of His Majesty's Government for service outside India'. They also accepted the government of India's view that 'the Indian Army should not be required permanently to provide large oversea garrisons'. The cost of such garrisons, moreover, 'should be borne by His Majesty's Government, or by the dependency or colony requiring their services'.[64] The imperial role of the Army in India continued to be a sensitive topic among Indian politicians. In March 1923 Rawlinson complained to Lord Derby (now Secretary for War) that the Under-Secretary of State for War (Walter Guinness) had referred in the House of Commons to the Army in India as 'an Imperial Reserve'. At once Rawlinson had been attacked in the Legislative Assembly 'and asked whether it was right for the Indian taxpayer to be charged with the maintenance of an Imperial Reserve. I got out of it as best I could!! *But* please ask Guinness *not* to repeat it'.[65]

The result of both spending cuts and the increasingly critical line taken by domestic Indian politicians over military questions was that the Army in India progressively became less and less of an imperial asset. So much so that in the 1930s the British government – as Worthington-Evans had feared in 1921 – agreed to pay subsidies for the maintenance and modernisation of the Indian armed forces.[66] It was perhaps apt that the costs of the process effectively initiated by India's massive contributions to the imperial war effort in 1914- 18, and confirmed by the calls made on Indian resources by London in the immediate post-war years, should eventually have settled firmly on to the shoulders of the British taxpayer.

Chapter 7

The defence of Suez

From the last quarter of the nineteenth century to the third quarter of the twentieth, Egypt with the Suez Canal occupied a singularly important position within the British empire. The canal was a vital link in the chain of imperial communications between Britain and the East, and a major artery for the world's merchant shipping fleets. In 1913 over twenty million tons of shipping (of which twelve was British) passed through the canal, incidentally earning a dividend of 1.3 million pounds on the British government's shares in the Canal Company.[1] In more general terms Egypt provided both a convenient base from which Britain's Near and Middle Eastern interests could be secured and a focus for British trade and investment throughout the region. Suez also had considerable symbolic significance. In a most satisfactory fashion British preeminence confirmed the supersession of the French who had long nursed imperial ambitions in the eastern Mediterranean. The canal itself represented a pleasingly profitable marriage of commerce and empire. The 'veiled protectorate', which had been established following the British occupation of Egypt in 1882 seemed, moreover, to strike a particularly happy balance between explicit formal control and potentially uncertain informal influence. The commonly-held British assumption that the country was of long-term strategic value was powerfully reinforced during the First World War. So much so that in 1917 the Director of Military Intelligence in Cairo described it as 'the keystone of our whole Near Eastern fabric'.[2] Yet, as in other parts of the empire, the wartime pressures imposed upon Egypt did much to undermine the uneasy and delicate political relationship between the British and their imperial subjects. Here too the catalyst of war accelerated local nationalism and began to erode the foundations of British control.

Following the British occupation the Sultan of Turkey had retained titular suzerainty over Egypt but after the Ottoman declaration of war against the Allies in November 1914 the British government unilaterally established a formal Protectorate over Egypt, introduced martial law and replaced the Turcophil Khedive Abbas Hilmi II with the less truculent Hussein who took the title of Sultan. The British administrative grip tightened during the war as Egypt was transformed into an enormous military base for Allied operations against the Ottoman Empire and a major clearing-house for supplies and reinforcements travelling to Europe from India and Australasia. The only direct threat to the Suez Canal by Ottoman forces was successfully repelled in February 1915 and thereafter the principal danger to Allied sea-communications came from the activity of enemy submarines.[3] The internal conditions of Egypt during the war gave little cause for concern to the British authorities. So secure, indeed, was Britain's position in 1917 that Milner made the unlikely assertion that 'Egypt will in future be as much a part of the British Empire as India or Nigeria'.[4] But in Egypt the war stimulated political and economic changes to such an extent that open revolt was to break out in 1919. The traditional Egyptian ruling class took offence at the increasing interference of British 'advisers' in domestic affairs. The subordination of the country's economy to military requirements dislocated traditional structures and privileges, while wartime inflation, conscription and compulsory purchase all fuelled the growing discontent.[5] Following the armistice, therefore, when the British seemed reluctant immediately to loosen their hold on the administration of Egypt it did not take much to transform latent social unrest into overt violence.

On 13 November 1918 a deputation led by Sa'ad Zaghlul, a veteran lawyer-politician who became the coryphaeus of Egyptian nationalism in the post-war period, asked the British High Commissioner, Sir Reginald Wingate, for complete independence. Wingate refused and also declined Zaghlul's further request for permission to travel to London to put his case personally to the British government. The High Commissioner, who had been acting under instructions from London, was, however, genuinely anxious to go at least some way towards meeting the legitimate national demands of the Egyptians and he eventually persuaded the Foreign Secretary to allow an official delegation of Egyptian ministers – not including Zaghlul – to go to London. But the ministers refused to go without Zaghlul on the very good grounds that in their absence he would be able to seize the initiative and secure for himself an unassailable position as the leading Egyptian politician. Nevertheless the British authorities remained determined that Zaghlul should not go to London, and at the beginning of March 1919, while Wingate was in England putting his conciliatory case to the Foreign Office, the Egyptian ministry resigned. Zaghlul immediately began to demand that the Sultan should postpone forming a new government until the British made some concessions to the nationalists. In the face of this agitation the acting High Commissioner, Sir Milne Cheetham, deported Zaghlul and his principal confederates to Malta, thus unintentionally providing the spark which set off revolt in Egypt.[6]

The first serious rioting broke out on 12 March and quickly spread throughout the country. But the army commander, Sir Edward Bulfin, efficiently suppressed the disorder with a rapid demonstration of overwhelming power and the full imposition of martial law. He was fortunate to have at his disposal large numbers of troops– many awaiting demobilisation – who comprised the residue of the British armies which had fought in Palestine and Syria. Thus he was able 'to take simultaneous action all over the country and also to dispense with a strong central reserve'. He had, moreover, the assistance of the RAF and 'at the most critical moment aeroplanes performed very useful service'. Within a month public order had been largely restored, although a general strike continued for some time.[7]

The violence of March 1919 greatly disturbed the decision-makers in London. Wingate was summarily replaced by Sir Edmund (later Lord) Allenby, who was Commander-in-Chief of the Egyptian Expeditionary Force and architect of the British victories in Palestine during 1917 and 1918. Nicknamed 'the Bull', he was the very model of a military proconsul. The new High Commissioner's immediate task of securing civil order was clear enough, but the longer-term problem of finding some mechanism by which Egyptian national feeling might be accommodated with imperial strategic requirements was not to be so simple.

Early in April 1919 Allenby reported to Balfour that although most outward disorder had been suppressed, 'causes of unrest and ill-feeling are as strong as ever and I can see no prospect of improvement under present conditions'.[8] He was convinced at this stage that no political settlement could be reached until law and order had been restored. Yet Allenby was not entirely blind to the political dimension of the Egyptian problem. 'This is not the moment for concessions', he wrote to Sir Henry Wilson, 'but it is a great pity that His Majesty's Government refused the Deputations last Winter. Egypt complains – with some truth – that she, who has been loyal throughout the War, is refused the right of being heard'.[9] Allenby, like Wingate before him, was coming to recognise that sooner or later Britain would have to go at least some way towards meeting the demands of the Egyptian politicians.

In the meantime, however, he had his hands full keeping order. He told Wilson that the Egyptian army and police could not in the last resort be relied upon and that he had not 'enough troops for a good margin of safety'. It was a familiar post-war tale. Since his soldiers were 'tired of war, and very bitter against the Egyptians for having stopped their demobilisation', he asked for an extra division of British infantry to be added to his command.[10] This was exactly what Wilson feared. Already he had written to the Foreign Office indicating 'that unless Egypt is kept quiet we shall be called on for more troops, and we shall have to send them which under present conditions will be a matter of extreme difficulty'. Towards the end of April he informed the Cabinet that 'insurrection in

Egypt and revolt in India ...' had resulted 'in urgent demands for reinforcements which are too well found and too insistent to ignore'.[11] Wilson managed to scrape together a division from garrison troops in France and Italy.[12] But it was barely enough to satisfy Allenby who took a very sombre view of the position in Egypt. On 21 April he observed to Wilson that outwardly order only prevailed 'due to the presence of my troops'. He envisaged retaining martial law 'for months to come' and saw little prospect of being able to reduce his garrison. 'Demobilisation', he added, 'must go on, or the troops will mutiny, and so I reiterate the necessity for a steady flow of reinforcements and drafts'.[13]

In London, both Wilson and Churchill were very nearly at their wits' end trying to solve the manpower shortage. On 20 May Wilson had a long talk with his Secretary of State about the problem. 'Men are getting very restless again especially in Egypt', he wrote in his diary that evening. 'We really must give up wasting a lot of good men in looking after & collecting stores in France'.[14] Three days later he wrote to Allenby to see if any manpower economies could be achieved in Egypt:

As you know we are in real difficulties at home in regard to finding troops for the different theatres and more especially for the technical services ... What struck both of us [Wilson and Churchill] was whether you could economise both in officers, and, especially, in transportation services, if you organised your forces more on the basis of a mobile police against internal disorders than on the divisional and corps organisation which is more fitted to compete with regular armies on the field ...

We are in such difficulties about finding absolutely essential troops for Ireland, yourself, Mesopotamia and India that we are continually casting about for ideas and expedients which would tend to economy, especially in transportation and technical services.[15]

But Allenby was not immediately able to help. Although the number of troops in the Egyptian Command (which included Palestine) had been reduced (mostly from demobilisation) in the first six months of 1919 from over 400,000 to just under 128,000,[16] no further reduction was possible until the British withdrew from Syria and Cilicia in favour of the French late in 1919, scaled down their military commitments in Palestine and, above all, until civil order was fully restored in Egypt. In March 1920 there were still over 100,000 imperial troops in the Egyptian Command, but from then on there were steady reductions until in April 1921 the figure stood at 41,000 troops, of which 25,000 were in Egypt itself.[17] By the middle of 1921 the British garrison in Egypt had settled to around 20,000 men, at which figure it was to remain for the rest of the year,[18] but it was a far cry from the pre-war garrison of about 6,000 men.

In order to lift the intolerable burden of a permanent military occupation of Egypt from the army it was clear to the policy-makers in London that some sort of political accommodation would have to be found which would ideally go some way towards restoring the *status quo ante* and render Egypt once again an apparently pliable and quiet client-state. Lord Curzon, who took charge of Egyptian policy while the Prime Minister and the Foreign Secretary were away in Paris at the Peace Conference, proposed at the end of March 1919 that a high-powered commission under the chairmanship of Lord Milner be appointed to enquire into the Egyptian question.[19] Apart from being Colonial Secretary and a 'sound' imperialist, Milner was something of an expert on Egypt. He was the only member of the Cabinet to have served in the Egyptian administration (Director-General of Accounts and later Under-Secretary for Finance, 1889–93) and also the author of *England in Egypt* (published 1892), the 'classic presentation of the English case in Egypt'.[20] Lloyd George and Balfour approved the suggestion[21] and in May Curzon announced it officially in the House of Lords. Because of delays in gathering together the necessary personnel the Milner Mission did not reach Egypt until the beginning of December by which time the nationalist 'Committee of Independence' had so successfully organised a comprehensive boycott that the only Egyptians the Mission were able to interview were officials connected with the Palace or the government.[22]

Shortly after his arrival in Egypt Lord Milner summarised British policy as being 'the exclusion from the affairs of Egypt of all foreign *political* influence except our own'. This was 'an absolutely necessary principle'. Although he was convinced that the Protectorate would have to come to an end, he seems to have regarded the meeting of nationalist demands as being little more than a question of semantics. 'It is possible', he wrote, 'that what *we* mean by "Protectorate" is not really incompatible with what *they* mean by "Independence" '. Towards the end of December 1919 he assured Lloyd George that the Egyptians cared more for the appearance of things than the substance and that the only problem was 'to find a way of making Egypt's relation to Great Britain *appear* a more independent & dignified one than it ever really can be without our abandoning the degree of control wh[ich], in view of native incompetence & corruption we are constrained to keep'.[23]

Milner and his colleagues remained in Egypt for three somewhat frustrating months. Exercised by nationalist intransigence, Milner came to the conclusion that a broad shift in British policy was required in order to break the deadlock which had existed since the end of the war. Military aspects of the Egyptian question reinforced this view. In February 1920 the Cabinet finance committee, searching as ever for economies in army expenditure, proposed that the permanent garrison in Egypt should not exceed 18,000 men. Milner was asked for his opinion. The 'absolute minimum' required for Egypt at the present time, he replied, was approximately 13,000 British and 18,000 Indian soldiers. This was the lowest possible figure which could be achieved 'without incurring grave risks', and the garrison thus reduced would be 'unable to spare men for any outside purpose'.[24] The enormous discrepancy between the Cabinet's 18,000 men and Milner's 31,000 clearly indicated that some adjustment in policy, either in London or Cairo, was essential. If reductions in military spending were given the highest priority by an economy-minded Cabinet, then this could only be done in Egypt by making political concessions to the forces of indigenous nationalism in order to secure internal order. When Milner sent the 'general conclusions' of his Mission to Curzon in May 1920, therefore, he proposed first of all that Egyptian independence should formally be accepted.[25]

Before drawing up his final report, however, Milner sought to hammer out the details of a concomitant treaty to secure 'essential' British interests in a series of negotiations in London with an Egyptian delegation led by Sa'ad Zaghlul himself. The result of these talks – held between June and August 1920 – was a memorandum, wrongly called an 'agreement' by some, for it was no more than a declaration of intent, which affirmed that Britain would recognise 'the independence of Egypt as a constitutional monarchy with representative institutions'. At the same time an alliance would be concluded between the two countries by which Egypt would render assistance to Great Britain in time of war, including 'harbours, aerodromes and means of communication for military purposes'. Great Britain was to retain a garrison on Egyptian soil 'for the protection of her Imperial communications', although this force was not to 'constitute in any manner a military occupation of the country, or prejudice the rights of the Government of Egypt'. Finally, on account of the 'special relations' between Britain and Egypt created by the alliance, the British minister would be 'accorded an exceptional position in Egypt and will be entitled to precedence over all other representatives'.[26]

This finely-balanced document seemed to provide nicely for both imperial strategy and Egyptian sensibility, but when the memorandum was prematurely leaked to the press a few days later, Churchill, supported by Wilson and Trenchard, immediately circulated a protest to the Cabinet. He had read the proposals for giving independence to Egypt 'with very great bewilderment'. He was concerned about the financial implications. Under Milner's terms the British army in Egypt was there solely to safeguard communications with the east, and that swept away altogether 'any claim which we might make for recovering any portion of the cost from the Egyptian Taxpayer'. He went on to say that giving Egypt a sovereign status outside the empire provided a distressing example for both Ireland and India. 'If we leave out the word "Egypt" . . . and substitute the word "Ireland",' he observed, 'it would with very small omissions make perfectly good sense, and would constitute a complete acceptance of Mr De Valera's demands'. Churchill urged that 'all demands to break away from the British Empire and British Crown should be perseveringly withstood'.[27] Sir Henry Wilson believed that 'the draft agreement, if confirmed, must have a far-reaching effect on the military situation of the British Empire'.[28] In his diary he wrote, 'It is a long step towards the ruin of our Empire'.[29] Egypt, like Ireland, was one of the places Wilson thought 'belonged' to Britain when he gave his invariable advice on imperial defence: 'Get out of the places that don't belong to you and hold on to those that do'.[30] Trenchard had more tangible reasons for complaint. In the post-war reorganisation of the air force Egypt had been selected as an 'ideal base' for imperial defence, and Trenchard hoped to station more than a quarter of his operational strength (seven out of twenty-five squadrons) in the country. 'The changed status of Egypt . . .', he noted to the Cabinet, 'is causing me considerable anxiety'. Egypt took an important place in the air force's training schemes and plans for future development and he hoped, therefore, that 'the new policy of the Government will not undo the work of construction to which we are committed'.[31] Allenby's reaction to the proposals was that they might very well necessitate an *increase* in the garrison, and he too thought that Milner's scheme would make 'another Ireland' out of Egypt.[32] What he – and everyone else – failed to see was that Egypt was already 'another Ireland'. He would have been more correct to observe a year later that Lloyd George with the Irish treaty had made 'another Egypt' out of Ireland, for following the Egyptian nationalist revolt of 1919 the British had been 'reduced to negotiating with men whom before 1914 they were accustomed to manage'.[33]

Milner, caught off-balance by the unexpected publication of the memorandum, soon replied to Churchill's criticisms. Rehearsing precisely the same argument that Gladstone had offered in support of Irish home rule, he declared that the proposed concessions to Egyptian nationalism were just and politic and 'calculated to strengthen and not to weaken our Imperial position'. He recognised the key position of Egypt in imperial communications, but saw that as no reason to 'own' the country. 'Is it not sufficient', he asked, 'if we have a firm foothold there?' Even Zaghlul 'was ready to admit our right to safeguard the Suez Canal'.[34] Churchill and his service chiefs, however, were not the only people alarmed by Lord Milner's proposals. Edwin Montagu thought that the British Empire was 'dead', that Milner had 'killed it by his Egyptian arrangement', and the Prime Minister was fearful lest the proposal for Egyptian independence should have an adverse effect in India.[35] Late in October 1920 Lord Beatty joined the band-wagon on behalf of the Admiralty and circulated a memorandum emphasising the extreme importance of the Suez Canal.[36] The Prime Minister of Australia, W. M. Hughes, telegraphed Lloyd George in November to protest about the proposals on the grounds that Egypt 'gateway to India, and East, including Australia', could not be handed over to elements who would probably, in his opinion, become hostile to the empire. 'I am of course aware', he continued, 'that it is intended to retain control of canal but quite sure effective control [of] this narrow and most vulnerable waterway cannot (be?) maintained when and if hinterland is in possession of hostile populations'. Lloyd George entirely concurred with Hughes 'as to supreme importance to the British Empire of keeping absolute control over the Suez Canal', assured him that the matter was receiving 'the earnest attention of the British Government' and suggested that the question be discussed at the imperial conference planned for June 1921.[37]

Lord Curzon put his official reaction to the Milner proposals in a Cabinet memorandum of 11 October which was much more favourable towards Milner than might have been expected. He accepted that a treaty of alliance was probably the best method of solving the problem of control in Egypt, but took issue with Milner over his estimate of 5,000 troops for the eventual imperial garrison in the country – not very different from the pre-war figure. 'The position of Egypt', asserted Curzon, 'renders it the inevitable and indispensable centre of British military strategy and operations in the Middle East' and the garrison, serving as an imperial reserve for the region, would have to be maintained at a high level. Two days later, nevertheless, he wrote privately to Balfour to say that the proposals had filled him 'with a good deal of alarm not merely for our position in Egypt, but for Palestine, Mesopotamia, Arabia & even India'.[38]

In the meantime, however, pressures other than imperial strategy or Egyptian politics were having their effect on the size of Lord Allenby's forces. At the beginning of November 1920 the War Office informed the Commander-in-Chief in India that they had approved a reduction in Egypt and Palestine of five Indian cavalry regiments and nineteen infantry battalions. They explained that the main reason for this, apart from economy, had been 'the paramount necessity of returning to India all troops due for repatriation at the earliest possible moment and reducing to a minimum the number of Indian troops employed outside India'. So important was this consideration that the War Office were 'prepared to accept a certain margin of risk in Egypt and Palestine, where, however, the situation and outlook now appears favourable'.[39] This was just a month after the Cabinet had learned of the Indian government's reluctance to supply extensive overseas garrisons from the Indian army.[40] Allenby had no choice but to acquiesce in the decision, but he placed on record his opinion that with a reduced garrison he would no longer have sufficient troops available to restore order in Egypt 'in the event of serious disturbance'.[41] Ten days later, after a revival of unrest, he asked for an extra eight battalions to be attached to his garrison. 'All this owing to Milner's rotten scheme', thought Wilson.[42]

The continuing drain on scarce military resources caused by the unsettled condition of Egypt had its effect on Cabinet attitudes. On 4 November a conference of ministers agreed 'that some alternative must be found to our present position in Egypt, the maintenance of which required the presence of a large military force'.[43] At the very end of the year, however, when it came to a 'full dress' debate on the Egyptian question, the Cabinet was deeply split over whether or not to approve Milner's proposals, and Lloyd George had to take the unusual step of taking a formal vote. Seven ministers backed Milner; five opposed him. Chamberlain, Fisher and Montagu, *inter alia*, supported the proposals. Worthington-Evans, Lloyd George, Churchill and Curzon (despite his memorandum of 11 October) were 'decidedly against', while Bonar Law reserved his judgment.[44] With no Cabinet consensus regarding the Milner proposals, throughout 1921 a debate continued on the extent to which the British government was able to concede Egyptian national demands while retaining the substance of her imperial strategic needs. Churchill, for example, urged that only minimal concessions be made, while in Egypt 'Adly Yeghen and the moderate nationalists, spurred on by Zaghlul's increasing extremism, refused to be fobbed off with anything less than complete independence. The full Milner Report, when it was published in the spring of 1921, astounded Egyptian opinion at the extent of the British concessions and as Wilson had correctly predicted when the proposals were first leaked, 'now it has been published we will never be able to get rid of it'.[45]

Churchill, nevertheless, would have been perfectly happy to have 'got rid of' the Milner Report and the unpalatable suggestion that Egypt should be granted sovereign status. In June 1921 he told Curzon that he was 'not at all prepared to sit still & mute & watch the people of this country being slowly committed to the loss of this great & splendid monument of British administrative skill & energy'. At the imperial conference the following month he assured the dominion leaders that the future status of Egypt was 'a matter of the actual vital existence of the structure of the British Empire', and declared that we could not afford 'to let ourselves be pushed out of our position in Egypt by the continuance of local agitations'.[46] During 1921 Allenby persevered with a policy of conciliating moderates and coercing extremists in the hope of creating an Egyptian ministry which would sign a formal agreement with Great Britain. As the series of desultory and abortive negotiations proceeded throughout the summer and autumn, however, both he and the majority of the British officials in Egypt came increasingly to the conclusion that the only way out of the political stalemate was for Britain unilaterally and unreservedly to grant independence to Egypt. But for the Egyptians 'independence' meant the withdrawal of the British garrison from Egypt proper to a base near the Suez Canal, and this was a pill which the intransigent imperialists in the British Cabinet found too bitter to swallow.

On 20 October, however, Curzon, who was nothing if not inconsistent with regard to Egypt, proposed to the Cabinet that a gradual withdrawal of British troops from Cairo and Alexandria to the Canal zone should be offered to 'Adly Yeghen. But both Lloyd George and Churchill firmly objected to the suggestion.[47] A few days later at the first (and only) meeting of the Cabinet 'sub-committee on situation in Egypt' Curzon repeated his proposal. Allenby (in London for consultation) expressed his opinion that now 'some form of independence' should be granted to Egypt, and that the principle should be acknowledged even if the current negotiations with 'Adly Yeghen broke down. Churchill, however, continued to cavil. 'He considered that an offer at the present time to withdraw our garrisons from Cairo and Alexandria would be an act of evacuation and an abrogation of our authority in Egypt which would have disastrous results'.[48] Herbert Fisher, another member of the sub-committee, disagreed and wrote to the Prime Minister to say so:

I fail to see how it makes any very material difference to our substantial hold upon Egypt whether the troops are within Cairo or Alexandria or within a striking distance of twenty-four hours from those two centres. We have to remember that whatever agreement we make we shall control the Sudan, the Canal and the Sea . . .

Zaghloul [sic] may, of course, upset any moderate Government which may be established . . . If so, we should be compelled to use force with the inevitable result that there would be a revulsion of Egyptian feeling in favour of constitutional government. All I am concerned with is to send Redmond back with a good offer for fear that we may have to deal with a Michael Collins.[49]

The Irish analogy was apt. Lloyd George, deep in negotiations with Sinn Fein, was prepared to be stern towards Egyptian (and Indian) nationalists in order to demonstrate to the restless Conservative backbenchers on whom his administration depended that he would not necessarily 'surrender' to the pressures of nationalism in every part of the empire. After a Cabinet on Egypt early in November Fisher noted in his diary: 'My impression is that PM is so anxious about Ireland that he dare not make concessions about Egypt'.[50] The successful conclusion of the Irish negotiations in December 1921 and the acceptance by the Irish delegation of the Crown and the empire led Churchill to hope that the Egyptians might do likewise. On the day that the Irish treaty was signed he wrote to Curzon to say that he did not 'wholly despair of the ultimate inclusion of Egypt in the general show'.[51]

Allenby too was generally more optimistic at the end of 1921. Tiring of Zaghlul's continued obstructionism, just before Christmas he deported him to the Seychelles. This set off some disorder but by 29 December

Allenby felt that the fire had 'almost burnt out'. 'I have great hopes for the future', he wrote to the young Archibald Wavell, 'All the best Egyptians are on my side'.[52] In January 1922 he outlined his general policy to Sir Henry Wilson:

The important point now is that Zaghlul and his co-exiles must not come back, and that His Majesty's Government makes no concession to him or his party. At the same time I want them to put into effect the policy outlined in the letter to the Sultan, of 3rd December; drop the word "protectorate", give them a constitution, retain all necessary safeguards, including British troops here, and make further concessions depending on circumstances.

I'll get a first class and friendly Ministry, and the Egyptian question will be far on towards settlement. Instead of the usual method of trying to conciliate our enemies, and carting our friends, we shall be conciliating our friends, rewarding those who have stood by us, and downing our enemies.

This being obviously the right thing to do, I can't get H.M.G. to do it. I've warned them that it's their last chance, and it will soon be too late even to do that. If I can't get it through, and that soon, I shall resign. Curzon is backing me, like a man.[53]

Allenby was understandably frustrated by the Cabinet's refusal to support what he regarded to be the only and obvious policy. Armed with an immediate and unilateral declaration of Egyptian independence as evidence of British good faith, he would be able to persuade the moderate nationalists he had been so assiduously cultivating to form a government with whom he could then work out a treaty containing the imperial safeguards which everyone on the British side agreed to be essential. London, however, held the position that no declaration of independence was possible until assurances had been received from the Egyptian side regarding those safeguards.

Faced with continued Cabinet vacillation, Allenby placed his resignation in the hands of the Foreign Secretary – 'the utterance of a mortified man', thought Curzon[54] – and he was summoned home to account personally for his attitude before the Cabinet. Lord Allenby arrived in London on 10 February and was at once plunged into a series of meetings to hammer out some viable Egyptian policy. Although Churchill declared that he would 'never agree' to Allenby's proposals and 'would fight to the end', Lloyd George, Curzon and Allenby eventually settled on a compromise which the Prime Minister presented to the Cabinet on 16 February.[55] This was the 'Allenby Declaration', published on 28 February, by which the British government conceded formal independence to Egypt while at the same time 'absolutely' reserving 'to the discretion of His Majesty's Government . . .

(a) The security of the communications of the British Empire in Egypt; (b) The defence of Egypt against all foreign aggression or interference, direct or indirect;

(c) The protection of foreign interests in Egypt and the protection of minorities; (d) The Sudan.[56]

Allenby 'has won all along the line', commented Wilson, '& the white flag is once more up over 10 Downing Street.'[57]

The Allenby Declaration was an enormous imperial red herring. After all the shouting it conceded little more than a constitutional nicety. The Colonial Secretary was at pains to point out to the dominion governments that it preserved fully 'the *status quo* with regard to the special interests of the British Empire in Egypt'.[58] It did not alter the essential British position which since 1882, with the exception of the wartime Protectorate, in Churchill's words, had 'rested on a fiction supported by force'.[59] Before 1914 Egypt had theoretically been a Turkish province; after 1922 it was theoretically independent. Consistently, however, the British retained a firm grip on the levers of power. Yet the Egyptians themselves seem to have been fooled for a time, although official recognition by the Egyptian government of Britain's 'special position' did not come until a twenty-year treaty was signed in July 1936. From 1922 moderate nationalist politicians were found who were prepared to work the system more or less within the British guide-lines. The instability and widespread disorder of the immediate post-war years died away.

By October 1922 the British garrison in Egypt had been reduced to only four battalions of infantry and three regiments of cavalry – much the same number of troops as before the war. Indeed, with the very real threat of war against Turkey, the War Office seriously considered reducing the garrison still further 'to the equivalent of two or three battalions'.[60] Such was the peaceful state of Egypt. It was not to last, of course, but for a time the political legerdemain of the Allenby Declaration, so painfully arrived at, did in 1922 what 20,000 troops and any amount of imperial bombast had failed to do in 1921 and the years before that.

The urgent wartime desire to protect the British position in Egypt and secure the Suez line of communications had been a major impetus behind the victorious campaign of Allenby's Egyptian Expeditionary Force which had followed the capture of Jerusalem in 1917 with that of Damascus, Beirut and Aleppo in October 1918. At the end of the war Britain enjoyed an unequalled military and political preponderance in the Arab lands of the Middle East. In Mesopotamia British control was complete; in the Arabian peninsula to the south a British-backed Arab army led by Sherif Husain of Mecca, King of the Hedjaz, had conquered all but a stubborn Turkish garrison in Medina. After the armistice the British government and their local agents faced the problem of how best to capitalise this new peace-time pre-eminence in the light of wartime promises, political expediency and strategic necessity. 'Politics in Palestine & Syria', wrote Allenby presciently in November 1918, are not going to be too easy in the future. Jews, Arabs, French, Italians, English & other nations, all think they have special interests and special claims and rights; and every known religion asserts itself, and adds knots to the tangle. However, I maintain the attitude of Gallio; and I concern myself only with the maintenance of order, and the establishment of an impartial, non-political administration.[61]

Allenby was wise to attempt to stay above politics, for the armistice in the Middle East opened a veritable Pandora's box of national, tribal and religious chaos, enhanced, if not largely caused, by the contradictory arrangements Britain had made during the war with Arabs, Jews and the French, among others. King Husain, who in 1916 led the Arab revolt against Turkey, understood from his correspondence with Sir Henry McMahon in 1915–16 that Great Britain would 'recognise and uphold' Arab independence both in the Arabian peninsula and also in parts of Palestine and Syria. The Jews, on the other hand, were encouraged by the Balfour Declaration of October 1917, by which they believed that Britain would favour and encourage the establishment of a 'national home' in Palestine. The French, who had historic interests in the Levant, had been granted Cilicia and the coastal zone of Syria and Lebanon by the Sykes-Picot Agreement in May 1916. Although the Syrian interior was to be no more than a French 'sphere of influence', it is clear that at the time the French regarded the distinction between the two parts of Syria as being only very minor. They had, certainly, a very different conception of the future administration of the region than that envisaged by King Husain.[62]

The British, then, in 1918 had the unenviable (and impossible) task of sorting out from their war-time tangle of political and moral commitments a viable Middle Eastern policy which might not entirely alienate the Arabs, nor irrevocably antagonise the French, and which, perhaps, might go some way towards satisfying the Zionists. This seemed scarcely possible to Sir Henry Wilson. 'We have made so many promises to everybody in a contradictory sense', he told Allenby, 'that I cannot for the life of me see how we can get out of our present mess without breaking our word to somebody'.[63]

Wilson was not alone in his opinion. Late in November 1918, when the Cabinet eastern committee met to prepare the British case towards Turkey for the peace conference, Lord Curzon observed that 'we have been a good deal embarrassed' by the undertakings given by McMahon to Husain. He had even less to say in favour of Sykes-Picot: 'That unfortunate Agreement, which has been hanging like a millstone round our necks . . . In May 1916 we were bound hard and fast by this deplorable Agreement, to which, as we know, the French seem disposed to adhere most tenaciously'. Arab opinion, moreover, had been inflamed by a declaration of 8 November 1918 outlining Anglo–French policy towards the Middle East which was apparently the first indication the Arabs had received that the French were expecting to gain a position of some authority in Syria.[64] A week later the committee turned to discuss Syria and Palestine in detail. Syria, declared Curzon, was 'the main source of possible conflict between ourselves on the one hand, and the French and Arabs on the other'. He reiterated his dissatisfaction with Sykes-Picot and noted that the Arabs were unhappy with the French claim to Syria. Ideally he himself would have preferred the French 'out of Syria altogether'. They were likely to be bad neighbours and 'in the event of trouble with the French in the future' their presence in Syria 'would undoubtedly impose heavy military responsibilities upon Egypt'. Curzon, nevertheless, was not prepared to carry any 'arrangement with the Arabs to the point of quarrelling with the French'. Lord Robert Cecil foresaw just such a quarrel should Great Britain attempt to exclude the French from Syria and he urged that Britain should 'go for some settlement which will give them some position in Syria, however unpleasant it may be to have them there'.[65] Thus it was to be. Later the same month, Lloyd George, who was anxious for Britain to retain both the supposed oil-rich Mosul *vilayet* in Mesopotamia, and Palestine, apparently agreed with Clemenceau that as a *quid pro quo* Britain would support French claims on the left bank of the Rhine, grant an equal share in the Mosul oil, and a free hand in Turkish Cilicia and Syria.[66]

Some of the more ambitious in the French *parti colonial* had also during the war put forward French claims to Palestine, but there was never any real possibility of Britain relinquishing the Holy Land; it was hers by right of conquest, she retained some moral obligations from the Balfour Declaration, and the Prime Minister was 'very vehement about our keeping Palestine'.[67] L. S. Amery, who could always be relied upon to find good reasons for the inclusion of almost any part of the world in the British Empire, was particularly anxious to retain the territory. 'Strategically Palestine and Egypt go together', he told Lloyd George. Palestine was 'a necessary buffer' to the Suez Canal, and it was most important to have control of a land through route from Egypt and the Mediterranean to Baghdad, 'both for rapidity of mutual support and in case of the danger of submarines in the Mediterranean or the Indian Ocean'.[68] Curzon was equally impressed with the strategic argument. 'Has not the whole history of the war shown us', he asked the eastern committee on 5 December, 'that Palestine is really the strategical buffer of Egypt, and that the Canal, which is the weak side of Egypt, if it has to be defended in the future, will have to be defended – as it has in this war – from the Palestine side?' Cecil, however, unremittingly gloomy at eastern committee meetings, thought there was 'not going to be any great catch about it . . . Because we shall simply keep the peace between the Arabs and the Jews. We are not going to get anything out of it. Whoever goes there will have a poor time'.[69] Time was to prove him correct. By August

1919, Curzon, displaying perhaps his 'lack of real strength of character',[70] had changed his mind about Palestine:

I am so convinced that Palestine will be a rankling thorn in the flesh of whoever is charged with its Mandate that I would withdraw from this responsibility while we yet can. There was a time when the soldiers told us that our possession of Palestine was necessary for the defence of Egypt, but they no longer hold this view . . . The Prime Minister clings to Palestine for its sentimental and traditional value, and talks about Jerusalem with almost the same enthusiasm as about his native hills.[71]

In September even Lloyd George and Allenby agreed that although Palestine 'had no economic value whatsoever', it could not now be given up 'without great loss of prestige'.[72]

The French, meanwhile, were pressing for a British military evacuation from the interior of Syria. At the end of 1918 Allenby had allowed a provisional Arab government to be set up under his 'Occupied Enemy Territory Administration East', which included a large 'somewhat indeterminate' area stretching from Aleppo to Damascus and the region later to become known as Trans-Jordan in the south.[73] In March 1919 General Clayton, then Chief Political Officer of the Egyptian Expeditionary Force, noting that British policies towards the French, Arabs and Jews were 'incompatible the one with the other', suggested that France be persuaded to give up Syria to Britain in exchange for Constantinople and a major sphere of influence in Turkey.[74] But these Arabophil sentiments cut little ice in London or Paris, and the dictates of *real-politik* demanded that France was appeased while the Arabs took the hindmost. There was some sympathy, however, for the Arab cause and the British attempted to compromise by restricting formal French occupation to the coastal region – now the Lebanon. In September 1919 it was announced that British forces would evacuate Syria in favour of a French administration on the littoral and a continuing Arab one in the interior. The Arabs regarded this 'with the utmost dismay'. King Husain's son Feisal told Lloyd George that the withdrawal of British troops from Syria was 'likely to lead to a catastrophe to the whole Arab World and to the Common Cause which the Allies are defending'.[75] But his protests were to no avail and the British troops began their evacuation at the beginning of November. Apart from the need to conciliate the French, the military strain of the Syrian occupation was beginning to tell on the army.

On 5 November Churchill described to the Cabinet the enormous British military responsibilities in the Middle East and observed that the forces there also contained the 'largest proportion of men who have been away from their homes for the longest time'. The General Staff, moreover, claimed that the evacuation of Syria would result in a reduction of some 25,000 troops in the Egyptian Expeditionary Force.[76] The withdrawal indeed caused the 'catastrophe' Feisal had predicted. In March 1920 the 'Second General Syrian Congress' had met in Damascus and declared Greater Syria to be an independent constitutional monarchy with Feisal himself as king, but the following month the San Remo Conference officially approved British and French mandates in the Middle East. Britain was to have Mesopotamia and Palestine, while France, to the dismay of the Arabs, was granted the Lebanon and all of Syria. In July, French forces under General Gouraud occupied Damascus, forced the Arab government to flee and by the end of the year had thoroughly consolidated their hold on the country.[77]

Britain's Palestine mandate included territories both west and east of the river Jordan. Feisal had claimed the western part – 'Trans-Jordan' – to be part of his Syrian kingdom but following his expulsion from Damascus he left it to the ambitions of his brother 'Abdullah. In the meantime the new mandate posed familiar problems of military control. In February 1920, Churchill noted that the Palestine garrison of 35,000 troops was costing nine million pounds a year which was 'of course, far beyond anything that Palestine can ever yield in return'. Lord Allenby and the General Staff, nevertheless, were in agreement that danger would result from 'any diminution'.[78] In May, the Director of Military Operations in London reinforced this view and emphasised that the apparent numerical size of the garrison was grossly misleading – as, it seemed, was the case with every other part of the army. He noted that the British units in Palestine were 'raw, untrained and unacclimatised and that a large percentage of their effective strength is at present employed in filling the gaps caused by demobilisation in the technical and administrative services'. Indeed, so weak were some units that 'for practical purposes, it may be taken that the British battalions in Palestine could only take the field at less than half their effective strength'.[79]

Sir Walter Congreve, GOC of the Egypt and Palestine Command, was equally concerned that due to the inadequacy of the local police force the troops in Palestine were 'dispersed all over the country to keep order'. Since this deprived him of 'an adequate reserve and the power of moving troops from the country in the event of their being required in Egypt', he suggested that a Palestine gendarmerie be formed 'at an early date'.[80] This idea was taken up enthusiastically by Colonel W. H. Deedes, civil secretary to Sir Herbert Samuel, the newly-appointed High Commissioner for Palestine. Such a force, he declared, could ease Congreve's military problems and be 'something a little more than Police and a little less than regular Troops'.[81] In August 1920 an interdepartmental committee in the Foreign Office considered the proposal. The Director of Military Intelligence, representing the War Office, said that his department was 'in general sympathy with the scheme, on the understanding that they were not called upon to bear any proportion of the cost'. It was a standard opening ploy. Colonel Deedes, however, thought that since the proposed force would 'enable the War Office to effect a reduction in the regular military garrison of Palestine' and thus produce a 'material economy', the Army Council might consider bearing the expense of the force until the Palestine administration was itself in a position so to do. But the Army Council were not thus disposed and suggested that 'if it were necessary for such a force to receive assistance from Imperial funds, such assistance would be an appropriate charge on the Consular and Diplomatic Vote'. The committee sought a ruling on the matter from the Treasury who further complicated the issue by stating 'that, in principle, the cost of the defence of Palestine, including the cost of the British garrison, should be a charge upon the revenues of that country'.[82] Since no-one seemed particularly anxious to pay for a British gendarmerie in Palestine, the scheme was quietly forgotten until Samuel revived it in December, once again as an alternative to a large permanent garrison of regular troops.

In 1920 there was as yet little evidence in Palestine of the intercommunal violence between Arabs and Jews which was later to become endemic. On his arrival in Jerusalem in July 1920 Sir Herbert Samuel was able to report to Curzon that the province was in a 'surprisingly satisfactory' state and 'the absence of any difficulties so far is as agreeable as it is unexpected'.[83] In the autumn, however, there were disturbances in Trans-Jordan and the French General Gouraud in Damascus, fearing that the unrest might spread to Syria, pressed Samuel to send in some British troops. 'I quite understand', wrote Samuel to London on 17 October, 'that after our recent experience in Mesopotamia, the War Office are very nervous in undertaking what may appear to be new commitments, but the conditions offer no analogy whatever'.[84] On 28 October he told Lloyd George that he doubted 'whether we can continue to keep order in Trans-Jordania with an establishment which consists of six British officers and nothing else at all'.[85] But that sort of small and inexpensive establishment was exactly to the tastes of both the War Office and the Cabinet who noted their hope in December that the 'present large military force' in Palestine would soon be reduced.[86] At the end of the month when Ronald Storrs, the Governor of Jerusalem, was home on leave, he tried to impress upon the authorities in London 'the vital importance of showing strength in Transjordania'. But his efforts were in vain, and he reported back to Samuel that he had 'really left no stone unturned – only there's nothing underneath them!'[87]

On 23 December the War Office informed the Egyptian Command that the Cabinet wished to reduce the size of the Palestine garrison. 'In view of the limited resources and population of that country' they had concluded that there could be 'no question' of maintaining a force on the present scale (15,000 troops). The Cabinet believed a garrison of 5,000 men to be the maximum possible 'and that the future of the country must be entirely reconsidered if a greater number is required'. The Foreign Office cabled Jerusalem for comment and Samuel replied by suggesting once again the idea of a Palestine Gendarmerie, which could be established 'on a less expensive footing than British troops'.[88] The General Staff were also consulted as to their views and concluded that a garrison of 5,000 'would be a highly dangerous experiment', but that one of 7,000 'would be a justifiable risk'. They also registered their continuing dissent from any extension of responsibilities in Trans-Jordan. In a covering memorandum, Churchill proposed to reduce the garrison to 7,000 forthwith, 'without prejudice to any further reductions which can be effected later on'.[89]

When Churchill became Secretary of State for the Colonies in February 1921, he exchanged the responsibility for reducing military expenditure for that of not only restricting the Colonial Office estimates but also incorporating Britain's new mandates in the Middle East in some sort of lasting settlement. In order to facilitate this task he gained Cabinet approval to create a wholly-new Middle Eastern department in the Colonial Office, which was to have particular responsibility for the Arab mandates and all matters affecting purely Arab affairs in the Middle East, in consultation, where necessary, with the Foreign and India Offices.[90] Churchill decided that the best way to work out a coherent policy for the region would be to hold a conference on the spot with the principal interested parties.

On 12 March 1921 he brought together in Cairo the chief British officials from Palestine, Mesopotamia, Persia, Somaliland and Aden. One of Churchill's aims was to redress in some measure the disappointments suffered by the Hashimite family of King Husain at the hands of the British. Husain's sons Feisal and 'Abdullah were to be put forward as candidates for the thrones of countries created under the British mandates: Feisal for Mesopotamia and 'Abdullah for Trans-Jordan. Churchill, however, proposed to London that a British military occupation would be necessary in order to secure 'Abdullah's new state. The suggestion was received with 'considerable misgivings' since it was argued by the War Office 'that this occupation would involve a military commitment, the extension and duration of which it was impossible to forecast'.[91] 'We discussed Winston's proposal sent from Cairo to occupy Amman & Trans-Jordania', wrote Wilson. 'I was opposed – & won – on the ground of expense & further commitments'.[92] In the end, Churchill, after discussions in Jerusalem with 'Abdullah himself (who did not want British troops in Amman) recommended that military assistance be given 'in the form of aerial support, and assistance in the organisation of local levies under British officers'. In the case of

Palestinian defence, the conference proposed that a local defence force be established to include both Jewish and Arab units.[93] Following the discussions in Cairo and Jerusalem in March 1921, Trans-Jordan was thereafter largely and no doubt thankfully ignored by ministers and officials in London. But as the Arabist H. St. J. Philby remarked in 1924, 'the only serious British interest in that country was, and still is, that it should not be a nuisance to its neighbours'.[94] This was very much the case from the spring of 1921 onwards.

In Palestine, however, there were problems of internal control. Serious riots broke out at Jaffa in May 1921 during which thirty Jews and ten Arabs were killed. An intelligence report blamed the disorder on the special position accorded to the Jews and warned that a much larger garrison than the present one would be required 'if the present British policy in Palestine is to continue unmodified'.[95] A month later Samuel wrote to Churchill: 'I cannot exclude from my mind the possibility of further disturbances, or, even, as my Military Advisors have warned me, of a general rising'.[96] In July the General Staff once again drew attention to 'the inadequacy of the British garrison in Palestine' and declared there to be 'three alternatives:- (1) An alteration of policy as regards Jewish immigration; (2) An increase in the British garrison; or (3) The acceptance of serious danger to the Jewish population'.[97] A fourth option, which was not considered, would have been to abandon Palestine altogether.

There was much sympathy for the Jewish cause in the British government. When Lloyd George was asked in March 1921 by a deputation of Indian Muslims if Palestine could not 'be left as an Arab State', the Prime Minister told them that was quite impossible. 'Oh no', he said, 'you could not go back on that. We are first of all committed to the Jew throughout the world on that subject; that is absolutely settled'.[98] Churchill was equally well-disposed towards Zionism, although he hesitated to support the more extreme Zionist demands (such as unrestricted Jewish immigration) when faced with the military cost of such policies. In August 1921 he told the Cabinet that the War Office estimates for the Palestine garrison during the coming year (1922–3) were £3,319,000. 'It cannot be doubted', he noted, 'that this expense is almost wholly due to our Zionist policy'.[99] The army, for their part were not altogether happy with the overall bias of British policy, as a memorandum from the General Staff in Cairo to the British garrison in Palestine made clear in October 1921:

> Whilst the Army officially is supposed to have no politics, it is recognised that there are certain problems such as those of Ireland and Palestine, in which the sympathies of the Army are on one side or the other.
> In the case of Palestine these sympathies are rather obviously with the Arabs, who have hitherto appeared to the disinterested observer to have been the victim of

the unjust policy forced upon them by the British Government.[100]

Military antipathy towards Zionist policies, coupled with the high cost of the Palestine garrison, at last drove Churchill to reconsider the idea of a quasi-military defence force. On 3 September he told Lloyd George that Palestine simply could not 'afford to pay for troops on the War Office scale' and put forward the case for 'a well British officered gendarmerie and police', which could be supported by 'aeroplanes and armoured cars under the Royal Air Force', Indian troops 'less in number than the present garrison and far cheaper', and, finally, by 'arming the Jewish colonies for their own protection'.[101] Conveniently, there was an entire police force already in existence which might be utilised, and later in September Churchill enthusiastically took up General Tudor's suggestion to transfer Black and Tans from Ireland to Palestine as soon as they could be spared.[102] Wisely, however, he did not propose to use the Black and Tans *in toto*. 'We should not send the Black and Tans as such', he wrote disingenuously to his military adviser, 'But raise a gendarmerie out of suitable elements, liberated in consequence of an Irish peace'.[103] In December the Cabinet accepted his proposals, including a 'Palestine gendarmerie of British nationality of a high individual status'.[104] The commander of the new force – General Tudor – and most of the officers came from the Auxiliary Division of the RIC. In the autumn of 1922 Tudor told Churchill that Palestine was 'a rest cure after Ireland'.[105] Thus Churchill solved the twin problems of 'defending' Palestine and saving money. He was able almost immediately to reduce the estimated cost of the forces in Palestine for 1922–3 to 'about £2,750,000', a point particularly noted in the findings of the Geddes committee.[106]

In the long run the British occupation of Palestine did nothing to enhance the security of Suez. Indeed, in the 1930s Palestine became a serious liability. Yet one of the main arguments originally advanced for occupying the territory and taking on the mandate was the positive contribution this would make to maintaining the British position in the Middle East. Similar arguments, with as it turned out considerably greater value, lay behind the more limited and circumspect British involvement along the flanks of the imperial route to the south and east of Suez. Before the war Britain's only real interest in the Arabian peninsula lay in securing imperial communications. This was well provided for in the east by a series of treaties with the Arab shaikhdoms of the Persian Gulf and in the south by formal annexations around the entrance to the Red Sea. The war itself, however, as elsewhere in the Ottoman dominions, stimulated an increased British involvement in the interior of Arabia. Not only did the British recognise and support the Sherif of Mecca as the leader of the Arab Revolt, but in 1915 they also – and this was a major departure from the traditional policy of non-intervention –

signed a treaty with ibn Sa'ud, the leading Arab chief in the western desert. After the war it was quite clear to the policy-makers in London and Delhi that the new independent Arab state promised to Husain should remain firmly within a British sphere of influence.

In December 1918 the Indian government declared itself to be 'vitally interested in the exclusion of all foreign influence from a country which lies off the main line of approach to India' and proposed that there should be 'a sort of Monroe Doctrine for Arabia'.[107] For Lord Milner the position was strikingly similar to that of Egypt:

The independence of Arabia has always been a fundamental principle of our eastern policy, but what we mean by it is that Arabia while being independent herself should be kept out of the sphere of European intrigue and within the British sphere of influence: in other words, that her independent native rulers should have no foreign treaties except with us.[108]

This policy was successfully pursued, principally through a continuation of the war-time subsidies paid to Husain, ibn Sa'ud and other less important chiefs, although it must be noted that no other power, great or otherwise, showed much interest in Arabia during the period in question. In stark contrast to the defence of British interests in other parts of the Middle East, Arabia was a shining example of informal rule being possible and formal rule dispensable.

The only possible drawback to Britain consolidating her position in Arabia lay in the ambitions of ibn Sa'ud to extend his rule throughout the whole peninsula. In May 1919 he defeated a Hashemite army led by Husain's son 'Abdullah at Turaba, less than a hundred miles from Mecca. Since both sides were in receipt of arms and money from different British departments, this raised the Gilbertian possibility of the India and Foreign Offices theoretically being at war. Although intermittent hostilities continued, ibn Sa'ud was largely deterred from pursuing his advantage by fear of losing his annual subsidy of £60,000. The post-war quest for economy in Britain brought criticism of the Arabian subsidies from the Treasury, but they were much less expensive than troops. Their continuation effectively postponed war in the Hedjaz until 1924, when ibn Sa'ud's subsidy was discontinued. Thereafter he felt free to pursue his vision of a 'Sa'udi Arabia', renewed hostilities against the Hashemites and in early 1926 became undisputed King of the Hedjaz.[109]

The only part of the Arabian peninsula over which Britain exercised formal control was the Aden Protectorate in the south-west. In 1918 India was nominally in charge of Aden, although during the war control of military affairs had been transferred to the War Office. India, nevertheless, both provided and paid for the garrison of almost 11,500 men. Before the war less than a thousand troops had sufficed and in 1919 the Indian administration began to press for reductions.[110] When Lord Rawlinson visited the port in November 1920 he was appalled by the size of the garrison and wondered why four battalions of infantry, native levies, artillery and supporting technical units (over 5,000 troops) were still being maintained in 'that hell on Earth'.[111] It was decided at the Cairo conference to reduce the garrison to three battalions, along with a flight of aeroplanes, although it was recognised that further reductions could not be effected until 'satisfactory relations' had been established with the neighbouring Imam of the Yemen. These recommendations, however, were also 'subject to a satisfactory agreement being reached on the question of financial adjustments between the Imperial Government and the Government of India'.[112]

This was easier said than done. Churchill hoped to transfer the administration of Aden to his new Middle Eastern Department, while at the same time retaining a contribution towards its cost from India. The Indian government, for their part, had no objection to the administrative transfer, but jibbed at the subsidy. In October 1921 Rawlinson told Wilson that the matter had been discussed in Council and they 'absolutely refused to accept Winston's proposal that we should pay fifty lakhs [about £300,000] a year, and have no voice in the control of the Aden situation'. When Churchill learned of this decision he sourly commented to Montagu that the Indian government refused to act 'except upon conditions which throw a heavy additional burden upon the British taxpayer'.[113] Between the wars, in fact, with India moving towards independence, London increasingly assumed control over Aden affairs and in 1937 a complete transfer of the administration was made to the Colonial Office. The financial problem was eased by shifting both the costs and the responsibility for local defence to the Air Ministry. In February 1922 a flight of RAF machines scored a notable success against Yemeni forces and as in other parts of the Middle East the RAF were able to provide both efficient and economical imperial policing in Aden. By 1930 the territory's defence was secured by a squadron of bombers, an armoured car section and a body of local levies.[114]

Across the Gulf of Aden from the protectorate in south Arabia was the British territory of Somaliland which for some years prior to the war had been troubled by the raiding activities of a tribe of dervishes led by the Mullah Muhammed ibn Abdullah Hassan. In December 1918 the GOC in Somaliland thought that the time was ripe for taking action against the 'mad Mullah'. Within two or three months, he told London, the Mullah's forces could be dispersed, principally through the use of 'aeroplanes and other modern appliances'. Nevertheless, he still considered that he would also require three battalions of the King's African Rifles, two 'well selected' Indian battalions and some Indian cavalry. But there were no troops to spare for so unimportant a territory and on Sir Henry Wilson's advice the War Cabinet agreed 'that it was most undesirable that we should become involved in any military activities in Somaliland'.[115]

In May 1919, however, shortly after having become Colonial Secretary, Lord Milner asked the CIGS if something could be done. Wilson declared that it was impossible and said (evidently off the top of his head) that it would take at least two divisions at prohibitive cost. 'The real trouble', wrote Milner later in the year, 'is that we have had such an overdose of war, that the mere mention of any new "expedition" gives the Government and especially the Chancellor of the Exchequer fits'.[116] Milner, therefore, cast around for a cheaper plan and came to the conclusion that the air force might be able to provide what the army could not. Trenchard, always anxious to 'prove' his young service, readily prepared a scheme which required only two battalions of troops in support of aeroplanes. In December Wilson finally assented to the 'Colonial Office and Air Ministry' plan for Somaliland, but only after Amery (then acting Colonial Secretary) and Trenchard had assured him 'that under no conceivable circumstances would they ask me for troops'.[117]

The operation, carried out at the beginning of 1920, was a complete success. A mixed force, including the Somaliland Camel Corps, a battalion of the King's African Rifles from Kenya and 'Z' unit of the RAF finally broke the power of the Somali dervishes. Although the Governor's official despatch on the operation asserted that 'the Royal Air Force . . . were the main instrument of attack and the decisive factor', and the Air Ministry enthusiastically claimed the success as theirs alone, the actual contribution made by 'Z' unit – which comprised only six aeroplanes – is debatable. Hastings Ismay, who commanded the Camel Corps throughout the campaign, believed that the role of the air force was greatly overrated and that independent air action only made 'a very slender contribution to the success of the campaign'.[118] But from the financial point of view the result was entirely satisfactory. In his memoirs Amery records the total cost as just £77,000 and declared it to have been 'the cheapest war in history'.[119]

Chapter 8

Persia and Mesopotamia

In mid-1918 Leopold Amery, 'the most dangerous amateur strategist we have got',[1] summarised for Lloyd George the imperial aspect of the war:

We have battled and will continue to battle our hardest for the common cause in Europe. But on behalf of that cause, as well as in defence of our existence, we shall find ourselves compelled to complete the liberation of the Arabs, to make secure the independence of Persia, and if we can of Armenia, and to protect tropical Africa from German economic and military exploitation. All these objects are justifiable in themselves and don't become less so because they also increase the general sphere of British influence, and afford a strategical security which will enable that Southern British World which runs from Cape Town through Cairo, Baghdad and Calcutta to Sydney and Wellington to go about its peaceful business without constant fear of German aggression.[2]

By the end of the year Amery's 'Southern British World' had come into being. Wartime strategy and a concern for imperial security had led Britain into establishing both formal and informal control – mostly formal – over a large part of the Middle East and the fringes of Central Asia.

British supremacy was everywhere amply confirmed by military force. Paralleling Allenby's Egyptian Expeditionary Force in the west of the region was the 350,000-strong Mesopotamian Expeditionary Force under the command of Sir William Marshall at Baghdad. By the time of the Turkish collapse at the end of October 1918 Marshall's troops had effectively occupied the whole of Mesopotamia, pushing on finally to take Mosul in the supposedly oil-rich north of the province several days after the armistice. The main body of Marshall's army was accompanied by an extraordinary collection of small semi-independent forces which together carried British control into Persia, Transcaspia and the Caucasus. At the head of the Gulf, small detachments of troops secured the Anglo-Persian Oil Company's installations at Abadan and throughout the Arabistan oil field. In the interior of southern Persia was the South Persian Rifles, a mixed British, Indian and Arab force, raised in 1916 and commanded by Sir Percy Sykes, an old Persia hand who had first come to the country in the early 1890s. In May 1918 it had been reinforced from India by the

'Bushire Expedition', and at the beginning of 1919 there was a total of some 10,000 troops in south Persia jointly paid for by the British and Indian governments. The Indian government were also responsible for the East Persia Cordon, based at Birjand, and General Wilfrid Malleson's intelligence mission ('Malmiss') at Meshed: approximately 1,500 men, supplied from the railhead of the British Indian railway at Duzdab, close to the Persian frontier with British Baluchistan. Soon after the creation of his Mission in mid-1918, Malleson advanced into Transcaspia and by December he had deployed a scattering of Indian troops along the railway from the Caspian port of Krasnovodsk to Askabad and Merv. Located around the south-eastern shores of the Caspian Sea was 'Norperforce', with headquarters at the Persian port of Enzeli, and by mid-November 1918 an advance force at Baku. The 3,000 or so soldiers in Norperforce were supported by both sailors and airmen. Surely one of the oddest 'sideshows' of the period was the Royal Navy Caspian Squadron based at Enzeli, Baku and Krasnovodsk. In January 1919 it comprised eight armed merchant ships, a number of wooden torpedo-boats and two seaplanes. At its maximum the force included about 1,200 officers and men of the navy and the RAF. Across the Caucasus from Baku was the final British force in south Russia: a full division from the 'Army of the Black Sea' which began disembarking at Batum on 22 December 1918 and was soon established along the railway to Tiflis and Baku.[3]

Wartime British interest in the Caucasus had been dominated particularly by a pressing desire to deny the region's enormous oil resources to the Central Powers. Yet, although the attraction of controlling the most productive oil field outside of North America remained a significant factor in policy-making following the armistice, the immediate rationale for the presence of British forces in south Russia was simply to keep order and to offer at least limited support to the nascent anti-Bolshevik governments at Tiflis (Georgia), Baku (Azerbaijan) and Askabad (Transcaspia). On 13 November 1918 the War Office strongly emphasised the importance of establishing British supremacy in the region and successfully sought Cabinet approval to occupy the Batum-Tiflis-Baku railway line in order to reinforce 'all the orderly elements in the Caucasus'. The following month the Indian government defined the main function of Malmiss as one of preventing Bolshevism 'from over-running Trans-Caspia from the north'.[4] Yet Delhi displayed no great firmness of purpose concerning Transcaspia. British policy, they asserted, demonstrating a hazy grasp of political geography, 'is not an Anti-Bolshevik campaign in Russia. We have, however, to keep the Bolsheviks out of regions east of the Black Sea. Our object is to assist the Russians to stand by themselves and to support and strengthen any existing organisations which show promise of maintaining law and order and are working in our interests'. Not only was this policy self-contradictory nonsense, but Delhi also undermined any possibility of success by limiting practical support to money and material only, adding the strict warning that 'our troops must on no account be committed to fresh enterprises which might lead to a difficult situation'.[5]

The general incoherence of both British and Indian policy was exacerbated by the lack of any central command for the various forces in the region. The Bushire Expedition, Malmiss and the East Persia Cordon troops were Delhi's responsibility. Norperforce came under the Mesopotamian command in Baghdad, while the Caucasus division was part of Sir George Milne's Black Sea army based in Constantinople. In January 1919, however, matters were simplified when Malmiss and the Norperforce troops at Baku and Krasnovodsk were transferred to Milne's command.[6] Milne, apparently unmoved by great strategic considerations, saw little justification for retaining any British forces in south Russia. This view was confirmed by a tour of inspection he made through the region at the beginning of 1919. 'The country and the inhabitants', he reflected while travelling between Tiflis and Baku, 'are equally loathesome and we seem to be accepting an enormous responsibility for no very great reason'. Milne was fully aware that a British withdrawal 'would probably lead to anarchy but', he added acidly, 'I cannot see that the world would lose much if the whole of the country cut each other's throats. They are certainly not worth the life of one British soldier'. A few days later, after meeting Malleson at Askabad, he observed in his diary that 'on our side the situation is quite unsound, military and political', and he immediately recommended that Malmiss be withdrawn to Krasnovodsk and Meshed.[7] On 8 February London agreed. By the beginning of April the withdrawals had been accomplished.[8]

Evacuation from the Caucasus, however, was not so straightforward, especially since the region was central to Curzon's planned system of buffer states along the frontiers of Soviet Russia. But not everyone agreed with him. In March Lord Robert Cecil raised the matter with Lloyd George. He noted that 'a certain section of the Government consider that the Caucasus is one of the gates to India, treating, I suppose, the Caspian, Transcaucasia and Afghanistan merely as a kind of private avenue leading up to the actual Indian frontier'. It was, he declared, 'a somewhat fantastic theory', and even if it were accepted, 'may we not enquire what conceivable hostile Power is likely to attempt to invade India at this stage of the world's history?' It was a thinly-veiled criticism of Curzon for building extravagant imperial structures on somewhat unsound foundations. As Cecil later remarked to the Prime Minister: 'For a clever man I know no one who is so almost invariably wrong as George Curzon, unless it be Winston!'[9] Edwin Montagu urged withdrawal more directly. 'Bring your men home', he advised Lloyd George. 'Bring them home from

Trans-Caspia, bring them home from Persia, bring them home as quickly as ever you can . . .'. He declared that he was 'as anxious as anybody in the world to see the end of the terrible menace of Bolshevism', but with a cool appreciation of the domestic ramifications of an over-adventurous foreign policy, he suggested that those who wanted to fight Bolshevism in Russia 'are against their will bringing it much nearer home'.[10]

Yet even Curzon himself was becoming concerned about the extent of the British military commitment. Milne, obliged by Curzon's policy to retain troops in the Caucasus and unable to follow his instinct to withdraw, now began to press London for additional forces on the grounds that his troops were currently too widely scattered for absolute safety. In mid-February, during a lengthy review of the position in south Russia, Curzon observed to the eastern committee that events seemed to be slipping out of the committee's grasp. The mere maintenance of law and order apparently involved an extended series of military operations. General Milne was now requesting reinforcements of two divisions. It appeared that the British government's responsibilities were increasing uncontrollably. There was only one ray of light: a suggestion made by Italian representatives at the Paris Peace Conference that they might assume responsibility for the Caucasus. Curzon was astounded. 'The Italians', he said, 'had as little to do with the Caucasus as he with the Peak of Teneriffe, and it had never occurred to him that they would come in . . . It almost looked like a joke, and to his mind it was a chimera'. In the meantime, however, the committee agreed that Milne should keep his military operations as limited as possible and they emphatically instructed that he should not 'get involved either in administrative or military responsibilities'.[11]

Caprice or not, the Italians seemed as good a straw as any to grasp at. Curzon, indeed, told Wilson that the Italian *and* the French Premiers had agreed to share the responsibility for the Batum garrison equally with Britain, pending the ultimate establishment of the city as a 'free port' under the League of Nations.[12] Possibly encouraged by these unexpected offers of assistance, in March the eastern committee ordered the War Office to draw up a plan for a general British evacuation from the Caucasus and the Caspian, 'to begin at once, the evacuation to be from east to west'.[13] Malmiss was duly moved back from Transcaspia, but further withdrawals were held up until the Allies sent forces to the region. This seemed increasingly unlikely. In May Wilson, who had in any case always regarded the scheme as 'somewhat sanguine', told Lloyd George that in conversation with the Italian Chief of Staff, he had gained 'a strong impression that the Italians did not intend to go . . . although General Diaz did not say so'.[14] Meanwhile exactly the same pressures were acting on the Army of the Black Sea as on every other part of the post-war army. General Kirke of the War Office told the eastern committee that 'from a military point of view the governing factor was manpower'. Nearly half of the troops at Constantinople and in the Caucasus were due for demobilisation, and there was a shortage of reinforcements available for the Middle East. 'Heavy calls', moreover, 'had recently been made upon them by General Allenby'. All in all the War Office 'wished to put an end as early as possible to the present position by which large numbers of British troops were locked up in the Caucasus'.[15] A date was fixed, 15 June, for the evacuation to begin. But because of Italian vacillation and Cabinet indecision the withdrawal was postponed, at first for a month at a time, and then indefinitely. Towards the end of August, however, Baku and the Caspian naval personnel were evacuated. 'Things are getting along', noted Milne in his diary.[16]

By about mid-October 1919 the only troops remaining in the Caucasus were three infantry battalions at Batum. But there the process of withdrawal stopped since hopes were still being nursed of gaining some help from the Allies. This was scant comfort for Sir Henry Wilson who had become resolutely opposed to continued involvement in the Caucasus. 'The real question for us', he told a conference of ministers in January 1920, 'was the defence of India and Mesopotamia. The command of the Caspian did not affect the defence of India unless we were prepared to hold the line Batoum [*sic*] – Baku – Krasnovodsk – Merv'. But this was exactly what Curzon had envisaged. Lloyd George, however, concurred with Wilson and stressed the over-riding necessity to reduce British commitments wherever possible. This was of particular importance since at a recent meeting of the industrial unrest committee he had gathered that there were not enough troops for keeping order at home. Curzon, nevertheless, dug in his heels and the garrison stayed.[17]

By this time Wilson was prepared to use almost any tactics to get the remaining troops away from Batum. Feeling within the government, moreover, was beginning to run strongly in favour of such a move. Early in February Wilson took advantage of Curzon's temporary absence on holiday in France to persuade the Cabinet to sanction evacuation. On his return Curzon responded with a sharp memorandum in defence of his regional policy. Withdrawal, he asserted, would be regarded as 'an act of betrayal' by the Caucasian states, and would 'bring to the ground with a crash the edifice which we and they have been at such pains to rear'. On 18 February he managed to get the decision reversed.[18]

During the early spring of 1920 Bolshevik forces steadily advanced southwards along the eastern Black Sea coast. This was sufficient justification for Wilson to give Milne complete authority to withdraw at any moment without reference back to London. Curzon was infuriated and complained bitterly to Bonar Law about Wilson's 'unpardonable abuse of authority'.[19] But the CIGS was not to be put off, and he kept up the pressure for evacuation. 'Batoum is getting into a mess', he wrote in his diary on 12 April, '& I have written F.O. for the 100th time saying I want to get out of it ... Our interference in everybody's business is madness'. Two days later Churchill agreed with Wilson that the garrison should be withdrawn.[20] Again there was delay. On 5 May:

Cabinet at 11.45 ... We discussed Batoum & to my disgust Curzon by a long winded jaw persuaded the Cabinet to allow our 2 Battns to remain on for the present. Winston did not fight. I did but was overruled. I am very disgusted as we shall now be kicked out, a most undignified proceeding.

Churchill did, however, make one attempt to reduce British commitments in the general area and asked if he might withdraw the garrison at Enzeli, but Curzon vetoed this as well.[21]

On 15 May Wilson learned from the British Military Attaché in Rome that no Italian troops would now be sent to the Caucasus.[22] Wilson wrote to inform Curzon noting, moreover, that the French proposed to 'send a black battalion' to Batum. 'May we come away now?' he asked. '*Batoum* – Bolt! Most certainly not!' replied Curzon. 'The French battalion is Algerian not actually black'. He had, he insisted, expected the Italians to back out, but the city could still be garrisoned with an English, an Indian and the Algerian battalion which could 'hold up our end a little longer until we learn what is going to happen'. Besides, 'Milne has got his orders to withdraw the moment there is any real danger – that is surely enough'.[23] In the face of further Red Army advances into south Russia, Curzon clearly thought that prompt action on the part of the local commander could prevent any direct conflict between British and Bolshevik forces.

But the very next day the vulnerability of the tiny British detachments scattered throughout the region was amply demonstrated. On 19 May Wilson received a wire from Teheran 'to say our garrison at Enzeli . . . had been surrounded by Bolsheviks and made prisoners! A nice state of affairs which will have a *bad* effect in the East. For months I have been begging the Cabinet to allow me to withdraw from Persia, & from the Caucasus. Now perhaps they will'. Next day he wrote to Curzon: 'Perhaps the "regrettable incident" at Enzeli which has now occurred & which will be followed by others may lead you to change your mind'.[24] Churchill similarly wrote to the Foreign Secretary urging an immediate withdrawal of all British troops both in Persia and the Caucasus:

I do not see that anything we can do now within the present limits of our policy can possibly avert the complete loss of British influence throughout the Caucasus, Trans-Caspia and Persia. If we are not able to resist the Bolsheviks in these areas, it is much better by timely withdrawals to keep out of harm's way and avoid disaster and shameful incidents such as that which has just occurred.[25]

On 4 June Churchill received the Prime Minister's permission to withdraw from Batum. Five days later the operation was completed.[26]

As Britain pulled in her horns in south Russia, the future of the British troops in Persia increasingly came under consideration. If India were not to be defended in the Caucasus and Transcaspia, the next line of defence lay in Persia and Mesopotamia. At a meeting of the eastern committee in January 1920 Sir Henry Wilson 'gave a lecture on a map showing the impossibility of standing on the forward lines in defence of India'. He defined the three possible lines as:

(a) Constantinople, Batum, Baku, Krasnovodsk, and Merv . . .
(b) Constantinople, Batum, Baku, Enzeli, Teheran, and Meshed . . .
The holding of this second line would require the same number of troops as the first alternative, *i.e.*, two divisions from Batum to Baku, and five divisions from Baku to Meshed.
Before describing the third alternative line, he wished to say that the War Office had definitely ruled out alternatives (a) and (b) as being impossible with the means at their disposal. We had not got seven divisions, nor was there any prospect of our being able to find them. Even if they could be found, their maintenance and reinforcement in these almost inaccesible regions would demand transport facilities which were not in existence and could not be procured.
(c) Northern Palestine, Mosul, some point about 100 or 50 miles from Khanikin. The force at Meshed, if and when attacked, to fall back upon Birjand.

This was the outside of what we could do. It was not even certain that we would be able to retain Mosul, but this point was still under consideration.

Wilson argued that the peace settlement in the region would very possibly 'leave the Turk dissatisfied and hostile, the Kurd restless and unquiet, and the Afghan unfriendly'. If either of the two more forward lines were to be held, it 'would mean that these threatening elements were in our rear'. Although the third line 'would mean the eventual loss of both North-East and North-West Persia', the CIGS bluntly asserted that this was 'unavoidable'.[27]

Not everyone was quite so reconciled to withdrawals from Persia. Since the end of the war Lord Curzon, in particular, had consistently pressed for the retention of a British 'presence' in the country. Hankey believed it was 'thanks almost entirely to Curzon' that Britain had 'responsibilities both civil and military [in Persia] we ought never to have assumed, and which have cost us tremendous sums'.[28] Curzon's concern, however, was not primarily military. British troops would stay in Persia only for so long as it took a stable anglophile Persian government to be established and it seems that he was happy to adhere to the old imperial principle (if Professors Robinson and Gallagher are to be believed) of 'extending control informally if possible, formally if necessary'.[29] In his book, *Persia and the Persian question*, he had emphasised the importance of maintaining the integrity of Persia. 'Any future triumphs that we may gain in Persia', he wrote upliftingly, 'will be won, not by powder and shot, not by bluster and bullying, not even . . . by bribes; but by the amicable stress of common interests, working in the direction of industrial development and domestic reform'.[30] But following the war the choice between informal and formal rule no longer obtained in much of the Middle East and British control had perforce to be maintained formally.

In December 1918 the eastern committee met to discuss the possibility of a complete withdrawal of British troops from Persia. Curzon thought this would be 'immoral, feeble and disastrous'. But after hearing from Mr. J. M. Keynes of the Treasury that expenditure in Persia was currently running at thirty million pounds a year, a figure which seemed 'out of all proportion to the objects attained', the committee, with Curzon concurring, decided that there should be immediate reductions and a search for a more permanent and less expensive arrangement.[31]

During the spring and summer of 1919 the British Political Resident in Teheran, Sir Percy Cox, painstakingly constructed an Anglo–Persian agreement which Curzon triumphantly presented to the Cabinet in August. Recognising that some of his colleagues would ask 'why Persia should not be left to herself and allowed to rot into picturesque decay', he re-affirmed his conviction that the geographical position of Persia, 'the magnitude of our interests in the country, and the future safety of our Eastern Empire' made it impossible for Britain to disengage. In the agreement, which bound His Majesty's Government 'to respect absolutely the independence and integrity of the country', Britain undertook to supply 'expert advisers' to assist the Teheran administration, and both personnel and material for a new military force to secure order 'in the country and on its frontiers'. So as to finance the proposed reforms London promised 'to provide or arrange a substantial loan for the Persian Government'.[32] In effect the agreement neatly established Persia as a British client state. But before it could come into operation it had to be ratified by the *Majlis* (Persian national assembly), the more nationally-minded elements of which characterised the agreement as little more than a British imperial trick. In the meantime the British and Indian troops which stayed in the country served to confirm the nationalists' suspicions that, despite Curzon's claims to the contrary, the ultimate British aim was domination rather than co-operation.

India, for whose benefit the Curzon–Cox policy was designed, voiced consistent doubts as to its lasting value. As early as January 1919 Delhi questioned the wisdom of 'pressing an elaborate network of British advisers' on to the Persian government. 'It would', they noted perceptively, 'savour too much of the Egyptian model not to raise the cry that the goal we have reached in Egypt is our ultimate goal in Persia'. Typically, they also warned 'that it will be our duty strenuously to resist any extension of India's financial commitments in Persian affairs'. In April the Viceroy argued that 'were Cox's scheme put into effect, chances of our ever being able to withdraw from Persia would insensibly decrease to zero'. On the contrary, military force (inevitably supplied from India) would be needed to support the pro-British politicians against the nationalists.[33] Although Montagu felt that the Anglo–Persian agreement represented 'our best chance' of avoiding 'the continual subsidies in which Indian revenues have been involved',[34] he was never able to alter the realistic Indian view that *any* formal British entanglement in Persia would sooner or later entail Indian expenditure of one sort or another. Delhi's misgivings were confirmed in late 1919 when London reacted to Bolshevik penetration by reinforcing Persia with Indian troops. Chelmsford immediately telegraphed Montagu to 'emphasise fact that neither our army in India nor our force in Mesopotamia has been organised with any idea of affording military support to Persia and are consequently inadequate for the purpose. To make them adequate', he added, 'would involve expenditure which we are quite unable to meet'.[35]

Over the turn of the year Bolshevik incursions from the north raised the real possibility of direct conflict between British and Soviet troops, a prospect which greatly alarmed the War Office. In November 1919 Henry Wilson told the eastern committee that the mere presence of Malleson's force at Meshed 'led the Persians to expect that we would assist them against a Bolshevik attack'. He took the matter up directly with the Foreign Office who, while conceding that the Anglo–Persian agreement did 'not commit His Majesty's Government to defend Persia against external aggression', stressed that it was 'very desirable, on political grounds, to protect Persia against the Bolshevik menace'. Three weeks later the War Office again approached the Foreign Office to enquire whether the government intended to defend Persia, or not. 'The protection of Persia', replied Curzon blandly, 'is at present a British interest as much as a Persian'.[36] However true that may have been, by the beginning of 1920 Montagu had evidently been persuaded by Chelmsford's consistent criticism that it was not particularly an Indian interest. He could not, he wrote to Curzon, be 'a party to defending India from the far side of Afghanistan while Afghanistan is in its present condition. I would stick within our Frontiers'.[37]

The extent to which Britain should – or, indeed, could – resist 'the Bolshevik onslaught on the Caucasian Republics, Persia and India' came up for consideration at the eastern committee on 12 January 1920. Since Curzon was attending meetings in Paris, the chair was taken by Austen Chamberlain. Wilson gave his lecture on the impossibility of holding forward lines of defence. Deftly taking advantage of Curzon's absence, he and Churchill persuaded the committee that evacuation from north and east Persia should be approved.[38] But in early February Curzon induced the Cabinet to restrict any immediate withdrawals to no more than the Malleson Mission and its supporting units. Even this limited reduction was subject to repeated delays. Despite continuing pressure from Delhi, in May the Cabinet approved only a partial evacuation from Meshed. Anxious as they were to comply, however, the Indian government were gallingly obliged to inform London that because of the local climate this would not be possible until the autumn.[39]

Although the War Office were keen to abolish Malmiss, they were for the meantime prepared to retain the Norperforce detachment at Enzeli. Churchill and the General Staff were inclined to fall in with Curzon's view that a precipitate evacuation from north Persia would 'have a deplorable effect on the political situation generally' and completely undermine any chance of the Anglo–Persian agreement succeeding. They agreed, therefore, that the Enzeli garrison – comprising barely a thousand men – should 'endeavour by bluff' to prevent Bolshevik attacks on the town.[40] Enzeli in early 1920 might be said to have been a microcosm of British imperial rule in the Middle East. But in May the Bolshevik occupation of Baku and advances along the south-west coast of the Caspian towards the Persian frontier led the War Office to re-assess their policy. On 13 May Wilson recommended evacuating Enzeli, '*unless His Majesty's Government are prepared to go to war with Russia*'.[41] Curzon responded by convening the eastern committee on 17 May. Perhaps in order to get his own back for the Malmiss decision in January, he invited neither Churchill nor Wilson, and in *their* absence secured a decision against evacuation.[42] Unfortunately, however, the bluff was called when on the very same day Bolshevik artillery shelled the town. So as to avoid 'certain defeat', the British garrison withdrew to Resht some thirty miles away.[43]

At a Cabinet meeting on 21 May Wilson, Churchill and even Lloyd George argued in favour of withdrawal from Persia. Curzon strongly disagreed and still held out hopes that his precious agreement would be ratified, thus obviating the need for the retention of British forces in the country. He was strongly supported by Lord Milner who had his own 'domino theory' for the region. If Persia were lost, he argued, 'we should lose Mesopotamia and then India was in danger'. The Cabinet as a whole seem to have been swayed by these points. They postponed any final decision concerning evacuation and agreed only to allow a concentration of Norperforce at Kasvin, about half way between Enzeli and Teheran.[44]

Milner, nevertheless, was so concerned about the question that he expanded his arguments in a paper circulated three days later. He worried that 'something like a panic seems to have seized on the public mind . . . at the discovery that we are incurring a military expenditure of 18 millions a year in Persia and Mesopotamia'. This high level of expenditure, he felt sure, was merely temporary. After all, was not the Sudan – 'a larger and more inaccessible country' – defended for less than two millions a year? With this in mind he thought that there was a danger of the Cabinet confusing the issue of 'the probable future cost of the retention of Mesopotamia as a mandated territory' with 'the present actual cost of maintaining our position and defending our interests in Mesopotamia and Persia, as long as the whole of the Near East . . . [is] . . . in a state of raging chaos'. He urged the necessity of taking a broad view of the Middle East where the only real solution was to gain some sort of accommodation, 'even if it were only a transient peace', with Russia, and to retain British influence, (and therefore British troops) in Persia:

It is evident that if we have no policy but that of gradual withdrawal, the Persians are bound to lose all faith [in us] . . . It is not primarily a question of helping an Ally, but of securing our own vital interests in Persia and saving all that we have already spent on that country from being wasted. A Bolshevik Revolution in Persia would involve consequences for the British Empire which it would be worth our while to spend not one, but many millions to avert.

Milner crowned his persuasive case by pointing out that Britain's economic interests in Persia were 'considerable' and in one important respect 'vital' – oil.[45]

The War Office, however, were not persuaded. In June 1920 Wilson again proposed the 'complete withdrawal of the British forces from Persia'. He asserted that 'a definite decision on the policy' was 'imperative; otherwise, not only will no reduction be possible in the present garrison but we shall also inevitably find ourselves committed to a process of gradual reinforcement which may entail unlimited liabilities'. He reminded ministers of the North Russian expedition 'which, beginning with a landing of 150 men at Murmansk, in the absence of definite policy absorbed nearly 20,000 British troops before it ended'. If the government did not intend to incur the heavy financial burden of maintaining a strong force in Persia, there was no other course open 'but to withdraw British and Indian troops entirely from Persia and to concentrate such forces as we have for the defence and security of those territories for which this country is directly responsible'. Wilson's assessment of the position was discussed at a Cabinet conference on 18 June, when both he and Churchill strove to put the Persian involvement into the perspective of Britain's global commitments. 'The Secretary of War and the C.I.G.S. placed on record their view that the military forces at the disposal of Great Britain were insufficient to meet the requirements of the policies now being pursued in the various theatres. An immediate curtailment of British responsibilities was indispensable if grave risk of disaster was not to be incurred'. But there was still opposition from both the Foreign and Colonial Secretaries. That night Wilson wrote in his diary that the proposal to abandon Persia had brought 'Milner & Curzon to their feet & it was quite clear they would resign if this were done'. No decision was taken but the Cabinet reserved the right to reconsider the situation 'if, at any time the General Officer Commanding considers that he cannot maintain the present position without reinforcements or without placing an undue strain on his forces'.[46]

Curzon's position was steadily being undermined by the failure of the *Majlis* to meet, let alone ratify the agreement. This was mainly due to a combination of the prevailing internal disorder with the Persian nationalists' healthy suspicion of British intentions and a widespread conviction that the agreement might reduce their country to semi-colonial status. Other explanations were provided from time to time. At one stage the Persian representative at the League of Nations assured H. A. L. Fisher that the delay had occurred because 'all votes have to be carried on donkeys'.[47] But by the middle of 1920 Curzon was beginning to falter in his hopes for a diplomatic solution of the military problem. 'We have no alternative', he wrote gloomily to Bonar Law, 'but to support the new Persian ministry, provided that it holds firm by the Anglo–Persian Agreement and plays the Game. If it does not there is no alternative but to allow Persia to go to ruin in her own way'.[48]

In August 1920 the continually heavy demands being made on the army throughout the empire stimulated renewed calls for evacuation from Persia. At a Cabinet finance committee meeting on 12 August Wilson and Churchill again 'went over all the military reasons for coming out of Persia' and again 'all the old arguments were produced by Curzon and Milner to remain'. Having once more postponed any final decision, and as if specially to highlight the extent of the empire's burdens, ministers went on to discuss the question of special emergency legislation to meet strikes at home and the possibility of withdrawing ten or twelve battalions from Ireland to reinforce Great Britain.[49] The Mesopotamian rebellion inevitably had an effect on Persia, and the GOC at Baghdad (Sir Aylmer Haldane) suggested that he might have to take troops away from the garrison in order to meet the emergency – a proposal which apparently caused 'consternation' in Teheran. 'I do hope you are following the increasingly grave developments in Mespota & Persia', wrote Churchill pointedly to Curzon at the end of the month. 'We are at our wits' end to find a single soldier'.[50] Wilson himself seems to have nursed hopes that the rebellion might provide sufficient excuse for a complete withdrawal, and, as had been the case with Milne in respect of the Batum garrison, he gave the GOC on the spot full authority to act without reference to London. 'I personally am very much in favour of coming out of Persia . . .' he wrote to Haldane,

but the Government won't hear of it, and so I have to keep on telegraphing you to remain there, although I always put in a proviso, to the great annoyance of the Foreign Office, that you have absolute power to come out of Persia if you deem it essential to save the situation in Mesopotamia. I hope you realise that I really mean this and that if at any time you think it necessary to withdraw the troops and the transport from Persia in order to re-establish yourself on a sound basis in Mesopotamia you won't hesitate to do so. I have told the Cabinet this over and over again and any time that you decide to do so I will back you at this end, nor would the Cabinet be in any position to resist.[51]

Despite Wilson's somewhat loaded assurances, in the end the decision to leave Persia was taken in London and on financial grounds. In December 1920 the Cabinet considered some draft resolutions on economy among which was a War Office proposal to evacuate the troops from Persia by the spring of the following year. This was agreed to in principle. 'The cry for retrenchment in this country is so strong', wrote Wilson three weeks later, 'that the Government will be forced to come away from Persia'.[52] So it was. At last, in January 1921, the final decision was made that the withdrawal of British troops was to commence 'on or about April 1st'. It was a bitter disappointment for Curzon, who retained fond hopes to the last that the evacuation might once more be postponed, but by this time the matter was a *chose jugée*. The move went ahead as planned and in June 1921 parliament was told that there were now no British troops in Persia 'beyond a few individual officers lent as instructors to the Persian Army and paid for by the Persian Government'.[53]

The arguments which Curzon and Milner had marshalled in favour of staying in Persia applied with equal, if not greater, force to Mesopotamia. Unlike Persia, however, and conveniently enough for British imperialists, Mesopotamia possessed no national tradition at all. The territory comprised the three former Turkish *vilayets* of Basra, Baghdad and Mosul, drawn together for convenience under an Anglo-Indian administration at Baghdad. It was thought to possess considerable strategic and economic value. Early in the war, while contemplating the eventual partition of the Ottoman empire, Lord Kitchener argued that it was 'imperative' for Britain to occupy Mesopotamia in order to forestall the Russians doing so. The one, prophetic, objection he raised to this course of action was the problem of supplying and paying for troops to garrison the country, but he dismissed this difficulty as merely temporary since Mesopotamia 'ought, after a short time ... to become self-supporting in view of its great natural wealth'.[54]

Kitchener gained enthusiastic support from the Admiralty. The occupation of Mesopotamia, they declared, was particularly important 'at a time when, as a dominant factor of sea power, coal, is giving way to oil'. With the territory under British control 'we have at our feet a complete solution of the new situation; for not only should we have an inexhaustible supply in our own hands, but we should have it at a point most desirable strategically – that is, at a point most remote from our home base'.[55] It was perhaps a little premature thus to assess

Mesopotamian potential, but for the Admiralty the oil already discovered in Persia and the favourable prognostications of the geologists provided a glint of that crock of black gold which would secure the Navy's fuel oil supply. Nevertheless it was only after considerable diplomatic manoeuvrings following the armistice that Britain gained control of Mosul, for by the Sykes-Picot Agreement of 1916 the Mosul *vilayet* had been assigned to France. Even so, the re-negotiation of Sykes-Picot seems not to have been done *primarily* to gain control over the oil since it was simply part of Balfour and Curzon's policy generally to reduce French influence in the region as a whole.[56]

The Admiralty, however, continued to stress the importance of Mesopotamian oil and they submitted papers to the eastern committee which Sir Henry Wilson understood to mean that the Mosul reserves in the future were going to be 'as important as the Welsh coalfields have been in the past'.[57] Since Mesopotamia actually produced very little oil at all at the time – there were some 'seepages' at a number of locations in the Mosul *vilayet* – hopes for petroleum production on any scale were largely speculative. In July 1919 a Board of Trade paper on 'the economic resources of Mesopotamia' noted that there was 'every reason to believe that the oil fields, which are continuations of a field now being exploited by the Anglo-Persian Company in Persia, are capable of very large development'.[58] Later the same year the General Staff preferred some specifically strategic reasons for the retention of Mesopotamia. The country, they observed, formed 'an important link in a chain of contiguous areas under British influence, extending from Egypt to India'. It was hoped that in the future this chain would be 'strengthened by a line of rail and air communications from west to east', extending, as it were, the familiar line 'from the Cape to Cairo' onwards to Karachi. This in turn would reinforce 'our position in India which, as our greatest possession in the East, may be likened to a most valuable appendage at the end of the chain'. The Staff also noted the importance of oil and asserted that, with the construction of a railway and pipeline to the Mediterranean, the position of England as a naval power there 'could be doubly assured, and our dependence on the Suez Canal, which is a vulnerable point in our line of communications with the East, would be considerably lessened'. This, the writers admitted, was 'at present little more than a visionary conception of our future Imperial policy', but they portentously added their conviction that 'the recent crossing of the Arabian Desert in a direct line from Damascus to Baghdad by a motor car is a positive index to the possibilities of the future'.[59]

Although Amery's 'Southern British World' was raising its attractive head even in the War Office, it was not long before imperial planners were disabused by the size, and cost, of this 'visionary conception'. In both civil and military terms British commitments in Mesopotamia seemed out of all proportion to the actual or potential benefits. A major difficulty arose from the lack of any strong central policy direction. In theory control of the civil administration was vested in the GOCinC, Mesopotamia, who from May 1919 to January 1920 was Sir George MacMunn. In practice, however, the administration was almost entirely in the hands of Colonel Arnold Wilson, who had been appointed Acting Civil Commissioner in April 1918. Apart from being subordinate to MacMunn (himself subject to War Office instructions), Wilson also received orders from the Secretary of State of India, 'in matters of policy', and the Indian government 'in certain matters of administration'.[60] In London, too, the Foreign Office insisted on having a major say in decision-making.

The broad outline of post-war policy in Mesopotamia was laid down in an Anglo–French declaration of 8 November 1918 which promised Allied assistance to set up 'indigenous governments and administrations' in the former Ottoman provinces.[61] Yet in the months immediately following the armistice both London and Delhi had more urgent concerns than the governing of Mesopotamia. In consequence Wilson and MacMunn were more or less left to do as they pleased. Neither man believed that the inhabitants were ready for self government. In July 1919 MacMunn observed that there were 'neither leaders, class nor opinion existing' able to take 'an advanced part' in the administration. The Arab majority was split between Shia and Sunni Islamic factions. There were substantial minorities of Kurds, Jews and Christians. Intrigue was 'rife' from pan-Arab, pan-Kurd, pan-Islam, Persian and Sherifian groups, 'and to these must be added Indian sedition and Russian Bolshevism'. In the GOC's opinion there was no alternative to the continuation 'for some time' of 'an accessible government by sympathetic political officers'.[62]

By the autumn of 1919 Wilson had perfected an elaborate and expensive 'Indianised administration'[63], fully staffed by district officers throughout Mesopotamia, but with little or no local participation. Matching the lavish civil administration was an equally generous military establishment which had developed during the war. One response to the disaster at Kut in 1917 had been a determination in the military high command that no part of their army should ever again run short of supplies of any kind. Inevitably this resulted in a massive over-provision of material throughout the command, a feature which carried on largely unchecked after hostilities had ceased. 'Sir George MacMunn's period of Command', wrote his successor as GOC, was 'a wildly extravagant one'.[64] Particularly costly was the provision of extensive permanent camps, including married quarters, for a substantial military garrison. Sir Arthur Hirtzel, assistant under-secretary at the India Office, described the officers' summer camp at Karind, nearly two hundred miles from Baghdad across the Persian frontier, as 'one of the least defensive [*sic*] items in an orgy of extravagance'. Hirtzel, however, gleaned some amusement from an anonymous poem on the subject which Arnold Wilson sent him in August 1920:

Half a lakh, half a lakh, half a lakh squandered
Up to the Persian hills G.H.Q. wandered . . .

Honour the brave and bold,
Taxpayer young and old,
Who although never told
Paid by the hundred:
Think of the Camp they made
Think of the water laid
On, and the golf links made
Think of the Bill we paid
Oh the wild charge they made!
Half a lakh squandered.

The humour, alas, was not much consolation for Austen Chamberlain, who found the rhyme 'too painfully true for me to enjoy it heartily'.[65]

Neither civil nor military profligacy in Mesopotamia could last indefinitely while British budgets were everywhere being trimmed. In September 1919 Churchill told Lloyd George that he was 'greatly concerned at the expense thrown upon us on account of Mesopotamia. In the current financial year it cannot be less than 25 millions', a cost which far exceeded 'any return that can be secured for many years from the province'. At an eastern committee meeting on 10 November Curzon, although strongly committed to the retention of Mesopotamia within a clearly British sphere of interest, expressed unease at the 'highly organised military administration'. It was 'inordinately expensive, and he would be glad to see it come to an end as soon as possible'. Yet he had no particular policy to offer beyond the hope that Sir Percy Cox – 'the only man to put it straight' – might solve the problems of Mesopotamia when he could be spared from Teheran, which would not in any case be before January 1920. A few days later Philip Kerr, one of Lloyd George's personal advisors in the 'Garden Suburb', warned that Britain was now faced with a possibly limitless commitment to the security of much of the region. Had the consequences been considered, he asked, of acquiring this new responsibility? 'Our army', he argued, 'is far more expensive than it was before the war, and is certainly not going to be any larger'. Can we, therefore, 'afford to add this gigantic land frontier, with the steady drain it must involve, to the British Empire?'[66]

Churchill certainly had his doubts, and while the eastern committee temporised he pressed on with reductions in Mesopotamian expenditure, a policy eased by the period of comparative peace enjoyed by the territory in late 1919 and early 1920. 'According to my latest returns', telegraphed Churchill to MacMunn on 9 September, 'you have at present in Mesopotamia 25,000 British troops, 81,000 native Indian troops, 18,000 local levies, 130,000 followers and 24,000 native labour; total 278,000'. The General Staff, he continued, had recently calculated that the provisional post-war garrison should amount to no more than 16,000 British and 49,000 Indian troops. It was necessary for MacMunn to get down to this figure at once:

> There can be absolutely no question of holding the present enormous forces at your disposal, and you must make the best military plan you can in the circumstances. I would remind you that under the Turks Mesopotamia not only paid its way but supplied a revenue to the Central Government. The military establishment you are maintaining at the present time would simply crush the province and possibly prove fatal to its retention by Great Britain. Its present cost is nearly 25 millions a year.

MacMunn protested that he was doing his best to reduce numbers, but that he was hampered by 'the disturbing conditions which the delay in settlement of former Turkish Empire has brought about'. By February 1920, nevertheless, the garrison had been brought down to 12,000 British and 53,000 Indian troops.[67] In the same month, when Sir Aylmer Haldane was setting out from England to take over the Mesopotamian Command, Churchill interviewed him and strongly emphasised the need to cut down expenses. Some time later after Haldane had reached Baghdad Churchill returned to this theme: 'The fate of the province', he told the GOC, 'depends, as I told you, entirely upon whether a reasonable scheme for maintaining order can be devised at a cost which is not ruinous'.[68]

In May Churchill circulated to the Cabinet a long paper containing memoranda by himself and Trenchard, a minute by Sir Henry Wilson and a note by the General Staff. 'I desire to draw the attention of my colleagues', wrote the Secretary of State, 'to the waste of money entailed by our present military and administrative policy in Mesopotamia'. He complained that there was an immense army in the country covering an enormous area at a vast cost and sharply pointed out that it was the Foreign Office, rather than the India or the War Office, which gave 'the directing impulse' to political policy in Mesopotamia. The civil political officers had penetrated to all parts of the territory and invariably expected military protection, resulting in the maintenance of 'considerable garrisons at posts remote from Baghdad'. Marshalling his ample powers of expression – not to say hyperbole – Churchill observed that the army was doing its best, but

the result of this vicious system is that a score of mud villages, sandwiched in between a swampy river and a blistering desert, inhabited by a few hundred half naked families,[69] usually starving, are now occupied, have been occupied for many months, and are likely to remain so occupied in the future unless policy is changed, by Anglo–Indian garrisons on a scale which in India would maintain order in wealthy provinces of millions of people.

Henry Wilson was less extravagant in his minute, simply describing the situation as 'very unsatisfactory', while the General Staff noted that the garrison could either be maintained at present levels 'with great strain' or reduced gradually. Arguably the most significant part of the paper was Trenchard's memorandum on 'a preliminary scheme for the military control of Mesopotamia by the Royal Air Force', which Churchill was increasingly coming to believe might solve the military problem of defending Mesopotamia.[70]

Churchill's unhappiness with the political and administrative aspects of Mesopotamian policy, and the evident absence of any progress towards a permanent government, found a response even in the Foreign Office. 'We are', minuted one official in June 1920, 'rapidly drifting in Mesopotamia into a position analogous to the vicious circle in Ireland'.[71] This was an ominous observation indeed, and all too prophetic, for by the end of the month rebellion had broken out. The rising was incoherent and incohate, but very widespread. 'What we are up against is anarchy, plus fanaticism', wrote Arnold Wilson. 'There is little or no Nationalism'. In part the violence was a response to the continued uncertainty about Mesopotamia's long-term future, and it undoubtedly expressed Arab disappointment and frustration with the Allies' unexpectedly imperious post-war policies. Another contributory factor was the very efficiency of Wilson's administration, especially that of his revenue collectors in the lower Euphrates valley.[72]

At the end of June 1920 an insurgent band of tribesmen attacked the British Political Office in Rumaithah, a small town on the Hillah branch of the Euphrates about half-way between Basrah and Baghdad. This, wrote Haldane, was the spark which 'lighted the fire of insurrection'.[73] Although the GOC had 9,800 British and 55,500 Indian troops in his Command at the time of the outbreak,[74] the effective force at his disposal was in fact only about 5,000 British and 25,000 Indian soldiers. Apart from those sick and in transit, there were 3,000 British and 23,000 Indian troops employed on non-combatant duties in 'various departmental services', including guarding several thousand Turkish prisoners-of-war.[75] Nor was this all. Sir Arnold Wilson provided a familiar and dreary catalogue of post-war military deficiencies. 'Owing to their extreme youth and inexperience', he telegraphed, most of the British troops could only be employed 'with advantage' on garrison duty. 'One of our great difficulties', he wrote on 26 July, 'is the fighting capacity of troops here'. Many soldiers had 'never fired a musketry course, much less seen a shot fired'.[76]

On 2 July Haldane suggested to the War Office that he might require reinforcements from India. The Indian government's reaction was somewhat cool, but they assured London that if the position were really serious they would supply what troops they could.[77] Haldane was certainly very worried. 'We are living on bluff and have been doing so for some weeks', he wrote in his diary at the beginning of August, 'and it is a trying game when the strain is prolonged'.[78] On 8 July he made the first substantive demand for reinforcements and such calls continued until 17 August. Between August and September 1920 some twenty battalions of infantry and numerous artillery units with supporting troops were sent from India to reinforce the command.[79] In the light of Haldane's difficulties Sir Henry Wilson went out of his way to tell Lloyd George that this was just what he had been prophesying and that what was essential was '*concentration* of forces'. He also asked if he might withdraw from Persia, but the Prime Minister said 'Curzon would not stand it'.[80] Naturally Wilson was short of troops, and a strain on the Army in India placed a consequent strain on the British army. Earlier in the month he had received an urgent call for more soldiers from Macready in Ireland. Wilson had approved a draft of three battalions and a brigade headquarters, but at the same time 'hoped S of S realised that these incessant demands would make us impotent in all other theatres'.[81]

Even at the height of the insurrection – which powerfully intensified the pressure for withdrawal, or at least a substantial reduction, of the garrison in Mesopotamia – there were still those who argued for the territory's retention on the grounds of imperial security. On 30 July 1920 Curzon circulated a 'note on the Mesopotamia–Persia situation' by Sir Percy Cox. 'I regard the maintenance of our present position in Mesopotamia as a factor of enormous importance to our general interests in the Middle East and India', wrote Cox. 'From the strategical point of view, the maintenance of British control in Mesopotamia seems to me to be an asset of the greatest importance'. He went on to stress the significance of Mesopotamia in communications with India, the oil in the region and concluded that 'our effective control in Baghdad strengthens enormously our position and facilitates the carrying out our policy in Persia'.[82] It was as well something did, fór Persia cannot be counted as one of the high spots of post-war diplomacy. Neither Cox's arguments, nor those of Curzon and Milner in the Cabinet, carried much weight with Churchill. In a letter to Lloyd George on 8 August he specifically blamed his two colleagues for the government's rejection of General Staff advice 'that we should take immediate and effective steps to contract and limit our responsibilities in this theatre'.[83]

On 18 August Sir Henry Wilson told Curzon that 'our military resources are practically exhausted', and although he heartily disagreed with the policy of staying in Mesopotamia, the General Staff would 'carry out the Government policy to the best of our ability'.[84] So the argument continued with no sign of coming near a solution, save that feared by Wilson when the supply of troops in the empire would finally run out. For the moment Curzon and Milner had their way, and Churchill was obliged to comply with their wishes. On 26 August he wrote to Lloyd George: 'With regard to Mesopotamia, I have told Henry Wilson that, now the Cabinet have definitely decided that we are to plough through in that dismal country, every effort must be made to procure vigorous action and decisive results'.[85] The rebellion dragged on until the early autumn, although Haldane steadily gained the upper hand from about the beginning of September. 'Aeroplanes', noted Arnold Wilson on 10 September, 'have been the saving of us. Without them I really believe we should have been out of Baghdad by now'. On 18 October Haldane told the CIGS that the worst was over.[86]

One result of the rebellion was the final abandonment of Wilson's Anglo–Indian administration. Sir Percy Cox was quickly posted to Baghdad as High Commissioner with a brief to establish a reliable Arab government. The rebellion also had the effect of bringing the India Office into line with the War Office in pressing strongly for withdrawal. On 9 October Edwin Montagu asked his colleagues not to approve the League of Nations mandate (under discussion at the time) on the grounds that it represented too many long-term liabilities:

It is almost superfluous to remind my colleagues that we have no money to spend in Mesopotamia; that we have no troops to send to Mesopotamia; that the Dominions have refused to help us there; that India, and I do not mean only the Indians, but the soldiers in India, including, I believe, the new Commander-in-Chief [Rawlinson] and the Government of India, are demanding the return of Indian soldiers and warn us of the grave political consequences if we try to enforce the Turkish peace by Indian mercenaries . . .

In these circumstances is it not rash to define the liabilities involved by our Mandate? If such a Mandate and such a programme are going to lead to the expenditure of more money, to the necessity of reinforcements or the maintenance of the present force, I, for one, would agree with the Secretary of War in demanding evacuation.[87]

Montagu's point about the shortage of troops was reinforced by a memorandum from the Director of Military Operations, 'concurred in by the C.I.G.S.', which pointed out that the events of the summer and autumn had demonstrated 'we ran things too fine and that a great disaster was only narrowly avoided'. In contrast to the optimistic and expansionist opinions advanced by the General Staff in 1919, the DMO's chief concern lay with immediate practical difficulties.

Our military position on the Tigris and Euphrates, and on the distant Persian Plateaux, [he declared] is thoroughly unsound, and must always be a potential cause of anxiety. Recent events have proved how precarious is the position of our scattered garrisons – widely dispersed in response to political necessities – at the end of long and vulnerable communications, without adequate reserves ready to strike promptly and quell trouble at the outset.[88]

In a series of meetings during December 1920,[89] ministers attempted to sort out the Mesopotamian tangle. They formally agreed to assume the mandate for the whole territory, although they were sorely tempted to withdraw from the Mosul and Baghdad *vilayets* and retain only lower Mesopotamia, Basra and the Persian oil-fields near the Gulf. There was, however, no possibility of an immediate evacuation for, as Bonar Law told the Cabinet on 13 December, 'we had to hold on to Mosul until the withdrawal of the force in North Persia', which could not happen until the spring 'owing to snow on the passes'. It was also decided that responsibility for Mesopotamian policy generally should be given to the new Middle Eastern department of the Colonial Office, which Churchill took over in February 1921, and which eventually solved the long-term problem of securing perceived British interests in Mesopotamia by a combination of old techniques and new technology: a suitably well-disposed Arab administration was installed and an air policing scheme introduced.

There was much opposition to the air scheme. Haldane was initially sceptical for both moral and practical reasons. 'I do not consider', he recorded in January 1921, 'that this country can be held and administered by a form of terrorism, which would involve the death by bombing of women and children ... Airplanes', he added, 'have not yet proved themselves to be reliable'. At London's request his staff compiled an assessment of how valuable aeroplanes had been during the insurrection. The report largely dismissed their usefulness and concluded that 'unsuccessful contact with troops, knowledge of existence of sufficient mobile garrisons and the sight of troops moving through the country are the only effective means of preventing or suppressing disorder'.[90] Viscount Peel, the Under-Secretary of State for War, although doubtful as to the value of air tactics, cynically observed that Haldane could employ whatever means he chose to keep order. 'Fortunately', he wrote, 'the great order of the sentimentalists have been too busy exploiting occasional outbreaks of Black & Tans in Ireland, & in ignoring Sinn Fein atrocities, to spare time for peace enforcing methods in Mespot.'.[91] Ignoring Haldane's hesitations, and Sir Henry Wilson's stiff criticism, Churchill pressed ahead with the scheme. On 18 August 1921, in the face of continued War Office opposition, he persuaded the Cabinet to approve his proposals. His colleagues were, after all, delighted both to have their cake *and* eat it. Thus the incubus of Mesopotamia was lifted from the army and, in due course, 'War Office responsibility for Iraq ceased from 1 October 1922'.[92]

Unlike Egypt, this military relief did not primarily depend upon an immediate solution to the problem of local political control. Churchill was sufficiently anxious to save money, and sufficiently confident in the RAF, to press ahead with the air defence scheme before finally coming to a satisfactory settlement with the Arab government he had established in Baghdad following the Cairo conference of March 1921. Although the Hashemite Prince Feisal was installed as King of Iraq in August 1921, negotiations continued for over a year until in September 1922 a treaty was agreed by which Feisal formally recognised British paramountcy.[93] One problem remained: the threat of Turkish aggression in the north of the country in support of anti-British and anti-Hashemite elements within Iraq. Following the expulsion of the Greeks from Asia Minor in September 1922, the victorious Kemalists turned towards the British in Iraq. Churchill's confidence in aerial power, however, was not misplaced. In October a Turkish-backed uprising among the Kurds of north Iraq was conclusively quashed. 'There is no doubt', averred the Air Officer Commanding, 'as to ability of air (?action) to deal effectively and economically with any situation which can reasonably be foreseen'.[94] But by this stage the belligerent policy at Chanak had precipitated the fall of Lloyd George's government and Lord Curzon had the last word, when, as Foreign Secretary in Bonar Law's new Conservative administration, he came to an amicable agreement with Kemal at the Lausanne conference between November 1922 and February 1923. As Sir Henry Wilson had maintained all along, the solution to Britain's problems in the Middle East lay above all in 'making love to the Turk'.

Conclusion

War, like any serious disease, is a difficult thing to shake off. Nothing illustrates this better than the predicament of the British empire following the First World War. Directly or indirectly, the war stimulated or exacerbated *all* of the problems which racked Britain and the empire after the armistice. This phenomenon was felt most keenly by the army which had, almost single-handed, to cope directly with the unsettled condition of the *post bellum* empire. In January 1919, therefore, it was perfectly understandable for Wilson and his colleagues to argue that the war was not yet over. It was certainly true that fighting did not universally cease when the guns fell silent on the Western Front.

In some regions, notably Russia, 'war' continued for some time. During the post-war years the British empire itself could hardly be described as a haven of peace. Violent nationalism was manifest in Ireland, India and Egypt; there was a major rebellion in Mesopotamia, a small war in Somaliland and a larger one on the North-West Frontier. Rioting seemed to have become endemic, and wherever violence broke out – in Liverpool or Lahore, Cork or Cairo – it was the army which was sent in to keep the peace. For a few years after the Great War it would be fair to describe the British empire as a 'military' empire. Never before had the 'defence of the empire' meant little more than police work for the army; never before had the British empire been a structure held together by military force in any large sense, nor had the army hitherto been cast in quite such a crucial role. In the 'good old days' before the war, imperial defence had largely been the prerogative of the Admiralty, but in 1918, while the navy was all dressed up with nowhere to go, the army, both at home and abroad, was stretched to the limit, pressed for economies by an anxious Treasury and given precious little freedom of action to deal with unrest as it saw fit.

The effects of the heady wine of victory at first tended to obscure any difficulties Britain might have to face in maintaining the empire. Like Pallas Athene from the head of Zeus, the British empire literally sprang fully-armed from the war. There, regrettably, the resemblance ceases. Yet many contemporary observers believed that the outstanding unity of the imperial military war effort constituted a rock on which to build post-war strategic planning. In a pamphlet published by the Royal Artillery Institution in June 1919, Colonel R. F. Cottrell argued that 'the maintenance of the *national spirit* and of *unity of purpose*', so amply displayed among the empire's white population, provided the essential basis for future imperial survival. As a corollary to this he suggested that inter-dominion and colonial organisation was 'now more important than ever before in history' and specifically proposed 'the unification of the means of defence of the various parts of the British Empire'. 'The very foundations of Imperial defensive policy', wrote General W. D. Bird in 1920, 'must be . . . unity of organisation among and control over the forces of the Empire'. He did, however, add the sensible observation that if such unity could not be achieved by a formal centralisation, it could be gained 'only by mutual and voluntary agreement'. General Sir John Davidson writing in the *Army Quarterly* was more forceful. The self-governing dominions and India, he declared, 'cannot stand aloof in matters of defence: on the contrary, with the growth of their power, they should assume their responsibilities in the Imperial Council and accept their proportionate burdens and liabilities'.[1] This was the view taken by the General Staff, as demonstrated for example by both their response to the Esher Report and their proposed topics for discussion at the 1921 imperial conference. But visionary assumptions that the high wartime level of imperial military co-operation would continue unchecked and, indeed, enhanced after the war simply constituted wishful thinking based on the false premise that there was a general community of military or strategic interest throughout the empire. Politicians and generals, mesmerised by the experience of the war, for a time believed in this illusion of common interest, but a moment's consideration of the fate before 1914 of 'imperial' military organisation – and 'imperial federation' – would soon have disabused them of such romantic notions. As Lord Peter Wimsey remarked in *Have his Carcase*, 'When Empire comes in at the window, logic goes out at the door'.

The dominions, in dashing War Office hopes of imperial military unity, were doing no more than picking up pre-war threads of autonomy. Even though the attitude of India was less certain, it became increasingly apparent that the 'Jewel of Empire' could not fully be relied upon to make a major contribution to imperial defence. Although before the war India had agreed to supply small imperial garrisons along the line of communications from Suez, and in the Far East, the use of Indian troops in any other circumstances seemed inevitably to stimulate acrimonious financial disputes with London. When the scale of Indian military involvement in the Middle East, as anticipated by the War Office, was enormously magnified after the war, it should not have been difficult to predict an adverse reaction in Delhi. But 'war imperialism' blinded the planners in London to peacetime realities and in particular the Indian government's reluctance to commit Indian troops or revenues for the maintenance of imperial, and more specifically British, interests in the Middle East. Clearly it was this sort of attitude which Wilson had in mind when he complained to Lord Cavan in January 1922 that 'India had already taken on the airs and graces of independence'.[2]

Here was the crux of the dilemma facing London. The need for internal political reform in India had to be balanced against the potential threat which such reform posed to the whole system of imperial defence. The traditional fabric of the imperial military system depended upon India not only as a reservoir of native troops but also, and more significantly, a cheap and convenient repository for a quarter of the British army.[3] After 1918, with Indian politicians less docile than of old, and the Indian constitution not so accommodating, the former satisfactory state of affairs was jeopardised. At first the British government refused to give way to Indian demands for a radical reassessment of imperial defence policy regarding India, or at the least a more equitable allotment of the military budget, but the mounting pressure that followed the war proved too great to resist. When referred to arbitration in the 1930s, the 'Garran tribunal' (1933) decided that His Majesty's Government should make a financial contribution (later settled at one and a half million pounds *per annum*) towards the costs of maintaining British troops in India.[4] This was the first, vital, break in the British position and a measure of the degree to which British imperial control was slipping away in India. Ten years previously London had been able to veto Delhi's plans for drastic reductions in the British garrison and concede only a token Indianisation scheme. At the time, therefore, the foundations of the British military apparatus in India remained secure.

The only area in which London was obliged to give way vis-a-vis Delhi was that of Indian Army service 'ex-India'. But it would be wrong to see this as necessarily a demonstration of *imperial* weakness. The decision to replace a large conventional garrison in Mesopotamia with the air-policing scheme turned more on considerations of expense than (*pace* Edwin Montagu) a carefully-weighed assessment of Indian political conditions. All the evidence suggests that politicians and generals in both Britain and India continued to believe unquestioningly that at a time of real emergency, such as the Mesopotamian rebellion in 1920, the Army in India would act as a general imperial military reserve, as indeed it did in 1939–45. Nevertheless Indian reluctance to provide a permanent and apparently unlimited supply of native troops was an increasingly important factor in defining the pace of imperial policy in the Middle East. Though Britain's Middle Eastern military empire could not long have survived the war, it would have lasted longer had the Indian government not raised such great difficulties over the supply of Indian troops for imperial garrisons. The process was to be repeated, and taken to its logical conclusion following the Second World War.

Arguably the single most important factor hastening the rapid dissolution of Britain's post-war military empire was the condition of the United Kingdom itself. Here was a theatre of operations in which the British government could not request, and the British army not expect, any direct assistance from the empire. Domestic affairs, moreover, as was always the case, took precedence over imperial matters so far as the British government was concerned. At home war-weariness and economic weakness stimulated calls for retrenchment and as it became progressively apparent to the Lloyd George government that political survival might depend on national economy, military spending was among the first to be cut. The War Office's ability to meet imperial commitments was additionally hampered by the needs of internal security in Great Britain at a time when, for many, revolution seemed to be just around the corner. But above all there was the problem of Ireland.

The restoration of order in Ireland was the largest single burden which the British army had to bear in the post-war years. In this it was only partially successful. Although there was no actual military defeat in Ireland, the prevailing weakness of the army, together with its domestic and imperial responsibilities, rendered it unable wholly to contain the Irish Republican Army. Yet until the summer of 1921, by which time this fact had evidently become apparent to Lloyd George, the British government persisted with a policy of repression which, despite the reinforcement of the Irish police, finally depended on the power of the military alone. In addition to the local frustrations of troops largely confined to a role 'in aid of the civil power', for the War Office Ireland represented a continual drain of men and material; it dislocated the 'Cardwell' system of supplying overseas garrisons and upset traditional patterns of routine training and recreation. The Irish ulcer steadily sapped the empire's military power and persuaded many British leaders that it was futile to counter violent nationalism solely with repression. No-one, it was frequently asserted, wanted 'another Ireland' in Egypt, India or anywhere else. Inevitably, therefore, the long-term 'defence of the empire' depended on the actions and abilities of politicians and diplomats rather than the tactics and prowess of soldiers or airmen. Most of the difficulties which beset the empire between 1918 and 1922 arose from the fact that this cardinal, though prosaic, truth was masked at first by the attractive glitter of 'war imperialism'.

This was especially true in the Middle East where the prosecution of war aims contributed towards the over-extension of Britain's peace-time military commitments. The British forces which remained in Russia and Persia after the armistice had all originally been despatched to meet real, but wartime, needs. Following the war, however, these specific needs became translated into more general concerns, such as the suppression of Bolshevism or the defence of India. For some time, moreover, the extensive employment of British troops in pursuit of these objectives remained largely unquestioned in London since Lloyd George's immediate concern was almost exclusively the establishment of a European peace settlement. One early critic of the ill-considered direction of British policy in the Middle East was General Sir H. V. Cox, the Military Secretary to the India Office. Late in 1918 he wrote a paper drawing attention to Lord Curzon's apparent policy of taking control, in one form or another, of 'the whole of the vast countries . . . from the east shore of the Mediterranean to the Black Sea and eastward to the Persian Gulf'. Cox believed 'that, from a military point of view, we are proposing to undertake far more than this country is able or willing for; unless she becomes a great military land Power which is most undesirable even if it were possible'.[5]

But British military control in the Middle East itself was only feasible *because* Britain had emerged from the war as 'a great military land power'. The problem facing both generals and politicians was to dismantle this military edifice as quickly and as safely as possible. Not even Lord Curzon disagreed with this. The question upon which opinions were divided was that of the *rate* at which formal British hegemony should be relinquished. Sir Henry Wilson and his colleagues in the War Office considered that a realistic assessment of British commitments in relation to disposable military resources clearly demonstrated the need for an immediate and substantial scaling-down of her global responsibilities. On the other hand the Foreign Office urged that there should be no precipitate withdrawals from for example Persia or Turkey where the eventual success of their policies seemed to depend upon the retention of a British military 'presence'. The War Office case, however, was the stronger. There was neither the money, nor the men, perhaps not even the will, for Britain militarily to underwrite either Curzon's grandiose plans for a *pax Britannica* in the Middle East, or Lloyd George's misconceived confidence in Greek ability to act as a counterpoise to a resurgent Turkey. As one gloomy observer put it in the spring of 1920:

It is not a question only of the impossibility . . . of finding money or men to take on more Empire, but of clear signs that we never are going to find either again. The fixed determination of our own people not to take military service except for their self preservation is as obvious as their failing Will to Power. The Empire has reached its maximum and begun the descent. There is no more expansion in us . . . we started in 1914 young and vigorous and we have come out in 1919 to find we are old and must readjust all our ideas.[6]

But the post-war empire was the novel creation of the Great War. It was an empire Britain could not afford. 'Because we lack money', wrote 'Boney' Fuller in 1922, 'we cannot increase the size of the army to fit the Empire; consequently there is only one thing we can do, namely, reduce the size of the Empire to fit our army'. Fuller offered two solutions: 'abandon large tracts of the Empire', or, 'increase our present speed of military movement so that our securities, through enhanced mobility, may be brought to balance our liabilities'.[7] Fuller's stark alternatives, however, which were designed to promote the attractions of mechanisation, were not the only choices available to the British government. Where possible there might be a reversion to the informal control which Britain had exercised over much of the Middle East before the war. To be successful this course of action depended on the British wooing pliant local collaborators who could be trusted with sufficient autonomy so as to relieve the army of its direct responsibilities for internal security while guaranteeing essential British strategic and commercial interests.

The policy was applied more or less effectively in Egypt, Trans-Jordan and Iraq. The same process, moreover, can be discerned in Ireland and India where, once the legitimacy of national aspirations was accepted, the British sought to solve their own actual or potential military difficulties by meeting the demands of the more moderate nationalists. The most notable failure of this policy was in Persia where the ironic fact that British troops were there in the first place undermined any chance of success. The peripheral anti-Bolshevik republics of south Russia, which Curzon clearly hoped would become British client states, were too short-lived for this ever to become a real possibility and the only factor which could have prolonged their life was a greater degree of military protection than Britain had the resources to provide. In Palestine the solution of informal rule did not obtain while Arabs and Jews refused to work together in any form of local self government. Within this pattern, the benefits of mechanisation were partially applied, but since the government did not entirely share Fuller's confidence in the merits of mechanical progress, it was only in Iraq and Trans-Jordan, where air defence schemes were applied, that 'enhanced mobility' featured prominently.

A few days before Christmas 1921 Sir Henry Wilson motored down to the Staff College at Camberley to deliver a short 'farewell address'. The title he gave his speech was 'The passing of the Empire'. Appropriately it summed up Wilson's feelings about his term as CIGS. His 'appreciation of the future of the British Empire', he told Rawlinson in February 1922, was 'of the very blackest'.[8] For Wilson the once-great British imperial system was on the verge of collapse, caused by a chronic inability to deal satisfactorily with internal discontent – that persistent lack of '*government*', most grievously illustrated in Ireland. But the Field

Marshal, maddened by his peculiar concern for Ireland, failed to perceive that what was happening was no more than a general reversion to traditional imperial techniques of control, albeit accelerated both by military weakness and the rising tempo of nationalism. Compared to the pinnacle of conquest in November 1918, the empire doubtless seemed greatly reduced by 1922, but in comparison to 1914 there was much for the imperial enthusiast to regard with pride. The acquisition of former German colonies had added a pleasing amount of red to the political map of the world; the Irish question had found an answer which, if not entirely satisfactory, was the best that could apparently be expected; violent nationalism had died down in India and Egypt, and by the middle of the following year a peace settlement with Turkey removed the last major irritant and confirmed Britain's enhanced position in the Middle East. The only blot on this agreeable imperial escutcheon was the retreat from Persia. Nevertheless, the exclusively-British Anglo–Persian Oil Company continued to work the oil fields in the south-west of the country.

By the end of 1922 Britain was well set on her inter-war path of strictly-limited international responsibilities, a policy of retrenchment, which, in the imperial sphere at least, paradoxically seemed to pose no threat to vital British strategic interests. It would not be true, however, to suggest that the post-war crises which beset the empire were no more than a series of colossal irritations which the 'weary Titan' took easily in his stride. The constant threat of military disaster was real enough and at times, as the Director of Military Operations observed after the Mesopotamian rebellion, 'we ran things too fine'.[9] Sir Henry Wilson sought earnestly to bring this point home to the Cabinet in what he regarded as his 'swan song',[10] the General Staff answer to Geddes:

We have definite evidence of a world-wide conspiracy fomented by all the elements most hostile to British interests – Sinn Feiners and Socialists at our own doors, Russian Bolsheviks, Turkish and Egyptian Nationalists and Indian Seditionists. Up to the present we have been lucky in not having experienced trouble in more than one theatre at the same time, but when it is remembered that the hostile combination is working with the connivance – if not under the active direction of – the German Foreign Office, it would be folly to ignore the probability of better co-ordinated attacks in the future.[11]

Sir Maurice Hankey had an alternative, though equally comprehensive, bogey to blame for the empire's difficulties:

The primary and original cause of our troubles in the East from Egypt, through Palestine, Mesopotamia, and Persia to India is President Wilson and his fourteen points, and his impossible doctrine of self determination. The adoption of this principle at the peace conferences has struck at the very roots of the British Empire all over the world from Ireland to Hong Kong, and has got us into a hideous mess.[12]

Whether it would be correct to lay the blame at the door of either the

Wilhelmstrasse or the White House is open to question, but it would seem that Hankey's identification of 'self determination', was closer to the truth. The maintenance of British control, formal or informal, anywhere in the world was to depend not on the power of her armed forces, even if available, but on the finesse of her local agents in not offending the susceptibilities of tender young nationalisms. Although the nationalist movements of the immediate post-war years largely ran out of steam in the 1920s, the weaknesses they briefly exposed in the imperial system and the responses they provoked from the British government provided a 'dry run' for the eventual disintegration of the empire following the Second World War. 'The truth is,' wrote Campbell-Bannerman in the aftermath of the South African War, 'we cannot provide for a fighting Empire, and nothing will give us the power. A peaceful Empire of the old type we are quite fit for'.[13] So it was to be in the 1920s when diplomacy and Britain's lingering imperial prestige, supplying power which simple military force could not provide, held the empire together. Twenty-five years later neither a 'fighting Empire' nor a peaceful one 'of the old type' were available as choices for the rulers of the British empire.

Notes

Chapter 1   The empire at war

1   Sir Charles Monro (CinC India) to Sir Henry Rawlinson (GOCinC IV Army), 12 Dec. 1918, Rawlinson MSS. 5201/33/79.

2   Dominions: 978,439 'total sent overseas or undergoing training, 1 Nov. 1918'. 'Statistical abstract of information regarding the armies at home and abroad, 1914–20', W.O. 161/82.
India: 239,561 ranks (including non-combatants) 'at the outbreak of war', plus 1,161,789 'recruited during the war up to 30 Sept. 1918', CAB. 24/70 G.T.6341.

3   *Conference of Prime Ministers*, 1921 cmd. 1474, p. 15.

4   Lucas (ed.), *The Empire at War*, I, p. v. Much of the information in this chapter is drawn from these volumes.

5   Ibid., p. 254.

6   Ibid., pp. 56–7.

7   Ibid., p. 54.

8   *Oxford Dictionary of Quotations*, p. 11 n. 9. Another version is quoted in Mansergh, *Commonwealth Experience*, p. 124.

9   'Copy extract report of the Indian Expenditure Commission', IOR L/F/7/783. I am grateful to Dr. B. R. Tomlinson of Birmingham University for this reference.

10   Lucas, *The Empire at War*, V, pp. 179, 163; Government of India, *India's Contribution to the Great War*, pp. 61–5; Mason, *A Matter of Honour*, p. 408.

11   261,067 soldiers (combatants only). 'Strengths by arms of the expeditionary forces', 16 Dec. 1918, Milner MS. dep. 145.

12   Note by E. S. Montagu, 13 Jan. 1919, Lloyd George MSS. F/172/1/1.

13   'Note on finance', c. Oct. 1918, Montagu MSS. AS/I/2/56; Dodwell, *Cambridge History of India*, VI, pp. 331, 484.

14   'Note on military aspects', c. Oct. 1918, Montagu MSS. AS/I/2/57; Government of India, *India's Contribution to the Great War*, p. 107.

15   There are useful accounts of imperial defence questions before the First World War in Gordon, *Dominion Partnership* and Mansergh, *Commonwealth Experience*, pp. 120–56.

16   Stanley, *Canada's Soldiers*, pp. 215–16, 270.

17   Barclay, *The Empire is Marching*, pp. 14–15.

18   Ibid., p. 40.

19 Jebb, *Imperial Conference*, I, pp. 354, 362–6; Gordon, *Dominion Partnership*, p. 160.
20 The best account of the pre-war period is in Gooch, *Plans of War*.
21 Bean, *The Story of Anzac*, p. 24; Barclay, *The Empire is Marching*, p. 58.
22 Duguid, *Canadian Forces in the Great War*, I, p. 7; Elton, *Imperial Commonwealth*, pp. 473–4.
23 Lucas, *The Story of the Empire*, p. 253.
24 Bonar Law to Lloyd George, 11 Dec. 1916, Bonar Law MSS. 50/20/9.
25 Hughes to Lloyd George and *vice versa*, 29 Dec. 1916 and 18 Jan. 1917, Lloyd George MSS. F/32/4/14 and 22.
26 Davis, *Irish Issues in New Zealand Politics*, pp. 131–2, 190–2.
27 Nicholson, *Canadian Expeditionary Force*, pp. 340–53; MacNaught, *History of Canada*, pp. 215–18; Barclay, *The Empire is Marching*, p. 73.
28 Lucas, *The Story of the Empire*, p. 260; *idem*, *The Empire at War*, III, pp. 402–3. In England the corresponding figure was 24% of the *male* population.
29 Lucas, *The Empire at War*, I, pp. 260–3, and IV pp. 151–99; 'The colonies and protectorates', paper prepared for Lord Milner, Jan. 1919, Milner MS. Eng. hist. c.699, fols. 123–33; 'Note on the possibility of employing African native troops overseas', 4 Feb. 1920, W.O. 32/5356 no. 4A.
30 Lucas, *The Empire at War*, I, p. 293.
31 Demangeon, *The British Empire*, pp. 189, 275.
32 Haig diary, 17 Mar. 1917, quoted in Blake, *Private Papers of Douglas Haig*, p. 214; Preston, *Canada and 'Imperial Defense'*, p. 469.
33 Mansergh, *Commonwealth Experience*, pp. 151, 173–5; Lucas, *The Story of the Empire*, p. 254.
34 W. H. Long to Lloyd George, 21 Mar. 1917, Lloyd George MSS. F/32/4/53.
35 Dodwell, *Cambridge History of India*, VI, pp. 486–8; Spear, *History of India*, II, pp. 184–90.
36 Norman, *History of Modern Ireland*, pp. 254–67; Ward, 'Lloyd George and Irish Conscription', pp. 107–29; Lucey, 'Cork public opinion', pp. 100–8.
37 Darwin, *Britain, Egypt and the Middle East*, pp. 60–74.
38 A concept developed by Darwin, ibid., especially pp. 161, 208.
39 Rawlinson to Sir Henry Wilson, 11 Nov. 1918, Wilson MSS. 13B/6.

Chapter 2 Weaknesses of the home base

1 See Howard, *The Continental Commitment*, chs. 1 and 2.
2 This point is discussed in Jeffery and Hennessy, *States of Emergency*, pp. 5–9.
3 Wilson diary, 15 Jan. 1920.
4 This argument is discussed with particular reference to post-1939 Britain in Kennedy, *The Realities behind Diplomacy*, chs. 7 and 8.
5 3,661,986 (*plus* 117,839 white troops in the Indian establishment), 'Monthly returns of the distribution of the army', July–Dec. 1918, W.O. 73/109.
6 Nov. 1919: 798,419 (Indian establishment, 80,533); Nov. 1920: 369,710 (62,206), 'Monthly returns . . .', W.O. 73/111, 113.
7 Milner to Lloyd George, 13 Nov. 1918, Lloyd George MSS. F/38/4/24.
8 Memo. by Secretaries for War and India, CAB. 24/69 G.T. 6292.
9 Wilson to Lord Cavan (GOCinC Italy), 18 Nov. 1918, Wilson MSS. 28B/20;

memo. by CIGS, 5 Dec. 1918, CAB. 24/71 G.T. 6434.

10 Fisher diary, 12 Nov. 1918, MS Fisher 13.

11 Graubard, 'Military demobilisation', gives a good general account of the problem.

12 Wilson diary, 6 and 9 Dec. 1918; draft note by Milner, 12 Dec. 1918, MS Milner dep. 46 fol. 94; Milner to Lloyd George, 4 Jan. 1919, Milner MS. Eng. hist. c. 696/2.

13 Wilson diary, 9 Jan. 1919.

14 Churchill to Lloyd George, 29 Dec. 1918, in Gilbert, *Churchill*, IV, Companion Part 1, p. 448.

15 Wilson diary, 10 Jan. 1919; Jones, *Whitehall Diary*, I. p. 72.

16 Lloyd George to Churchill, 18 Jan. 1919, Lloyd George MSS. F/8/3/2.

17 Addison to Lloyd George, 24 Jan. 1919, ibid., F/1/5/4.

18 Churchill to Lloyd George, 27 Jan, 1919, ibid., F/8/3/8.

19 CAB. 23/9 W.C. 521 and appendix; also Churchill to Lloyd George, 29 Jan. 1919, in Gilbert, *Churchill*, IV, Companion Part 1, pp. 494–6.

20 Wilson diary, 25 Jan. 1919.

21 Ibid., 4 Jan. 1919.

22 Ibid., 6 Jan. 1919.

23 Sir Edmund Allenby (High Commissioner for Egypt) to Wilson, 17 May 1919, Wilson MSS. 33B/16.

24 'The military situation throughout the British Empire', 3 May 1919, CAB. 24/78 G.T. 7182.

25 Wilson diary, 9 Jan. 1919.

26 'The military situation . . .', 3 May 1919, CAB. 24/78 G.T. 7182.

27 'Strength of the British army', appendix B, 5 Nov. 1919, CAB. 24/92 C.P. 55.

28 11 May 1920, CAB. 23/21/29(20) appendix II, appendix.

29 Memo. by AG, 23 Oct. 1920, CAB. 24/114 C.P. 2006.

30 Wilson diary, 10 Sept. 1920. Beatty was First Sea Lord.

31 Chelmsford to Edwin Montagu (S. of S. for India 1917–22), 8 July 1919, Chelmsford MSS. E.264, vol. 11, p. 26.

32 Wilson diary, 12 Mar. 1920; Hankey diary, 27 Mar. 1920.

33 Jones, *Whitehall Diary*, III, p. 27.

34 Rawlinson to Wilson, 10 Mar. 1921, Wilson MSS. file 13D/1. There were, moreover, fewer British troops in India in 1920 (64,000) than there had been in 1913 (75,000).

35 Coalition MPs, 473; others, 234 (including 73 abstentionist Irish members).

36 Chamberlain to Hilda Chamberlain (sister), 24 Mar. 1919, Chamberlain MSS. AC 5/1/122.

37 *Revised statement of army expenditure 1919–20*, 1919 cmd. 378; *Army estimates 1914–15*, House of Commons papers 1913, li, p. 12.

38 *Revised statement . . .*, 1919 cmd. 378; Cabinet finance committee 11th meeting, 22 Oct. 1919, CAB. 23/71.

39 Chamberlain to Churchill, 30 Jan. 1919, Chamberlain MSS. AC 24/1/24.

40 Churchill to Lloyd George, 1 May 1919, Lloyd George MSS. F/8/3/46.

41 Memo. by Chamberlain, 18 July 1919, G.T. 7729, Addison MSS., Box 4, folder 297.

42 Memo. by Addison, 28 July 1919, ibid.

43 War Cabinet meeting, 5 Aug. 1919, CAB. 23/15/606A.

44   Ibid., 15 Aug. 1919, CAB. 23/15/616A. Similar guidelines were laid down for the navy. See Macdonald, 'Lloyd George and the search for a postwar naval policy'.

45   Wilson diary, 15 Aug. 1919.

46   'Summary of army estimates 1920–21', 7 Feb. 1920, CAB. 24/97 C.P. 585. The finally-published estimate was £125 million. See *Army Estimates 1920–21*, 16 Mar. 1920, House of Commons papers 1922, xii, pp. 4–5.

47   Memo. by Chamberlain, 7 June 1920, CAB. 24/107 C.P. 1413.

48   Darwin, *Britain, Egypt and the Middle East*, p. 33.

49   'Proposed committee on national expenditure', 7 Aug. 1920, CAB. 24/110 C.P. 1753; Gilbert, *Churchill*, IV, p. 768.

50   'Estimates circular 1921–22', 1 Oct. 1920, Addison MSS. Box 53.

51   'Resolutions of economy as announced by the Chancellor of the Exchequer during the debate on national expenditure, 9 Dec. 1920', CAB. 24/116 C.P. 2274.

52   £29,750,000. Memo. by Secretary for War, 10 Dec. 1920, CAB. 24/116 C.P. 2232.

53   Hankey diary, 3 Jan. 1921.

54   Woolwich East in Mar. 1921 and Hackney South in Aug. 1922 (both won by Coalition Unionists). Craig, *British Parliamentary Election Statistics*, p. 21.

55   See Cowling, *The Impact of Labour*, chs. 2–6, and Morgan, *Consensus and Disunity*, chs. 8–10.

56   'Home Office weekly report on revolutionary organisations in the U.K.', no. 112, 30 June 1921, CAB. 24/125 C.P. 3100.

57   Chamberlain to Sir George Lloyd (Governor of Bombay), 11 Apr. 1921, Chamberlain MSS. AC 18/1/20.

58   Fisher diary, 2 Aug. 1921, MS Fisher 18.

59   Wilson diary, 24 Oct. 1921.

60   CAB. 24/131 C.P. 3570.

61   Wilson to Maj.-Gen. Sir C. J. Sackville–West (Military Attaché in Paris), Wilson MSS. 12G/70, and Wilson diary, 22 Dec. 1921.

62   Memo. by General Staff, 20 Jan. 1922, CAB. 24/132 C.P. 3619.

63   Memo. by Worthington-Evans, 4 Feb. 1922, ibid., C.P. 3682.

64   Report of Churchill committee, 4 Feb. 1922, ibid., C.P. 3692. The pre-war army estimates actually totalled more than £27 million. The annual average for the three estimates 1912–13 to 1914–15 was £28,362,712, and that for the ten years 1905–06 to 1914–15 was £27,851,502.

65   Mowat, *Britain between the Wars*, p. 131.

66   Grigg, *Prejudice and Judgment*, p. 69.

67   Wilson diary, 23 Dec. 1921 and 1 Jan. 1922.

68   Cavan, 'Recollections hazy but happy', ch. 15, p. 2, Cavan MSS.

69   Wilson diary, 10 Nov. 1918.

70   From Nov. 1918 this information was contained in a 'Fortnightly report on pacificism and revolutionary organisations in the U.K. and morale abroad'. In April 1919 this changed into a weekly 'Report on revolutionary organisations in the U.K.', collated by the Home Office Directorate of Intelligence (Report no. 1, 30 Apr. 1919, CAB. 24/78 G.T. 7196).

71   See Kendall, *The Revolutionary Movement in Britain*, pp. 190–2.

72   Critchley, *History of Police in England and Wales*, pp. 186–9. A more

popular account of both police strikes will be found in Reynolds and Judge, *The Night the Police went on Strike*.

73 McLean, 'Popular protest and public order'; Middlemas, *The Clydesiders*, pp. 92–6.

74 Hankey diary, 12. Oct. 1919.

75 'The employment of troops in industrial disturbances', 12 Nov. 1919, CAB. 24/93 C.P. 111.

76 Wilson diary, 6 Oct. 1919.

77 Ibid., 3 Jan. 1920.

78 'Capacity of the army to assist the civil power', 3 Jan. 1920, CAB. 24/96 C.P. 472.

79 Rawlinson diary, 14 Jan. 1920, Rawlinson MSS. 5201/33/29. At this time Rawlinson was GOCinC Aldershot Command.

80 Wilson diary, 15 Jan. 1920.

81 CAB. 23/35/S.10; Wilson diary, 16 Jan. 1920; Hankey diary, 24 Jan. 1920.

82 Memo. by Hankey, 17 Jan. 1920, Lloyd George MSS. F/24/2/3.

83 Hankey diary, 24 Jan. 1920.

84 Conference of ministers, 18 Jan. 1920, CAB. 23/35/S.11; Wilson diary, 19 Jan. 1920.

85 Wilson diary, 22 Jan. and 2 Feb. 1920; Rawlinson diary, 28 Jan. 1920, Rawlinson MSS. 5201/33/29.

86 Riddell, *Intimate Diary*, p. 203.

87 Home Office report, week ending 2 Sept. 1920, CAB. 24/111 C.P. 1830. On ex-servicemen generally, see Ward, 'Intelligence surveillance of British ex-servicemen, 1918–20'.

88 Wilson diary, 6 and 10 Sept. 1920.

89 Ibid., 15 Sept. 1920.

90 Ibid., 21 Oct. 1920.

91 Hankey diary, 22 Oct. 1920.

92 Wilson diary, 20 Feb. 1921.

93 Ibid., 28 Feb. 1921.

94 Ibid., 31 Mar. 1921.

95 Ibid., 2 April 1921.

96 CAB. 23/25/17(21).

97 Wilson diary, 7 April 1921.

98 CAB. 23/25/22(21) appendix V.

99 Wilson to Sackville-West, 14 Apr. 1921, Wilson MSS. 12G/25.

100 Fisher diary, 4 Apr. 1921, MS Fisher 18. Thomas was General Secretary of the National Union of Railwaymen. Wilson records Lloyd George saying that Thomas claimed 'Jesus Christ could not now stop this revolutionary Movement'. Wilson diary, 4 Apr. 1921.

101 The lock-out dragged on until 1 July when the miners gave in to the owners' proposals.

102 Rawlinson to Wilson, 27 Apr. 1921, Wilson MSS. 13D/16.'Frocks' was a slang term for politicians. It was short for 'frock-coats'.

103 Memo. by General Staff, 20 Jan. 1922, CAB. 24/132 C.P. 3619.

104 Kendall, *The Revolutionary Movement in Britain*, pp. 194–5.

Chapter 3   Imperial problems old and new

1 'Other ranks' only: Canada 138,296; Australia, 94,520; New Zealand, 22,668; South Africa, 8,176; total, 263,660. 'Strengths by arms of the Expenditionary Forces . . . estimated up to 16 Dec. 1918', MS Milner dep. 145.

2 Memo. by Sir Henry Wilson, 11 Dec. 1918, W.O. 106/315 no. 47 (circulated to Cabinet as G.T. 6459); Imperial War Cabinet meeting, 12 Dec. 1918, CAB. 23/42/42.

3 Hughes and Botha to Lloyd George, 5 March and 1 Apr. 1919, Lloyd George MSS. F/28/3/6 and F/5/5/5.

4 Chief of the General Staff, Ottawa, to W.O., 23 Dec. 1918, MS. Milner dep. 143 fol. 191; Borden to Lloyd George, 13 Feb. 1919, Lloyd George MSS. F/5/3/9; Churchill to Wilson 5 Mar. 1919, in Gilbert, *Churchill*, IV, Companion Part 1, p. 572.

5 Jack Gallagher's phrase. See Gallagher, 'Nationalisms and the crisis of empire, 1919–1922', and *The Decline, Revival and Fall of the British Empire*, pp. 86–99.

6 Memo. by Col. W. R. Robertson (later CIGS), 17 Jan. 1902, W.O. 106/48 paper E3/1.

7 Howard, *The Continental Commitment*, pp. 19–20.

8 Wilson diary, 5 Nov. 1918.

9 Cabinet eastern committee 40th meeting, 2 Dec. 1918, CAB. 27/24.

10 Memo. by CIGS, 13 Nov. 1918, CAB. 24/70 G.T. 6311.

11 Memo. by Lord Curzon, 9 Aug. 1919, CAB. 1/28/24.

12 An argument for the great importance of oil will be found in Kent, *Oil and Empire*; a quite contrary view in Darwin, *Britain, Egypt and the Middle East*, pp. 258–65. A good general book on the topic is Longrigg, *Oil in the Middle East*.

13 Memo. by First Sea Lord, 25 Jan. 1919, CAB. 24/74 G.T. 6703.

14 Wilkinson, 'The influence of oil', p. 114.

15 Wilson (quoting Sir Philip Chetwode) to Sir Charles Sackville-West (Military Attaché, Paris), 11 Aug. 1921, Wilson MSS. 12G/50.

16 Riddell, *Intimate Diary*, p. 118. For Lloyd George's earlier opinions, see Imperial War Cabinet meetings, 12 and 23 Dec. 1918, CAB. 23/42/42 and 45.

17 Memo. by Montagu, 17 December 1918, CAB. 24/72 G.T. 6529.

18 War Cabinet meeting, 14 Nov. 1918, CAB. 23/8 W.C. 502.

19 4 Dec. 1918, CAB. 29/2 P.42.

20 S. of S. to Viceroy, 8 Apr. 1920, Montagu MSS. D.523, vol. 4, p. 20.

21 Viceroy to S. of S., 12 Feb. 1920, Chelmsford MSS. E264, vol. 6, pp. 32–3.

22 Chamberlain to Sir George Lloyd (Governor of Bombay), 13 Apr. 1921, Chamberlain, MSS. AC 18/1/23.

23 17th meeting (6 July), Imperial Meetings 1921, vol. I, Lloyd George MSS. F/118.

24 'The future of Cyprus', 3 Jan. 1919 and note by Long, 9 Jan. 1919, CAB. 29/2 P. 86 and P. 90.

25 Milner to Lloyd George, 16 May 1919, Lloyd George MSS. F/39/1/21 (copy to Wilson, Wilson MSS. 11/21); Wilson diary, 16 May 1919.

26 Lee, *Imperial Military Geography*, p. 79. See Lowe and Marzari, *Italian Foreign Policy*, pp. 170–1.

27 Note by Curzon, 16 Oct. 1918, CAB. 24/67 G.T. 6015; Colonial Office memo., Oct. 1918 and India Office memo. 4 Dec. 1918, CAB. 29/2 P. 47 and P. 42.

28 Memo. by Amery, enclosed in Amery to Wilson, 22 Dec. 1918, Wilson MSS. 8/20. For a full account of the Tanganyika question, see Louis, *Great Britain and Germany's Lost Colonies*, pp. 117–60.

29 A summary of some of the principal agreements will be found in Nicolson, *Curzon*, pp. 83–7. There is a good general account of the Middle Eastern peace-making in Dockrill and Goold, *Peace without Promise*, ch. 4.

30 Wilson to Sackville-West, 11 Oct. 1919, Wilson MSS. 12E/7.

31 Cabinet eastern committee meetings Nov. 1918–Jan. 1919, CAB. 27/24. The minutes of its successor, the inter-departmental conference on Middle Eastern affairs (IDCE), are in the Curzon MSS. F.112/275.

32 'A note of warning about the Middle East', 25 Mar. 1919, CAB. 24/77 G.T. 7037.

33 Curzon to eastern committee (16th meeting), 24 June 1918, CAB. 27/24.

34 Wilson to Churchill, 2 Apr. 1919, Wilson MSS. 18A/23; Churchill to Balfour, 12 Aug. 1919, Balfour Add. Mss. 4964.

35 Montagu to Lloyd George, 16 Apr. 1919, Lloyd George MSS. F/40/2/50.

36 Milner to Montagu, 30 Aug. 1919, Montagu MSS. AS/I/6/167.

37 Lloyd George to Montagu, 25 Apr. 1920, ibid., AS/I/12/262. The full text of the Treaty of Sèvres will be found in *British and Foreign State Papers* (1920), cxiii, pp. 652–776.

38 26 June 1920. Riddell, *Intimate Diary*, p. 208.

39 D'Abernon, *An Ambassador of Peace*, I, p. 38.

40 Lloyd George's description in an interview with Gen. Ironside, July 1920. Ironside, *High Road to Command*, p. 92.

41 Wilson diary, 18 and 24 June 1920.

42 Cabinet memo. by Churchill, 23 Nov. 1920, in Gilbert, *Churchill*, IV, Companion Part 2, p. 1249.

43 There is an account of these, and subsequent, attempts to come to an accommodation with the nationalist Turks in Darwin, *Britain, Egypt and the Middle East*, pp. 208–42. There are other useful accounts of Asia Minor during this period in Llewellyn Smith, *Ionian Vision* and Howard, *The Partition of Turkey*.

44 'The military situation in Turkey', 26 May 1921, CAB. 24/123 C.P. 2981; 31 May 1921; Cabinet minutes, CAB. 23/25/44 (21) and Wilson diary.

45 Lloyd George MSS. F/209/2. Telegrams were sent to Australia, Canada, Newfoundland, (which offered support, but had no troops), New Zealand and South Africa. See also conference of ministers, 19 Sept. 1922, CAB. 23/39 no. 140.

46 'Future military operations in Russia', 24 Feb. 1920, W.O. 106/316 no. 11. Circulated to Cabinet as G.T. 6885.

47 Memo. by CIGS, 13 Nov. 1918, CAB. 24/70 G.T. 6311; Cabinet minutes, 31 Dec. 1918, CAB. 23/42/48.

48 Churchill to Lloyd George and *vice versa*, 13 and 16 Feb. 1919, Lloyd George MSS. F/8/3/14 and 18.

49 Churchill to Lloyd George, 17 and 27 February 1919, ibid., F/8/3/19 and 21.

50 Enclosed with Lloyd George to Churchill, 30 Aug. 1919, ibid. F/9/1/15. Denikin commanded anti-Bolshevik forces in the Crimea and south Russia.

51 Churchill to Lloyd George, Sept. 1919, Lloyd George MSS. F/9/1/17.

52 Gilbert, *Churchill*, IV, p. 330. The full text of the letter is in *idem, Churchill*, IV, Companion Part 2, pp. 870–2.
53 Monday, 22 Sept. 1919, Lloyd George MSS. F/9/1/20.
54 Kedourie, 'Sa'ad Zaghlul', p. 151.
55 There is a good account of the north Russian intervention in Ironside, *Archangel*.
56 Rawlinson to Wilson, 16 Aug. 1919, and Wilson to Churchill, 1 Sept. 1919, Wilson MSS, 13B/15 and 18A/45.
57 Cabinet minutes, 11 June 1920, CAB. 23/21/35(20).
58 Churchill's 'picturesque phrase'. Hankey diary, 31 May 1920.
59 24 Jan. 1920. Riddell, *Intimate Diary*, p. 163.
60 Ullman, *Anglo–Soviet Relations*, III, p. 373.
61 Carr, *Bolshevik Revolution*, III, pp. 262–3. There is a detailed treatment of Soviet policy 1917–27 in Kapur, *Soviet Russia and Asia*.
62 Cabinet minutes, 17 Nov. 1920, CAB. 23/23/61(20).
63 'Reply of British Government to M. Krassin's note of June 29th, 1920', 30 June 1920, Davidson MSS. 'Russia 1919–23' Box.
64 A full account of the negotiations will be found in Ullman, *Anglo–Soviet Relations*, III.
65 26 Apr. 1919. Circulated to the Cabinet on 3 May, CAB. 24/78 G.T. 7182.
66 CAB. 24/107 C.P. 1467.
67 Note on the 1920–21 army estimates, 7 Feb. 1920, CAB. 24/97 C.P. 586.
68 Memo. relating to the army supplementary estimate, Dec. 1920, CAB. 24/116 C.P. 2232. The original estimate for 1920–21 had been £125,000,000.
69 Wilson diary, 2 Apr. 1921.
70 Note by CIGS, 5 Aug. 1920, Philby MSS. Box VI, file 3.
71 This catalogue does not include the 15,000 British troops in Mesopotamia.
72 Wilson to Robertson, 30 Mar. 1921, Wilson MSS. 23/7.
73 Note by CIGS, 5 Aug. 1920, Philby MSS. Box VI, file 3.
74 Wilson diary, 13 Mar., 15 July and 5 Aug. 1920; Wilson to Rawlinson and Haldane, 2 April and 28 Dec. 1921; Wilson MSS. 13C/26 and 55/5.
75 Wilson to Haldane, 28 Dec. 1921, Wilson MSS. 55/5.

Chapter 4 Searching for imperial manpower

1 Hankey to Balfour (copy to Sir Henry Wilson), Nov. 1920, Wilson MSS. 6/42C.
2 Viceroy to S. of S., 2 Dec. 1918, Chelmsford MSS. E.264. vol. 9, pp. 467–8.
3 Ibid., 8 Dec. 1918, IOR L/MIL/3/2510, p. 4025.
4 Ibid., 31 Dec. 1918, Chelmsford MSS. E.264, vol. 9, p. 531.
5 Chamberlain to Curzon, 17 Sept. 1919, Curzon MSS. F.112/209.
6 Montagu to Chelmsford, 17 Oct. 1919, Montagu MSS. D.523, vol. 3, p. 218.
7 Chelmsford to Montagu, 31 Dec. 1919, ibid., vol. 9, pp. 413–4.
8 Viceroy (Army dept.) to S. of S., 6 Feb. 1922, and *vice versa*, 14 Feb. 1922, IOR L/MIL/3/2514, no. 1121 and /2534, M.1348/1922.
9 Lytton to Montagu, 14 Aug. 1922, Montagu MSS. AS/I/6/160(5).
10 'Despatch on the operations against the Kuki tribes of Assam and Burma', June 1919, W.O. 106/58.
11 Viceroy to S. of S., 20 Aug. 1919, Chelmsford MSS. E.264, vol. 11, pp. 188–9.

12 Ibid., 6 Oct. 1919, 23 Mar. and 4 Sept. 1920, Chelmsford MSS, E.264. vol. 11, pp. 321–2, vol. 12, pp. 274–5, and vol. 13, pp. 214–15.
13 Ibid., 30 Jan. 1921, Chelmsford MSS. E.264, vol. 14, p. 109.
14 'Military policy in Mesopotamia', 26 Aug. 1920, copy of telegram from S. of S. for War to GOCinC, Mesopotamia, CAB. 24/111 C.P. 1814.
15 Viceroy to S. of S., 7 July 1920, Chelmsford MSS. E.264, vol. 13, p. 24.
16 'Supply of overseas garrisons from the Indian Army', 3 Sept. 1920, CAB. 24/111 C.P. 1844.
17 S. of S. to Viceroy, 29 Jan. 1919, Chelmsford MSS. E.264, vol. 10, p. 39.
18 Viceroy to S. of S., 7 Apr. 1920, ibid., vol. 12, p. 311.
19 Ibid., 17 Dec. 1920, ibid., vol. 13, p. 511.
20 Ibid., 19 Feb. 1921, ibid., vol. 14, p. 168.
21 Ibid., 2 Nov. 1920, ibid., vol. 13, pp. 380–1.
22 Mason, *A Matter of Honour*, pp. 418, 425, 441–2.
23 Viceroy to S. of S., 2 Nov. 1920, Chelmsford MSS. E.264, vol. 13, pp. 380–1.
24 S. of S. to Viceroy, 18 Feb. 1921, ibid., vol. 14, p. 89.
25 Viceroy to S. of S., 13 Jan. 1921, ibid., pp. 35–6; S. of S. to Viceroy (Army dept.) and *vice versa*, 3 Feb. and 12 Mar. 1921, IOR L/MIL/3/2533, M.1068/730 and /2513, p. 586.
26 S. of S. to Viceroy (Army dept.), 29 Dec. 1921, IOR L/Mil/3/2533, no. 6531.
27 Viceroy to S. of S., 30 Mar. 1921, Chelmsford MSS. E.264, vol. 14, p. 294; *Legislative Assembly Debates*, vol. I, no. 15, pp. 1683–1762, enclosed in IOR L/MIL/7/10822.
28 Viceroy (Army dept.) to S. of S. (2 parts), 6 May 1921, IOR L/MIL/3/2513, p. 958.
29 Ibid., 6 June 1921, ibid., p. 1140.
30 Rawlinson to Wilson, 8 June 1921, Wilson MSS. 13D/28.
31 Evinced by their attitude to possible dominion reinforcements. See below p. 60.
32 Rawlinson to Wilson, 4 Jan. 1922, Wilson MSS. 13F/32.
33 'Reinforcements for Mesopotamia', 9 Sept. 1920, CAB. 24/111. C.P. 1843.
34 Cabinet minutes, CAB. 23/22/51(20). The texts of the telegrams sent on 18 Sept. will be found in CAB. 24/111 C.P. 1875.
35 New Zealand reply, 20 Sept. 1920; Australia, 24 Sept.; Canada, 26 Sept. CAB. 24/111 C.P. 1876, 1892, 1893.
36 CAB. 23/22/53(20); Colonial Secretary to Officer administering the government of New Zealand, 1 Oct. 1920, CAB. 24/112 C.P. 1940.
37 See Higham, *Armed Forces In Peacetime*, pp. 59–63, and Holland, *Britain and the Commonwealth Alliance*, pp. 15–17.
38 Memo. by General Staff, 23 Feb. 1921, Lloyd George MSS. F/118, vol. III, E.3.
39 'Imperial military defence: summary prepared in the War Office', 11 June 1921, ibid., E.34.
40 Preston, *Canada and 'Imperial Defense'*, pp. 527–8.
41 IDCE 15th meeting, 10 Apr. 1919, Curzon MSS. F.112/275.
42 Churchill to Wilson, 11 Jan. 1920, W.O. 32/5356, no. 1A.
43 W.O. to C.O., 14 Jan. 1920, and 'Note on possibility of employing African native troops overseas', enclosed in W.O. to C.O. and F.O., 4 Feb. 1920, ibid., nos. 2A and 4A.
44 C.O. to W.O., 4 Feb. 1920, ibid., enclosed after no. 4A.
45 F.O. to W.O., 10 Feb. 1920, ibid., no. 5A.

46 Sir Lee Stack to Lord Allenby, 13 Mar. 1920, enclosed in Allenby to Lord Curzon, 27 Mar. 1920, and minute by J. Murray, 9 Apr. 1920, F.O. 371/5023/E2899.

47 Kirke to DMO, 1 and 30 Mar. 1920, W.O. 32/5356, nos. 6A and 7.

48 W.O. to C.O., enclosing 'Employment of African troops overseas', 6 Apr. 1920, ibid., nos. 7A and 7B.

49 Kirke to DMO, 14 Apr. 1920, ibid., no. 9A.

50 DMO to deputy CIGS, 16 Apr. 1920, ibid., no. 9.

51 Churchill to Milner, 23 Apr. 1920; C.O. to W.O., 25 May 1920; W.O. to C.O., 29 Sept. 1920 and 29 Jan. 1921, ibid., nos. 15A, 17A, 30A and 34B.

52 'External employment of troops raised in mandatory territory', 22 Dec. 1920, CAB. 24/117 C.P. 2361.

53 Cabinet meeting, 20 Apr. 1921, CAB. 23/25/25(21).

54 Instructions by S. of S. for committee on Mesopotamia, 8 and 9 Jan. 1921, W.O. 32/5234, nos. 1 and 2. The French raised over 600,000 imperial troops during the war. See Andrew and Kanya-Forstner, *France Overseas*, p. 140.

55 Report of committee on Mesopotamia. In the draft report (16 Jan. 1921) this passage read: 'as they have no caste system, are easily disciplined, and have not been infected by Bolshevik propaganda', W.O. 32/5234, nos. 15A and 3A (draft report).

56 Memo. by deputy DMO, 11 Jan. 1921, W.O. 32/5234 no. 15A, appendix V.

57 Report of committee on Mesopotamia, W.O. 32/5234, no. 15A.

58 Churchill to Austen Chamberlain, 16 Feb. 1921, in Gilbert, *Churchill*, IV, Companion Part 2, pp. 1356–7.

59 Grant to DMO, 9 June 1921, W.O. 32/5356, no. 43A.

60 Report on possible employment of east African troops overseas, 7 Sept. 1921, ibid., no. 55A.

61 Creedy to Under S. of S. C.O., ibid., no. 61A.

62 The whole question of using African troops for imperial defence is covered in Killingray, 'The idea of a British Imperial African Army'.

63 Memo. by Sykes, 9 Dec. 1918, MS. Milner dep. 145.

64 French (CinC Home Forces) to Lloyd George, 18 Apr. 1918, Lloyd George MSS. F/48/6/7.

65 Cabinet minutes, CAB. 23/24/15(21) and Wilson diary, 24 Mar. 1921; Townshend, *The British Campaign in Ireland*, p. 171.

66 Note on the unrest in Egypt, 9 Apr. 1919, CAB. 1/28/17.

67 'A brief narrative of the hostilities with Afghanistan', Sept. 1919, IOR L/MIL/7/16907; despatch by CinC India on the Third Afghan War, 1 Nov. 1919, W.O. 106/58.

68 G. F. Archer (Governor of Somaliland) to L. S. Amery (acting Colonial Secretary), 15 May 1920, enclosed in C.O. to I.O., 20 July 1920, IOR L/MIL/7/14634.

69 Churchill to Austen Chamberlain, 31 Jan. 1919, Chamberlain MSS. AC 24/1/25.

70 Churchill to Lloyd George, 1 May 1919, Lloyd George MSS. F/8/3/46.

71 Memo. by A. T. Wilson, 16 Apr. 1919, W.O. 32/5222 no. 1.

72 Note by Col. Nugent, G.S., 4 May 1919, ibid., no. 2.

73 DMO to deputy CIGS, 14 May 1919, ibid.

74 Minute by Churchill, 17 May 1919, ibid., no. 5.

75   23 Mar. 1920, CAB. 1/29/15.
76   'Mesopotamia', 1 May 1920, CAB. 24/106 C.P. 1320.
77   A. T. Wilson to Sir A. Hirtzel (deputy Under Secretary, I.O.), 24 May 1920, A. T. Wilson Add. MSS. 52455.
78   IDCE 37th meeting, 13 Apr. 1920, Curzon MSS. F.112/275.
79   Report of committee on Mesopotamia, 21 Jan. 1921, W.O. 32/5234, no. 15A.
80   Report on Middle Eastern conference, April 1921, C.P. 2866, Worthington-Evans MS. Eng. hist. c.919; Cabinet meeting, 18 Aug. 1921, CAB. 23/26/70(21); Churchill, *The Aftermath*, pp. 464–5.
81   Wilson diary, 2 Dec. 1921; Wilson to Rawlinson, 5 Oct. 1921, Wilson MSS, 13E/29.
82   Boyle, *Trenchard*, p. 387.
83   'Weekly appreciation of matters of naval interest', nos. 62 and 76, weeks ending 21 Feb. and 29 May 1920, CAB. 24/99 C.P. 733 and 24/106 C.P. 1385.
84   Wilson diary, 26 May 1920.
85   'Defence of Irish coastguard stations', 27 May 1920, CAB. 24/106 C.P. 1353.
86   CAB. 23/21/33(20), appendix II.
87   Long to Lloyd George, 29 June 1920, Lloyd George MSS. F/34/1/29.
88   Cabinet meeting, 2 June 1921, CAB. 23/26/47(21); memo. by Admiralty, 6 Oct. 1921, CAB. 24/128 C.P. 3372.
89   W.O. to F.O., 27 July 1920, Milner MS. Eng. hist. c.701 fols. 37–8.
90   He commanded troops in aid of the civil power both in south Wales in 1910 and Belfast in 1914. He was Commissioner of the Metropolitan Police, 1918–20, and GOCinC Ireland, 1920–22.
91   Quoted in Report on the Irish administration by Sir Warren Fisher, 12 May 1920, Lloyd George MSS. F/31/1/32.
92   'Protection', 23 Jan. 1920, CAB. 24/96 C.P. 490.
93   Conference of ministers, 2 Feb. 1920, CAB. 23/20/10(20), appendix I.
94   Cabinet meeting and conferences of ministers, 6, 8, 9 and 12 April 1921, CAB. 23/25/22(21) and appendixes III–V and IX.
95   Strictly the soubriquet applies only to the early British ex-service recruits to the RIC (from Nov. 1919 onwards) who, owing to a shortage of police uniforms, wore a mixture of RIC bottle green and service khaki dress.
96   Wilson diary, 2 Nov. 1920.
97   Report of committee on Mesopotamia, 21 Jan. 1921, W.O. 32/5234, no. 15A.
98   Boyle, *Trenchard*, p. 422.

Chapter 5   The Irish ulcer

1   Nicolson, *King George V*, p. 353.
2   Mansergh, *The Irish Question*, pp. 88, 120, 191.
3   Wilson diary, 4 Nov. 1913.
4   Baillie-Grohman, 'Flashlights on the past' (typescript autobiography), Baillie-Grohman MSS.; Diary of Lady Lilian Spender, 1 Nov. 1921, Spender MSS. D.1633/2/25. There is a good, brief, account of the Curragh incident in Jalland, *The Liberals and Ireland*.
5   24 Mar. 1914. Quoted in Fergusson, *The Curragh Incident*, p. 93.
6   Wilson diary, 29 Mar. 1914 and 4 May 1920.
7   Cabinet memo., 1 Sept. 1920, Jones, *Whitehall Diary*, III, p. 38.

8 Hancock, *Smuts*, II, pp. 49–61.
9 Wilson diary, 6 Dec. 1921.
10 Macardle, *The Irish Republic*, p. 110.
11 Harris, 'The other half million', pp. 101–10. It is a somewhat generous estimate.
12 Boyce, *Englishmen and Irish Troubles*, p. 43.
13 *Report of the Royal Commission on the Rebellion in Ireland, 1916*, 1919, cd. 8279.
14 Report by Lord French, 26 Nov. 1918, CAB. 24/70 G.T. 6391.
15 Townshend, *The British Campaign in Ireland*, pp. 33–9. This is a very good book indeed and I have relied heavily upon it for charting the development of British policies up to the truce in July 1921.
16 January 1919: 9,300 police. The authorised strength of the RIC was about 10,200. Townshend, op. cit., p. 28.
17 Memo. by CIGS, 26 Apr. 1919, CAB. 24/78 G.T. 7182.
18 Memo. by Lt.-Gen. Sir Frederick Shaw, enclosed in French to Macpherson, 17 May 1919, Lloyd George MSS. F/46/1/5.
19 Cabinet memo. by W. H. Long, 4 Dec. 1919, and French to Lloyd George, 29 Dec. 1919, Lloyd George MSS. F/31/1/17. Byrne's future was, indeed, in the colonies. He was Governor of the Seychelles, 1922–7; of Sierra Leone, 1927–31; Governor and C-in-C, Kenya, 1931–7.
20 Lloyd George to French, 30 Dec. 1919, Lloyd George MSS. F/31/1/17.
21 Lloyd George to Bonar Law, 30 Dec. 1919, Bonar Law MSS. 98/5/23.
22 Churchill to Robertson, 21 July 1919, Robertson MSS. I/31/2.
23 Wilson to Churchill, 12 Oct. 1919, Wilson MSS. 18B/21.
24 Wilson diary, 24 July 1917.
25 Ibid., 16 Oct. 1919.
26 Asquith to Lloyd George, 6 July 1916, Lloyd George MSS. E/2/23/2.
27 Quoted in Townshend, *The British Campaign in Ireland*, p. 20. It is perhaps worth noting that Macready himself came from an Irish family.
28 Robertson to Wilson, 15 Jan. and 25 Feb. 1920, Wilson MSS. 1/36 and 1/42; Wilson diary, 11 Feb. 1920.
29 Churchill to Lloyd George, 11 Oct. 1919 and 29 Feb. 1920, Lloyd George MSS. F/9/1/36 and F/9/2/10.
30 Macready, *Annals of an Active Life*, II, p. 425; Churchill to Secretary, CIGS, 25 Mar. 1920, Wilson MSS. 18B/31.
31 Churchill to Wilson, 4 Apr. 1920, Wilson MSS. 18B/33; to Clementine Churchill, 27 March 1920, Gilbert, *Churchill*, Companion vol. IV, part 2, p. 1059; to Robertson, 1 Apr. 1920, Robertson MSS. I/31/6.
32 Wilson diary, 29 Mar. 1920.
33 Ibid., 13 Jan. 1920; Fisher diary, 22 July 1920, MS Fisher 16; see also Holmes, *The Little Field-Marshal*, pp. 356–8.
34 Macready to Long, 23 Apr. and 1 May 1920, Lloyd George MSS. F/34/1/19 and Bonar Law MSS. 102/5/10.
35 Churchill to Lord Stamfordham, 13 May 1920, Gilbert, *Churchill*, Companion vol. IV, part 2, p. 1096.
36 Townshend, *The British Campaign in Ireland*, pp. 81–2.
37 Greenwood to Bonar Law, 8 May 1920, Bonar Law MSS. 103/3/1.
38 Chamberlain to Lloyd George and Bonar Law, 12 May 1920, and Report by Sir

Warren Fisher, Lloyd George MSS. F/31/1/32.

39 Macready, *Annals of an Active Life*, II, pp. 473, 479.

40 'Capacity of the army to assist the civil power', 7 Jan. 1920, CAB. 24/96 C.P. 472; 'Note of conversation at 10 Downing Street', 30 Apr. 1920, CAB. 23/21/23(20)A.

41 CAB. 23/21/29(20) appendix A; Wilson diary, 11 May 1920; Hankey diary, 23 May 1920.

42 'Formation of a special force for service in Ireland', CAB. 24/106 C.P. 1317; Townshend, *The British Campaign in Ireland*, pp. 46, 110–11.

43 CAB. 23/21/33(20).

44 Note by General Staff, 9 June 1920, in CAB. 24/107 C.P. 1467.

45 Wilson diary, 18 June 1920; Wilson to Churchill, 18 July 1920, Wilson MSS. 18C/8.

46 Jones, *Whitehall Diary*, III. p. 27.

47 Wilson diary, 10 Sept. 1920. The diary note refers to 'last Monday'.

48 'The internal situation and military precautions', 13 Sept. 1920, CAB. 24/111 C.P. 1853.

49 1,526. The number of men in the RIC proper was 14,212, along with 1,126 in the unarmed Dublin Metropolitan Police. 'Weekly survey of the state of Ireland for week ended 27 June 1921', CAB. 24/125 C.P. 3087.

50 6 June 1920, Riddell, *Intimate Diary*, p. 202.

51 Wilson diary, 1, 7 and 10 July 1920.

52 A good argument for the primacy of public opinion in influencing policy will be found in Boyce, *Englishmen and Irish Troubles*.

53 'Note of conversation', 30 Apr. 1920, CAB. 23/21/23(20)A. It has been argued that the British government were unwilling to declare a state of war in Ireland since this would mean recognising the *Dáil Éireann* as a belligerent authority and thus Irish claims to national sovereignty. Hancock, *Survey*, pp. 123–4.

54 Hankey diary, 23 May, 1920.

55 Jones, *Whitehall Diary*, III, pp. 19–20.

56 Ibid., pp. 28, 33.

57 CAB. 23/23/59(20)A; Hankey diary, 13 Nov. 1920.

58 Wilson diary, 22 Nov. 1920.

59 Ibid., 30 Nov. 1920.

60 Jones, *Whitehall Diary*, III, p. 41; CAB. 23/23/65(20)A.

61 CAB. 23/23/79(20)A; Fisher diary (MS Fisher 16) and Hankey diary, 29 Dec. 1920.

62 CAB. 23/23/81(20). Proclaimed 4 Jan. 1921.

63 Wilson to Rawlinson, 5 Jan. 1921, Wilson MSS. 13C/6; Report by Sir Warren Fisher, 11 Feb. 1921, Lloyd George MSS. F/17/1/9.

64 Cabinet meeting, 4 Apr. 1921, CAB. 23/25/17(21); Conferences of ministers, 8 and 9 Apr. 1921. CAB. 23/25/22(21), appendixes V and VIII; Wilson diary, 13 and 19 Apr. 1921.

65 The four members of the 'opposition' were unionists returned by the Dublin University constitutency.

66 CAB. 24/123 C.P. 2964.

67 Ibid. C.P. 2965.

68 Cabinet meeting, 24 May 1921, CAB. 23/25/41(21).

69   Wilson to Sackville-West (British Military Attaché in Paris), 28 May 1921, Wilson MSS. 12G/38.
70   Townshend, *The British Campaign in Ireland*, p. 196.
71   Jones, *Whitehall Diary*, III, pp. 76–85; Nicolson, *King George V*, pp. 351–4.
72   Wilson diary, 11 July 1921.
73   Ibid., 13 and 18 Aug. 1921.
74   Cabinet meeting, 20 July 1921, CAB. 23/26/60(21).
75   Wilson diary and Fisher diary (MS Fisher 18), 5 Aug. 1921; Cabinet committee on Ireland meetings, 17 and 18 Aug. 1921, CAB. 27/130 C.I.P.2; Cabinet meeting, 25 Aug. 1921, CAB. 23/26/72(21).
76   Macardle, *The Irish Republic*, pp. 535–7. The full text of the treaty is contained in pp. 880–5.
77   3 Dec. 1919, CAB. 23/18/10(19).
78   Col. W. W. Ashley, Coalition Unionist MP for Fylde, in the House of Commons, 20 May 1920, 129 H.C. Deb. 5s, col. 1728.
79   29 July 1920, Lloyd George MSS. F/225/10; 4 Aug. 1920, Jones, *Whitehall Diary*, III, p. 36.
80   25 May 1921, CAB. 23/25/42(21).
81   Conference on Ireland regarding naval defence, 13 Oct. 1921, Lloyd George MSS. F/25/2/32. See also Hawkings, 'Defence and the role of Erskine Childers'.
82   Macardle, *The Irish Republic*, p. 881.
83   Rawlinson to Wilson, 8 Dec. 1921, Wilson MSS. 13F/26; Cabinet meeting, 6 Dec. 1921, CAB. 23/27/90(21); 14 Dec. 1921, 149 H.C. Deb. 5s, col. 48.
84   Wilson diary, 7 Dec. and 21 Mar. 1921.
85   Ibid., 5 July 1921.
86   Ibid., 3 Nov. 1921.
87   Derby to Lord Rawlinson, 31 Dec. 1921 and 11 Feb. 1922, Derby MSS. D.605/15–16.
88   22 June 1922. Callwell, *Sir Henry Wilson*, II, pp. 346–7. A more complete account of the circumstances surrounding Wilson's death will be found in R. Taylor, *Assassination*!
89   Memoranda on Ireland, 5 Apr. 1922, CAB. 23/30/23(22), appendixes I and II; Jones, *Whitehall Diary*, III, pp. 206–13. See also Committee of Imperial Defence sub-committee on Ireland meetings, 1–2 June 1922, CAB. 16/42.
90   Chamberlain to Churchill, 11 May 1922, Chamberlain MSS. AC 35/1/11.
91   Macready, *Annals of an Active Life*, II, pp. 651–9.
92   CAB. 23/32/68(22), appendix II.
93   Report of the 'Churchill committee', 4 Feb. 1922, CAB. 24/132, C.P. 3692.

Chapter 6   India

1   25 Nov. 1920, Wilson MSS. 13C/2.
2   A. J. Balfour to the Cabinet, 6 Sept. 1905. Quoted in Judd, *Balfour*, p. 61.
3   'A brief narrative of the hostilities with Afghanistan in 1919', IOR L/MIL/7/16907; Despatch by C-in-C, India, on the Third Afghan War, 1 Nov. 1919, W.O. 106/58.
4   Chelmsford to Curzon, 6 Nov. 1919, Curzon MSS. F.112/209.
5   S. of S. to Viceroy, 8 Apr. 1920, Chelmsford MSS. E.264, vol. 6, pp. 14–15.
6   Dobbs to A. T. Wilson, 26 May 1920, A. T. Wilson Add. MSS. 52458.

7 Initialled 1 March 1921. *British and Foreign State Papers* (1923 part II), cxviii, pp. 10–11.

8 Rawlinson to Wilson, 1 June 1921, Wilson MSS. 13D/26. Viceroy to S. of S. (telegram), 19 Oct. 1920, CAB. 24/112 C.P. 1996.

9 Rawlinson to Wilson, 8 June 1921, Wilson MSS. 13D/28. In March 1921 the Soviet government had also concluded an agreement with Kemalist Turkey. See Kapur, *Soviet Russia and Asia*, p. 103.

10 Rawlinson to Wilson, 23 Nov. 1921, Wilson MSS. 13F/19. The treaty, signed on 22 Nov. 1921, is in *British and Foreign State Papers* (1921), cxiv, pp. 174–9. Dobbs received a knighthood for his efforts.

11 Dodwell, *Cambridge History of India*, VI, pp. 403–31; Morison, *From Alexander Burnes to Frederick Roberts*, pp. 1–32.

12 Report of committee on Indian charges for forces in east Persia, Feb. 1921, W.O. 32/5808. For 1902 agreement see above, pp. 3–4.

13 Spear, *History of India*, II. pp. 185–8.

14 Wilson diary, 11 Jan. 1921.

15 Rawlinson to Wilson, 9 Jan. 1921, Wilson MSS. 13C/13.

16 Low, 'Government of India and the first non-co-operation movement', p. 321.

17 Hardy, *Muslims of British India*, pp. 185–7.

18 Dodwell, *Cambridge History of India*, VI, p. 481; memo. by Montagu, 15 Oct. 1920, CAB. 24/112 C.P. 1987.

19 Gordon, 'Noncooperation', p. 129.

20 A committee chaired by Mr Justice Rowlatt in 1918 had recommended the measures. There is a good general account of this period in Rumbold, *Watershed in India*, especially ch. 8.

21 Martial law was lifted from the Punjab (except on the railways) in June. Viceroy to S. of S., 17 June 1919, Chelmsford MSS. E.264, vol. 10, p. 470.

22 Viceroy to S. of S., 18 Apr. 1919, ibid. vol. 10, no. P.5342.

23 Wilson diary, 19 and 23 Apr. 1919.

24 Viceroy to S. of S., 5 May 1919. Chelmsford MSS. E.264, vol. 10, p. 285.

25 Ibid., 6 and 10 May 1919, pp. 286 and 309.

26 Government of India, *The Army in India*, pp. 221–2.

27 1914: 81,000 British and 152,000 Indian; Nov. 1918: 64,023 British and 388,599 Indian. Figures from *The Army in India*, p. 219 and War Office, *Statistical Abstract of Information regarding the Army at Home and Abroad*, W.O. 161/82.

28 Memo. by C-in-C India, 24 Dec. 1919, enclosed in Chelmsford to Montagu, 31 Dec. 1919, Montagu, MSS. D.523, vol. 9, pp. 403–16.

29 Majumdar, *Struggle for Freedom*, pp. 313–14; Spear, *History of India*, II, p. 191; Gordon, 'Non-cooperation', pp. 129–53.

30 Hankey diary, 22 Feb. 1920.

31 Report of the Army in India Committee, 1919–20, 22 June 1920, CAB. 24/112 C.P. 1980.

32 Chelmsford to Montagu, 12 Feb. 1919, Montagu MSS. D.523, vol. 8, p. 26.

33 Rawlinson to Derby, 25 Nov. 1920, Derby MSS. D.605/1. Rawlinson had landed at Bombay on 21 Nov.

34 Rawlinson to Wilson, 3 Dec. 1920, Wilson MSS. 13C/3.

35 S. of S. to Viceroy, 18 Jan. 1921, Chelmsford MSS. E.264, vol. 14, p. 50.

36 Viceroy to S. of S., 22 Jan. 1921, ibid., p. 33.

37   Viceroy to S. of S., 30 Mar. 1921, ibid., pp. 293–4; *Legislative Assembly Debates*, vol. I. no. 15, enclosed in IOR L/MIL/7/10822.
38   Rawlinson to Derby, 30 Mar. 1921, Derby MSS. D.605/5.
39   Rawlinson to Sir Charles Monro, 21 Sept. 1920, Rawlinson MSS. 5201/33/22.
40   Gopal, *British Policy in India*, p. 65.
41   Memo. by Montagu, 15 Oct. 1920, CAB. 24/112 C.P. 1987.
42   Moore, *The Crisis of Indian Unity*, pp. 21–2; Low, 'Government of India and the first non-co-operation movement', pp. 305–18.
43   Rawlinson to 'Douglas' (Haig?), 10 May 1921, Rawlinson MSS. 5201/33/22.
44   'The defence of India', memo. by general staff, 10 May 1921, CAB. 16/38 vol. II, I.M.R./14 appendix III.
45   'Indian journal', 10 July 1921, Rawlinson MSS. 5201/33/23.
46   Rawlinson to Wilson, 12 July 1921, Wilson MSS. 13E/19.
47   Viceroy (Army dept.) to S. of S., 21 July 1921 (2 parts), IOR L/MIL/3/2513 p. 1512. The proceedings of the Rawlinson committee are in CAB. 16/38 vol. II, I.M.R./14.
48   Rawlinson to Wilson, 31 July 1921, Rawlinson MSS. 5201/33/32.
49   Viceroy (Army dept.) to S. of S., 4 Aug. 1921, IOR L/MIL/3/2513, p. 1631.
50   Griffiths, *To Guard my People*, pp. 288–92; Mackinnon, 'The Moplah rebellion', pp. 260–77.
51   Rawlinson to Wilson, 23 Nov. 1921, Wilson MSS. 13F/19.
52   Viceroy (Army dept.) to S. of S., 28 Nov. 1921, IOR L/MIL/3/2513, p. 2374.
53   Viceroy (Army dept.) to S. of S., 6 Feb. 1922, IOR L/MIL/3/2514 no. 1121.
54   The proceedings of the 'Indian military requirements sub-committee' are in CAB. 16/38 vol. I.
55   Fisher diary, 10 Feb. 1922. Fisher was a member of the sub-committee.
56   S. of S. to Viceroy, 14 Feb. 1922, IOR L/MIL/3/2534 M.1348/1922 no. 1.
57   Ibid., no. 2.
58   'Indian journal', 28 July 1922, Rawlinson MSS. 5201/33/22.
59   Reading to Peel, 3 Aug. 1922, Reading MSS. E.238, vol. 5, p. 112.
60   Rawson, 'The Role of India in Imperial Defence', p. 46.
61   'Future military expenditure', Aug. 1921, CAB. 27/164 G.R.C. (D.D.) 8.
62   Rawlinson to Wilson, 21 July 1921, Wilson MSS. 13E/8; Longer, *Red Coats to Olive Green*, p. 194.
63   Quoted in Maurice, *Rawlinson*, p. 313.
64   Report of 'Indian military requirements subcommittee', 22 June 1922, CAB. 16/38 vol. I, paper 130–D.
65   Rawlinson to Derby, 22 Mar. 1923, Derby MSS. 920.DER (17)/29/4.
66   Rawson, 'The Role of India in Imperial Defence', pp. 55–67, 280–334.

Chapter 7   The defence of Suez

1   Farnie, *Suez Canal*, pp. 751, 757.
2   Note by Brig.-Gen. G. F. Clayton, 22 July 1917, 'Documents collected for the special mission to Egypt', vol. I, p. 162, MS. Milner dep. 444.
3   Five out of the thirteen million tons of Allied and neutral shipping sunk by submarine during World War I were lost between Gibraltar and Port Said. Farnie, *Suez Canal*, pp. 534–5, 540, 546–7.
4   Memo. by Milner to the Egyptian administration committee, 31 Oct. 1917,

CAB. 27/12.
5 Darwin, *Britain, Egypt and the Middle East*, pp. 60–74.
6 Kedourie, 'Sa'ad Zaghlul', pp. 139–51.
7 Note on the unrest in Egypt by Sir Ronald Graham, 9 Apr. 1919, CAB. 1/28/17; Gwynn, *Imperial Policing*, pp. 65–82.
8 Allenby to Balfour, 4 Apr. 1919, Wilson MSS. 19–12.
9 Allenby to Wilson, 16 Apr. 1919, ibid., 33B/12A.
10 Ibid.
11 Wilson to PUS, Foreign Office, 7 Apr. 1919, Wilson MSS. 19/12; memo. by CIGS, 26 Apr. 1919, CAB. 24/78 G.T. 7182.
12 Wilson diary, 25 Apr. 1919.
13 Allenby to Wilson, 21 Apr. 1919, Wilson MSS. 33B/13.
14 Wilson diary, 20 May 1919.
15 Wilson to Allenby, 23 May 1919, Wilson MSS. 33B/15.
16 Dec. 1918: 416,527, 'Strengths by arms of expeditionary forces', MS. Milner dep. 145; Aug. 1919: 127,800, 'Note on British military commitments', W.O. 106/316 no. 26.
17 March 1920: 107,353, 'Statistical abstract', W.O. 161/82; April 1921: Egypt, 25,015; Palestine, 16,042, 'Monthly returns of the distribution of the army', April 1921, W.O. 73/114.
18 See 'Monthly returns', June–Dec. 1921, W.O. 73/114, 115.
19 Curzon to Balfour, 29 Mar. 1919, Curzon MSS. F.112/208 (a).
20 Gollin, *Proconsul in Politics*, p. 26.
21 Balfour to Curzon, 6 Apr. 1919, Wilson MSS. 19/12.
22 Marlowe, *Anglo-Egyptian Relations*, p. 239.
23 Memo. by Milner, 22 Dec. 1919, Curzon MSS. F.112/213(a); Milner to Lloyd George, 28 Dec. 1919, Lloyd George MSS. F/39/1/52.
24 Minutes of Cabinet finance committee, 9 Feb. 1920, CAB. 24/98 C.P. 659; Allenby to Curzon, 18 Feb. 1920, F.O. 371/4991/E309. The totals in this telegram, however, were all 'establishment' figures, and therefore considerably in excess of actual numbers.
25 'General conclusions of the report of the special mission to Egypt', 3 May 1920 (sent to Curzon on 17 May), MS. Milner dep. 451. This was circulated to the Cabinet by Curzon on 12 Oct. 1920, CAB. 24/112 C.P. 1960.
26 Memo. on 'the result of conversations between Lord Milner . . . and Zaghloul Pasha', enclosed in Milner to 'Adli Yeghen (Egyptian Prime Minister) 18 Aug. 1920, MS. Milner dep. 450.
27 'The Egyptian proposals', 24 Aug. 1920, CAB. 24/111 C.P. 1803.
28 Ibid.
29 Wilson diary, 24 Aug. 1920.
30 Quoted in Wavell, *Allenby in Egypt*, p. 52; also Wilson to Rawlinson 2 Apr. 1921; to Haldane, 28 Dec. 1920; to Arnold Robertson, 30 Mar. 1921; to Sir W. N. Congreve, 10 Dec. 1921; Wilson MSS. 13C/26, 55/5, 23/7, 52B/40.
31 'The Egyptian proposals', CAB. 24/111 C.P. 1803. See also Boyle, *Trenchard*, pp. 333, 354.
32 Wilson diary, 6 Sept. 1920.
33 Kedourie, 'Sa'ad Zaghlul', p. 152.
34 Memo. by Milner, 16 Sept. 1920, CAB. 24/111 C.P. 1870.
35 Fisher diary, 5 and 13 Oct. 1920, MS Fisher 16.

36   27 Oct. 1920, CAB. 24/114 C.P. 2034.

37   Hughes to Lloyd George, 18 Nov. 1920, and reply, 24 Nov. 1920, Lloyd George MSS. F/28/3/47 and F/39/3/32.

38   Memo. by Curzon, 11 Oct. 1920, CAB. 24/112 C.P. 1960; Curzon to Balfour, 13 Oct. 1920, Balfour Add. MSS. 49694.

39   W.O. to CinC India, repeated GHQ Egypt, 2 Nov. 1920, F.O. 371/4981/E15263.

40   See above pp. 55–6.

41   GHQ Egypt to WO, 13 Nov. 1920, F.O. 371/4981/E15263.

42   Wilson diary, 22 Nov. 1920.

43   CAB. 23/23/62(20) appendix III.

44   Cabinet meeting, 29 Dec. 1920, CAB. 23/23/79(20); also Fisher diary.

45   Kedourie, 'Sa'ad Zaghlul', p. 155; Wilson diary, 24 Aug. 1920. There is a copy of the Milner Report (1921 Cmd. 1131) in MS. Milner dep. 451.

46   Churchill to Curzon, 13 June 1921, Curzon MSS. F.112/219; 6 July, 'Imperial meetings, 1921', vol. I, Lloyd George MSS. F/118.

47   20 Oct. 1921: Fisher diary and Cabinet meeting CAB. 23/27/81(21).

48   Cabinet sub-committee on Egypt, 24 Oct. 1921, CAB. 27/134.

49   Fisher to Lloyd George, 28 Oct. 1921, Lloyd George MSS. F/16/7/72.

50   Fisher diary, 4 Nov. 1921, MS Fisher 14.

51   Churchill to Curzon, 6 Dec. 1921, Curzon MSS. F.112/219.

52   Allenby to Wavell, 29 Dec. 1921, Allenby MSS. DS 43.1.A5.

53   Allenby to Wilson, 21 Jan. 1922, Wilson MSS. 33C/9.

54   Curzon to Lloyd George, 10 Feb. 1922, Lloyd George MSS. F/13/3/6.

55   Wavell, *Allenby in Egypt*, p. 75; Wilson diary, 12 Feb. 1922; Cabinet meeting, 16 Feb. 1922, CAB. 23/29/10(22).

56   Circulated to the Cabinet 25 Feb. 1922, CAB. 23/29/14(22) appendix II.

57   Wilson diary, 17 Feb. 1922.

58   Churchill (telegram) to Governors-General of Canada, Australia, New Zealand and the Union of South Africa, 27 Feb. 1922, Lloyd George MSS. F/10/2/56.

59   Cabinet memo. 30 Dec. 1924. Gilbert, *Churchill*, V, Companion Part I, p. 317.

60   Minute by J. Murray, 9 Oct. 1922, F.O. 371/7900/E10681.

61   Allenby to Wilson, 16 Nov. 1918, Wilson MSS. 33A/30.

62   Kedourie, *In the Anglo-Arab Labyrinth*, pp. 65–158; Andrew and Kanya-Forstner, *France Overseas*, chs. 4–7.

63   Wilson to Allenby, 5 June 1919, Wilson MSS. 33B/17.

64   Cabinet eastern committee 39th meeting, 27 Nov. 1918, CAB. 27/24.

65   Ibid., 41st meeting, 5 Dec. 1918.

66   Andrew and Kanya-Forstner, *France Overseas*, pp. 174–5.

67   Fisher diary, 20 Aug. 1919, MS Fisher 13.

68   Memo. on Palestine, enclosed in Amery to Lloyd George, 19 Oct. 1918, Lloyd George MSS. F/2/1/31.

69   Cabinet eastern committee 41st meeting, CAB. 27/24.

70   Harold Nicolson to Walford Selby, 22 May 1934, Allenby MSS. DS 43.1.A5.

71   Curzon to Balfour, 20 Aug. 1919, Curzon MSS. F.112/208(a).

72   Conference of ministers and officials at Trouville, 10 Sept. 1919, CAB. 21/153. Quoted in Ingrams, *Palestine Papers*, pp. 77–8.

73 Wavell, *Allenby in Egypt*, p. 28.
74 Memo. by Clayton, 11 Mar. 1919, Lloyd George MSS. F/205/3/9.
75 Sherif Feisal to Lloyd George, 9 Oct. 1919, ibid., F/59/10/5.
76 'Strength of the British army', 5 Nov. 1919, CAB. 24/92 C.P. 55.
77 Andrew and Kanya-Forstner, *France Overseas*, pp. 215–19, 228–30.
78 'Note on the army estimates 1920–21', 7 Feb. 1920, CAB. 24/97 C.P. 586.
79 'The military situation in Palestine', 7 May 1920, F.O. 371/5119/E4349.
80 GOC Egypt to WO, 1 May 1920, enclosed in WO to FO, 29 May 1920, Milner MS. Eng. hist. c.701, fols. 31–3.
81 Memo. by Col. Deedes, c.June 1920, ibid., fols. 23–7.
82 Inter-departmental committee on Middle Eastern affairs, 1st, 10th and 12th meetings, 10 Aug., 7 Sept. and 12 Oct. 1920, F.O. 371/5277/E9762, E11460 and E13174.
83 Samuel to Curzon, 12 July 1920, Samuel MSS. correspondence vol. III.
84 Samuel to Lord Stamfordham (private secretary to King George V), 17 Oct. 1920, ibid.
85 Samuel to Lloyd George, 28 Oct. 1920, Lloyd George MSS. F/44/8/3.
86 Cabinet meeting, 9 Dec. 1920, CAB. 23/23/67(20).
87 Storrs to Samuel, 28 Dec. 1920, Samuel MSS. correspondence vol. III.
88 WO to GOC Egypt, 23 Dec. 1920, enclosed in War Office to FO, 24 Dec. 1920; F.O. to Samuel and *vice versa*, 23 and 27 Dec. 1920; F.O. 371/5257/E 16036 and E16108.
89 'Proposed reduction in the garrison in Palestine', 26 Jan. 1921, CAB. 24/118 C.P. 2430.
90 Mejcher, 'British Middle Eastern policy', p. 101.
91 Churchill to Lloyd George, 18 Mar. 1921 and *vice versa*, n.d. (c.22 Mar. 1921), Lloyd George MSS. F/9/3/20.
92 Wilson diary, 22 Mar. 1921.
93 'Report on Middle Eastern conference held in Cairo and Jerusalem, March 12th to 30th, 1921', Worthington-Evans MS. Eng. hist. c.919. Circulated to the Cabinet in CAB. 24/126 C.P. 3123.
94 Philby, 'Trans-Jordan', p. 302.
95 'The situation in Palestine', 9 June 1921, CAB. 24/125 C.P. 3030.
96 Samuel to Churchill, 13 June 1921, F.O. 371/6372/E7438.
97 Note by General Staff, 8 July 1921, CAB. 24/126 C.P. 3129.
98 Notes on a deputation to the Prime Minister, 24 Mar. 1921, Lloyd George MSS. F/172/1/10.
99 Memo. by Churchill, 11 Aug. 1921, CAB. 24/127 C.P. 3213.
100 29 Oct. 1921, Lloyd George MSS. F/86/8/4.
101 Churchill to Lloyd George, 3 Sept. 1921, ibid. F/9/3/86.
102 Gilbert, *Churchill*, IV, p. 635.
103 Churchill to Col. R. Meinertzhagen, 10 Oct. 1921. Gilbert, *Churchill*, IV, Companion Part 3, p. 1645.
104 Conference of ministers, 21 Dec. 1921, CAB. 23/27/93(21) appendix III, see also memo by Churchill, Nov. 1921, CAB. 24/131 C.P. 3515.
105 Tudor to Churchill, 1 Oct. 1922. Gilbert, *Churchill*, IV, Companion Part 3, p. 2061. See also Duff, *Bailing with a Teaspoon*, p. 19.
106 Interim report of committee on national expenditure, 14 Dec. 1921, CAB. 24/131 C.P. 3570.

107 'Indian desiderata for peace settlement', 4 Dec. 1918, CAB. 29/2 P. 42.
108 Milner to Lloyd George, 16 May 1919, Lloyd George MSS. F/39/1/21.
109 Gathorne-Hardy, *International Affairs*, pp. 127–8; Troeller, *The Birth of Sa'udi Arabia*, pp. 216–31; Philby. 'The triumph of the Wahhabis', pp. 293–319.
110 S. of S. to Viceroy, 17 Oct. 1919. Montagu MSS. D. 523, vol. 3, p. 218. The complexities of the Aden administration question may be followed in Gavin, *Aden*, especially ch. X.
111 Rawlinson to Wilson, 16 Nov. 1920; also 'Indian Journal', Rawlinson MSS. 5201/33/22 and 23.
112 Report on Middle Eastern Conference, Apr. 1921, Worthington-Evans MS. Eng. hist. c.919.
113 Rawlinson to Wilson, 5 Oct. 1921, Wilson MSS. file 13F; Churchill to Montagu, 8 Oct. 1921, Montagu MSS. AS/I/3/68.
114 Gavin, *Aden*, pp. 262–3, 281–2.
115 Gen. A. R. Hoskins to WO, 22 Dec. 1918, MS. Milner dep. 143; War Cabinet meeting, 24 Jan. 1919, CAB. 23/9 W.C. 519.
116 Boyle, *Trenchard*, p. 366; Milner to Sir Reginald Wingate (Cairo), 7 Aug. 1919, Milner MS. Eng. hist. c.702 fol. 187.
117 Boyle, *Trenchard*, pp. 366–7; Wilson diary, 2 Dec. 1919. See also *The Leo Amery Diaries*, vol. I, p. 263.
118 G. F. Archer to Milner, 15 May 1920, enclosed in CO to IO, 20 July 1920, IOR L/MIL/7/14634; Ismay, *Memoirs*, pp. 34–5. Ismay adds, however, that even if the Air Staff claims were ill-founded, 'it is quite certain that they were justified a hundredfold if they did anything to strengthen the case for an independent Air Force'.
119 Amery, *My Political Life*, II, p. 202.

Chapter 8 Persia and Mesopotamia

1 Sir P. Chetwode (deputy CIGS) to Wilson, 25 Jan. 1921, Wilson MSS. 58A/14.
2 'British war aims', 8 June 1918, Lloyd George MSS. F/2/1/24.
3 Accounts of these various forces may be found in: Barker, *The Neglected War*; Sykes, *History of Persia*, Vol. II (3rd edn); Dickson, *East Persia*; Malleson, 'The British Military Mission to Turkestan'; Ellis, *The Transcaspian Episode*; 'Q.L.', 'The Transcaspian expedition'; Tod, 'Operations in Transcaspia'; Norris, 'The navy in the Caspian'; and Nicol, *Uncle George*.
4 Memo. by DMO, 13 Nov. 1918, CAB. 24/69 G.T. 6274; Note on the Malleson Mission by Sir H. V. Cox, 20 Dec. 1918, IOR L/MIL/5/806/31.
5 Government of India telegram, 17 Nov. 1918, quoted in GHQ Baghdad to Norperforce, 25 Nov. 1918, Advanced Norperforce War Diary 1918–19, appendix no. 38, W.O. 95/5045.
6 GHQ Mesopotamia G.S. War Diary, 15 Jan. 1919, W.O. 95/4967.
7 Milne to Wilson, 22 Jan. 1919, Wilson MSS. 37/5; Milne diary, 27 Jan 1919, quoted in Nicol, *Uncle George*, p. 205.
8 IDCE 5th meeting, 8 Feb. 1919, Curzon MSS. F.112/275; Malleson, 'The British Military Mission to Turkestan', p. 102. Krasnovodsk was evacuated three months later.
9 Cecil to Lloyd George, 9 Mar. and 15 May 1919, Lloyd George MSS. F/6/6/15

and 46.

10 Montagu to Lloyd George, 14 Feb. 1919, ibid., F/40/2/35.
11 IDCE 6th meeting, 13 Feb. 1919, Curzon MSS. F.112/275.
12 Curzon to Wilson, 25 Feb. 1919, Wilson MSS. 20A/29.
13 IDCE 11th meeting, 6 Mar. 1919, Curzon MSS. F.112/275.
14 Wilson to Milner, 28 May 1919, Milner MS. Eng. hist. c.702 fols. 179–80;
    Wilson to Lloyd George, 14 May 1919, Lloyd George MSS. F/47/8/14.
15 IDCE 19th meeting, 22 May 1919, Curzon MSS. F.112/275.
16 22 Aug. 1919, quoted in Nicol, *Uncle George*, p. 211.
17 Conference of ministers, 18 Jan. 1920, CAB. 23/35 S.11.
18 Conference of ministers, 3 Feb. and Cabinet meeting, 18 Feb. 1920, CAB
    23/20/10(20) appendix II and 11(20); memo. by Curzon, 9 Feb. 1920, CAB
    24/97 C.P. 594.
19 Curzon to Bonar Law, 4 Mar. 1920, Davidson MSS.
20 Wilson diary, 12 and 14 Apr. 1920.
21 Ibid, 5 May 1920; Gilbert, *Churchill*, IV, p. 393.
22 Maj.-Gen. J. Duncan to DMI, 15 May 1920, enclosed in Wilson to Curzon, 17
    May 1920, Wilson MSS. 20A/40. The Military Attaché in Rome does not seem
    to have been very efficient for the Italian decision not to send troops to Batum
    was made in June 1919. See Nitti, *Peaceless Europe*, pp. 147–8, and Stern,
    'Britain, Italy and the Versailles settlement', pp. 164–7.
23 Wilson to Curzon and *vice versa*, 17 and 18 May 1920, Wilson MSS. 20A/40
    and 43.
24 Wilson diary, 19 May 1920; Wilson to Curzon, 20 May 1920, Wilson MSS.
    20A/44.
25 Churchill to Curzon, 20 May 1920, Curzon MSS. F.112/215.
26 Wilson diary, 4 June 1920; Nicol, *Uncle George*, p. 214.
27 12 Jan. 1920: Wilson diary and IDCE 34th meeting, Curzon MSS. F.112/275.
28 Hankey diary, 31 Dec. 1920.
29 Gallagher and Robinson, 'The imperialism of free trade', p. 13.
30 Curzon, *Persia*, II, p. 621.
31 Cabinet eastern committee 48th meeting, 30 Dec. 1918, CAB. 27/24.
32 Memo. by Curzon, 9 Aug. 1919. CAB 1/28/24. The published version of the
    agreement itself is in *British and Foreign State Papers* (1919) cxii, pp. 760–1.
    There is a useful account of Anglo-Persian matters during the immediate
    post-war period in Ullman, *Anglo-Soviet Relations*, III, pp. 349–94.
33 Viceroy to S. of S., 27 Jan. and 24 Apr. 1919, Chelmsford MSS. E. 264, vol. 10,
    pp. 64–6 and 256.
34 S. of S. to Viceroy, 11 June 1919, Montagu MSS. D.523, vol. 3, p. 131.
35 Viceroy to S. of S., 28 Dec. 1919, Chelmsford MSS. E.264, vol. 11, p. 527.
36 IDCE 32nd meeting, 18 Nov. 1919, Curzon MSS. F.112/275; WO–FO
    correspondence, 26 Nov.–20 Dec. 1919, F.O. 371/3866/E155806 and E162479.
37 Montagu to Curzon, 5 Jan. 1920, Montagu MSS. AS/I/12/268.
38 IDCE 34th meeting, 12 Jan. 1920, Curzon MSS. F.112/275.
39 S. of S. to Viceroy, 10 Feb. and 5 May, and *vice versa*, 21 Feb. and 13 May
    1920, Chelmsford MSS. E. 264, vol. 12, pp. 80, 245, 153–5 and 445.
40 WO to GOC, Mesopotamia, 25 Feb. 1920, in 'Summary of events in
    North-West Persia, 20 May 1920', appendix C, F.O. 371/4904/C11.
41 Original italics. General Staff memo., 13 May 1920, ibid, appendix E.

42   IDCE 38th meeting, 17 May 1920, and Churchill to Curzon, 20 May 1920, Curzon MSS. F.112/275 and 215.

43   Haldane diary, 18 May 1920; GHQ Baghdad to WO, 20 May 1920, GHQ Mesopotamia War Diary, appendix 12, W.O. 95/4968.

44   21 May 1920: Wilson diary, Fisher diary, and Cabinet meeting, CAB. 23/21/30(20).

45   Memo. by Colonial Secretary, 24 May 1920, CAB. 24/106 C.P. 1337.

46   'British military liabilities: minute by the CIGS', 9 June 1920, CAB. 24/107 C.P. 1467; memo. by Hankey, 17 June 1920, Lloyd George MSS. F/24/2/38; Wilson diary, 18 June 1920; conference of ministers, 18 June 1920, CAB. 23/21/38(20) appendix I.

47   Fisher diary, 24 Nov. 1920, MS Fisher 16.

48   Curzon to Bonar Law, 30 June 1920, Bonar Law MSS. 99/2/16.

49   12 Aug. 1920: Wilson diary and Cabinet finance committee 27th meeting, CAB. 27/71.

50   GHQ Mesopotamia to WO, 3 Aug. 1920, F.O. 371/4905/E3119; Churchill to Curzon, 31 Aug. 1920, Curzon MSS. F.112/215.

51   Wilson to Haldane, 24 Aug. 1920, Wilson MSS. 55/2.

52   Cabinet meeting, 8 Dec. 1920 CAB.23/23/67(20); Wilson to Haldane, 28 Dec. 1920, Wilson MSS. 55/5.

53   Wilson diary, 4 Jan. 1921; S. of S. to viceroy, 5 Jan. 1921, Chelmsford MSS. E.264, vol. 14, pp. 7–8; Curzon to Norman (British minister in Teheran), 3 Jan. 1921, and FO to WO, 13 Jan. 1921, F.O. 371/6399/E2 and E600; notes for a parliamentary question, 15 June 1921, F.O. 371/6426/E6922.

54   Memo. by Kitchener, 16 Mar. 1915, Lloyd George MSS. C/16/2/3.

55   Admiralty memo. 17 Mar. 1915, ibid., C/16/2/4.

56   Kent, *Oil and Empire*, pp. 13, 137–57; Darwin, *Britain, Egypt and the Middle East*, p. 262.

57   Cabinet eastern committee 42nd meeting annex, 9 Dec. 1918, CAB. 27/24.

58   Board of Trade memo., 23 July 1919, Lloyd George MSS. F/195/4/2.

59   'The situation in Mesopotamia', appendix I, 12 Nov. 1919, CAB. 24/93 C.P. 120.

60   Note on the organisation of the civil administration of Mesopotamia, 1 Sept. 1919, Philby MSS. Box VI, file 1. Wilson was acting Civil Commissioner in place of Sir Percy Cox who had been temporarily posted as British Minister at Teheran.

61   The full text of the declaration is given in Antonius, *The Arab Awakening*, pp. 435–6, which gives 7 Nov. 1918 as the date of publication. Col. Wilson, however, gives 8 Nov. See Wilson to S. of S. for India, 15 Nov. 1919, A. T. Wilson MSS. 69/79/1.

62   GOC Baghdad to WO, 22 July 1919, GHQ Mesopotamia War Diary July 1919 appendix 7, W.O. 95/4967.

63   Curzon's phrase in undated note on Mesopotamia file, Curzon MSS. F.112/257. Wilson's own account of the administration is in his book, *Mesopotamia 1917–20*, especially pp. 170–85.

64   Haldane dairy, note following entry for 8 Apr. 1920.

65   Wilson to Hirtzel, 26 Aug. 1920, A. T. Wilson Add. MSS. 52455; Hirtzel to Chamberlain (enclosing the rhyme), 8 Oct. 1920; and Chamberlain to Ida Chamberlain, 5 Nov. 1920, Chamberlain MSS. AC 23/1/13–14 and 5/1/186. Sir

Aylmer Haldane collected a second rhyme, which was specifically, and nastily, directed against Sir George MacMunn. Entitled 'Squandermania in Mesopotamia', it begins:
When I became king of the castle,
My name is GEORGE, by the way,
Said I, "'Tis a nice little parcel
For which the Public shall pay . . .
You have heard of half a lakh squandered
When to Persia G.H.Q. went,
But the money on this scheme I wasted
Is to me a fine monument . . ."
Haldane diary, following entry for 8 Apr. 1920.

66 Churchill to Lloyd George, Sept. 1919, Lloyd George MSS. F/9/1/17; IDCE 30th meeting, 10 Nov. 1919, Curzon MSS. F.112/275; Kerr to Lloyd George, 15 Nov. 1919, Lloyd George MSS. F/89/4/23.

67 S. of S. to GOCinC Mesopotamia, 9 Sept. 1919, and *vice versa*, 12 and 25 Sept. 1919; minute by deputy CIGS, 26 Mar. 1920, W.O. 32/5227 nos. 1A, 2A, 3A and 27.

68 Haldane diary, 6 Feb. 1920; Churchill to Haldane, 1 April 1920, Haldane MSS. Acc. 2070 no. 11.

69 The population of Mesopotamia was estimated at 2,200,000 Arabs and 500,000 Kurds. Note by DMO, 15 Apr. 1920, W.O. 32/5806 no. 2A.

70 'Mesopotamia', 1 May 1920, CAB. 24/106 C.P. 1320.

71 Minute by Hubert Young, 9 July 1920, F.O. 371/5227/E7725.

72 Wilson to MacMunn, 10 Sept. 1920, A. T. Wilson Add. MSS. 52457; Darwin, *Britain, Egypt and the Middle East*, pp. 198–9.

73 30 June 1920. Haldane, *The Insurrection in Mesopotamia*, p. 73.

74 23 June 1920. There were a further 3,700 British and 10,500 Indian troops in Persia. Notes for a parliamentary question, 29 June 1920, F.O. 371/5075/E7483.

75 Estimate by GHQ Baghdad of troops available on 1 July 1920, quoted in IO to FO, 3 Sept. 1920, F.O. 371/5229/E10872; Haldane, *The Insurrection in Mesopotamia*, p. 64; *idem, A Soldier's Saga*, p. 379.

76 Wilson to IO, 9 July 1920; to Sir Arthur Hirtzel, 26 July; and to Capt. G. C. Stephenson (liaison officer for Mesopotamia, IO), 26 July; A. T. Wilson Add. MSS. 52455 and 52456.

77 S. of S. to Viceroy, 2 July 1920, and *vice versa*, 7 July 1920, Chelmsford MSS. E.264 vol. 13, pp. 2–3 and 24.

78 Haldane diary, 4 Aug. 1920.

79 S. of S. to Viceroy, 9 July 1920, Chelmsford MSS. E.264 vol. 13, p. 34; Haldane, *The Insurrection in Mesopotamia*, pp. 343–4.

80 Wilson diary, 15 July 1920.

81 Ibid., 7 July 1920.

82 Note by Cox, 24 July 1920, CAB. 24/110 C.P. 1715.

83 Churchill to Lloyd George, 8 Aug. 1920, Lloyd George MSS. F/9/2/37.

84 Wilson to Curzon, 18 Aug. 1920, Wilson MSS. 20B/6.

85 Churchill to Lloyd George, 26 Aug. 1920, Lloyd George MSS. F/9/2/41.

86 Wilson to MacMunn, 10 Sept. 1920, A. T. Wilson Add. MSS. 52457; Haldane to Sir Henry Wilson, 18 Oct. 1920, Wilson MSS. 55/3.

87   Memo. by Montagu, 9 Oct. 1920, CAB. 24/112 C.P. 1948.
88   'The situation in Mesopotamia', 10 Dec. 1920, CAB. 24/116 C.P. 2275.
89   Cabinet conferences, 1 and 3 Dec. 1920, CAB. 23/23/82(20), appendix II and
     23/23/70(20) appendix IV; Cabinet meetings, 8, 13, 17 and 31 Dec. 1920, CAB.
     23/23/67(20), 69–70(20), 72(20) and 82(20). See also Wilson diary, 13 Dec., and
     Hankey diary, 15 Dec. 1920.
90   Haldane diary, 14 Jan. 1921; Report on value of aeroplanes, 3 Feb. 1921,
     Haldane diary 1921, pp. 89A–C.
91   Peel to Haldane, 11 Mar. 1921, Haldane MSS, Acc. 2070, no. 10, ff. 11–12.
92   Cabinet meeting, 18 Aug. 1921, CAB. 23/26/70(21); Undated minute on
     'Middle East' file, W.O. 237/14 no. 1047.
93   High Commissioner, Iraq, to Colonial Secretary and *vice versa*, 10 and 11
     Sept. 1922, Curzon MSS. F.112/223.
94   Air Officer Commanding, Iraq, to Air Ministry, 30 Oct. 1922, F.O.
     371/7772/E11903.

Conclusion

1   Cottrell, *Imperial Defence*, pp. 2–3; Bird *The Direction of War*, p. 17;
     Davidson, 'The defence of the British empire', p. 246.
2   Wilson diary, 11 Jan. 1922.
3   26% in Dec. 1921. 65,501 (India and Aden) out of 252,838. 'Monthly returns',
     W.O. 73/115.
4   See Rawson, 'The Role of India in Imperial defence', pp. 55–63.
5   'British case for the peace conference', 8 Dec. 1918, IOR L/MIL/5/806/28.
6   D. G. Hogarth (Director of the Arab Bureau in Cairo, 1916–18) to Gertrude
     Bell, 11 Apr. 1920. A. T. Wilson Add. MSS. 52458.
7   Fuller, *The Reformation of War*, p. 192.
8   Wilson diary, 21 Dec. 1921; Wilson to Rawlinson, 6 Feb. 1922, Wilson MSS.
     13F/37.
9   See above p. 152.
10   Wilson to Rawlinson, 11 Jan. 1922, Wilson MSS. 13F/29.
11   Memo. by General Staff, 20 Jan. 1922, CAB. 24/132. C.P. 3619.
12   Hankey diary, 3 Jan. 1921.
13   Campbell-Bannerman to Mr Bryce, 26 Jan. 1903, quoted in Spender,
     Campbell-Bannerman, II, p. 88.

Bibliography

A. Primary sources

1. Official Records, coded as in references

Cabinet Office papers, Public Record Office, Kew

CAB. 1 Miscellaneous records

CAB. 2 Committee of Imperial Defence minutes

CAB. 4 Committee of Imperial Defence memoranda

CAB. 16 Ad-hoc sub-committees of the Committee of Imperial Defence

CAB. 21 Registered files

CAB. 23 Minutes and conclusions of Cabinet meetings and conferences of ministers

CAB. 24 Cabinet papers and memoranda, G.T. series (to 1919) and C.P. series (1919 onwards)

CAB. 27 Cabinet committees

CAB. 29 Peace ('P') series of printed Cabinet papers, 1916–20

Foreign Office papers, Public Record Office, Kew

F.O. 371 General correspondence (political)

India Office Records, British Library India Office Library and Records, London

L/F/783 Government of India Finance Department papers relating to payment for Indian troops employed out of India

L/MIL/3/– Government of India Army Department, secret and confidential telegrams

L/MIL/5/– and L/MIL/7/– Military collection miscellaneous material

War Office records, Public Record Office, Kew

W.O. 32 Registered files: general series

W.O. 73 Monthly returns: distribution of the army

W.O. 106 Directorate of Military Operations and Intelligence papers

W.O. 161 Miscellaneous unregistered records

W.O. 162 Adjutant-General's Department papers

W.O. 237 War Office committees: abstract of the recommendations of commissions, committees and conferences relating to army affairs

2. Private papers

Addison, Christopher, Bodleian Library, Oxford

Allenby, Field Marshal Lord, St. Antony's College, Oxford

Baillie-Grohman, Vice-Admiral H. T., Imperial War Museum

Balfour, A. J., British Library
Cavan, Field Marshal Lord, Churchill College, Cambridge
Chamberlain, Sir Austen, Birmingham University Library
Chelmsford, Lord, India Office Library and Records
Curzon, Lord, India Office Library and Records
Davidson, J. C. C., House of Lords Record Office
Derby, Lord, 2 collections: India Office Library and Records (MSS Eur. D.605) and Liverpool City Library (920. DER. 17)
Fisher, H. A. L., including Fisher diary, Bodleian Library, Oxford
Haldane, Gen. Sir Aylmer, including Haldane diary, National Library of Scotland, Edinburgh
Hankey, Sir Maurice, including Hankey diary (HNKY 1/5), Churchill College, Cambridge
Law, Andrew Bonar, House of Lords Record Office
Lloyd George, David, House of Lords Record Office
Milner, Lord, 2 collections: MS. Eng. hist. c.691–703 and 'MS Milner', Bodleian Library, Oxford
Montagu, Edwin, 2 collections: India Office Library and Records (MSS Eur. D.523) and Trinity College, Cambridge (AS/I/–)
Philby, H. St. J. B., St. Antony's College, Oxford
Rawlinson, Gen. Lord, National Army Museum
Reading, Lord, India Office Library and Records
Robertson, Field Marshal Sir William, Liddell Hart Centre for Military Archives, King's College, London
Samuel, Sir Herbert, House of Lords Record Office
Spender, Sir Wilfrid and Lady Lillian, Public Records Office of Northern Ireland
Wilson, Sir A. T., British Library
Wilson, Field Marshal Sir Henry, including Wilson diary (microfilm), Imperial War Museum
Worthington-Evans, Sir Laming, Bodleian Library, Oxford

B. Published and other sources cited in references

(The place of publication is London unless otherwise noted)

Amery, L. S., *My Political Life*, vol. II, Hutchinson, 1953
Amery, L. S., *The Leo Amery Diaries* (ed. J. Barnes and D. Nicholson), vol. I, Hutchinson, 1980
Andrew, C. M., and A. S. Kanya-Forstner, *France Overseas: the Great War and the Climax of French Imperial Expansion*, Thames and Hudson, 1981
Antonious, George, *The Arab Awakening*, Hamish Hamilton, 1938
Barclay, Glen St. J., *The Empire is Marching: a Study of the Military Effort of the British Empire 1800–1945*, Weidenfeld and Nicolson, 1976
Barker, A. J., *The Neglected War: Mesopotamia 1914–18*, Faber and Faber, 1967
Bean, C. E. W., *The Story of Anzac*, 2nd edn, Angus and Robertson (Sydney), 1933
Bird, W. D., *The Direction of War: a Study of Strategy*, Cambridge University Press, 1920
Blake, Robert (ed.), *The Private Papers of Douglas Haig 1914–19*, Eyre and Spottiswoode, 1952
Boyce, D. G., *Englishmen and Irish Troubles*, Jonathan Cape, 1972

Boyle, Andrew, *Trenchard*, Collins, 1962

Busch, Briton Cooper, *Britain, India and the Arabs*, University of California Press (Berkeley and London), 1971

Callwell, C. E., *Field Marshal Sir Henry Wilson, His Life and Diaries*, 2 vols., Cassell, 1927

Carr, E. H., *The Bolshevik Revolution 1917–1923*, vol. III, Penguin edn., 1966

Churchill, W. S., *The Aftermath*, Macmillan edn, 1941

Cole, D. H., *Imperial Military Geography*, 2nd edn, Sifton Praed, 1924

Cottrell, R. F., *Imperial Defence after the War*, Royal Artillery Institution (Woolwich), 1919

Cowling, Maurice, *The Impact of Labour 1920–24*, Cambridge University Press, 1971

Craig, F. W. S. (ed.), *British Parliamentary Election Statistics 1918–68*, Political Reference Publications (Glasgow), 1968

Critchley, T. A., *A History of Police in England and Wales*, Constable, 1967

Curzon, G. N., *Persia and the Persian Question*, 2 vols., facsimile of 1892 edn, Frank Cass, 1966

D'Abernon, Lord, *An Ambassador of Peace*, 3 vols, Hodder and Stoughton, 1929–30

Darwin, John, *Britain, Egypt and the Middle East*, Macmillan, 1981

Davidson, Sir J. H., 'The defence of the British empire', *Army Quarterly*, vol. 1 (1921), pp. 241–62

Davis, Richard P., *Irish Issues in New Zealand Politics 1868–1922*, University of Otago Press (Dunedin), 1975

Demangeon, Albert, *The British Empire: a Study in Colonial Geography*, Harrap, 1925

Dickson, W. E. R., *East Persia: a Backwater of the War*, Edward Arnold, 1924

Dockrill, M. L. and Douglas Goold, *Peace without Promise: Britain and the Peace Conferences, 1919–23*, Batsford, 1981

Dodwell, H. H. (ed.), *The Cambridge History of India, vol VI: the Indian Empire 1858–1918*, Cambridge University Press, 1932

Duff, D. V., *Bailing with a Teaspoon*, John Long, 1953

Duguid, A. F., *Official History of the Canadian Forces in the Great War 1914–19*, vol. I, King's Printer (Ottawa), 1938

Ellis, C. H., *The Transcaspian Episode 1918–19*, Hutchinson, 1963

Elton, Lord, *Imperial Commonwealth*, Collins, 1945

Falls, Cyril, *The First World War*, Longmans, 1960

Farnie, D. A., *East and West of Suez: the Suez Canal in History 1854–1956*, Clarendon Press (Oxford), 1969

Fergusson, Sir James, *The Curragh Incident*, Faber and Faber, 1964

Fuller, J. F. C., *The Reformation of War*, Hutchinson, 1923

Gallagher, J. A., and R. E. Robinson, 'The imperialism of free trade', *Economic History Review*, 2nd ser. vi (1953), pp. 1–15

Gallagher, John, 'Nationalism and the crisis of empire, 1919–1922', in C. Baker *et al.* (eds.), *Power, Profit and Politics*, Cambridge University Press, 1981 (also *Modern Asian Studies*, vol. 15 part 3, 1981)

Gallagher, John, *The Decline, Revival and Fall of the British Empire* (ed. Anil Seal), Cambridge University Press, 1982

Gavin, R. J., *Aden under British Rule 1839–1967*, C. Hurst, 1975

Gilbert, Martin, *Winston S. Churchill*, vol. IV, Heinemann, 1975

Gilbert, Martin, *Winston S. Churchill*, vol IV, Companion parts 1–3, Heinemann, 1977

Gollin, A. M., *Proconsul in Politics: a Study of Lord Milner in Opposition and in Power*, Anthony Blond, 1964

Gooch, John, *The Plans of War. The General Staff and British Military Strategy c.1900–1916*, Routledge and Kegan Paul, 1974

Gopal, S., *British Policy in India 1858–1905*, Cambridge University Press, 1965

Gordon, Donald C., *The Dominion Partnership in Imperial Defense 1870–1914*, Johns Hopkins Press (Baltimore), 1965

Gordon, Richard, 'Non-cooperation and council entry 1919 to 1920', in John Gallagher *et al.* (eds.), *Locality, Province and Nation: Essays on Indian Politics 1870–1940*, Cambridge University Press, 1973

Government of India, *India's Contribution to the Great War*, Calcutta, 1923

Government of India, *The Army in India and its Evolution*, Calcutta, 1924

Graubard, S. R., 'Military demobilisation in Great Britain following the First World War', *Journal of Modern History*, xix (1947), pp. 297–311

Griffiths, Sir Percival, *To Guard My People: the History of the Indian Police*, Benn (London and Bombay), 1971

Grigg, P. J., *Prejudice and Judgment*, Jonathan Cape, 1948

Gwynn, Sir C. W., *Imperial Policing*, Macmillan, 1934

Haldane, Sir Aylmer, *A Soldier's Saga*, William Blackwood (Edinburgh and London), 1948

Haldane, Sir Aylmer, *The Insurrection in Mesopotamia, 1920*, William Blackwood (Edinburgh and London), 1922

Hancock, W. K., *Smuts: the Fields of Force 1919–50*, Cambridge University Press, 1968

Hancock, W. K., *Survey of British Commonwealth Affairs vol. I: Problems of Nationality 1918–36*, Oxford University Press, 1937

Hardy, P., *The Muslims of British India*, Cambridge University Press, 1972

Harris, Henry, 'The other half million', in O. Dudley Edwards and Fergus Pyle (eds.), *1916: the Easter Rising*, MacGibbon and Kee, 1968

Hawkings, F. M. A., 'Defence and the role of Erskine Childers in the treaty negotiations of 1921', *Irish Historical Studies*, xxii (1981), pp. 251–70

Higham, Robin, *Armed Forces in Peacetime: Britain 1918–40, a Case Study*, G. T. Foulis, 1962

Holland, R. F., *Britain and the Commonwealth Alliance 1918–39*, Macmillan, 1981

Holmes, Richard, *The Little Field Marshal: Sir John French*, Jonathan Cape, 1981

Howard, Harry N., *The Partition of Turkey, a Diplomatic History 1913–23*, Fertig (New York), 1966 edn.

Hyam, Ronald, *Britain's Imperial Century*, Batsford, 1976

Ingrams, Doreen (ed.), *Palestine Papers 1917–22; Seeds of Conflict*, John Murray, 1972

Ironside, Lord, *Archangel 1918–19*, Constable, 1953

Ironside, Lord (ed.), *High Road to Command. The Diaries of Maj-Gen. Sir Edmund Ironside 1920–22*, Leo Cooper, 1972

Ismay, Lord, *Memoirs*, Heinemann, 1960

Jalland, Patricia, *The Liberals and Ireland; the Ulster Question in British Politics to 1914*, Harvester Press, 1980

Jebb, R., *The Imperial Conference*, 2 vols., 1911

Jeffery, Keith, and Peter Hennessy, *States of Emergency: British Governments and Strikebreaking since 1919*, Routledge and Kegan Paul, 1983

Jones, Thomas (ed. K. Middlemas), *Whitehall Diary*, vols. I and III, Oxford University Press, 1969 and 1971

Judd, Denis, *Balfour and the British Empire*, Macmillan, 1968

Kapur, Harish, *Soviet Russia and Asia 1917–21*, Michael Joseph, 1966

Kedourie, Elie, *In the Anglo-Arab Labyrinth: the MacMahon–Husayn Correspondence and its Interpretations 1914–1939*, Cambridge University Press, 1976

Kedourie, Elie, 'Sa'ad Zaghlul and the British', in A. Hournai (ed.), *St. Antony's Papers No. 11*, Chatto and Windus, 1961, pp. 139–60

Kendall, Walter, *The Revolutionary Movement in Britain 1900–21*, Weidenfeld and Nicolson, 1969

Kent, Marian, *Oil and Empire: British Policy and Mesopotamian Oil 1900–1920*, Macmillan, 1976

Kennedy, J. N., 'The anti-Bolshevik movement in south Russia, 1917–20', *Journal of the Royal United Service Institution*, lxvii (1922), pp. 600–21

Kennedy, Paul, *The Realities behind Diplomacy*, Fontana, 1981

Killingray, David. 'The idea of a British imperial African army', *Journal of African History*, vol. 20 (1979), pp. 421–36

Klieman, Aaron S., *Foundations of British Policy in the Arab World: the Cairo Conference of 1921*, Johns Hopkins Press (Baltimore and London), 1970

Knollys, D. E., 'Military operations in Trans-Caspia, 1918–19' *Journal of the Central Asian Society* xii (1926), pp. 90–110

Lee, J. Fitzgerald, *Imperial Military Geography*, 2nd edn, Clowes, 1922

Llewellyn Smith, M., *Ionian Vision*, Allen Lane, 1973

Longer, V., *Red Coats to Olive Green*, Allied Publishers (New Delhi), 1974

Longrigg, S. H., *Oil in the Middle East*, 3rd edn., R.I.I.A./Oxford University Press, 1968

Louis, W. R., *Great Britain and Germany's Lost Colonies, 1914–19*, Oxford University Press, 1967

Low, D. A., 'The government of India and the first non-co-operation movement 1920–22', in R. Kumar (ed.), *Essays in Gandhian Politics*, Oxford University Press, 1971

Lowe, C. J., and F. Marzari, *Italian Foreign Policy 1870–1940*, Routledge and Kegan Paul, 1975

Lucas, Sir Charles (ed.), *The Empire at War*, 5 vols., Royal Colonial Institute, 1921–6

Lucas, Sir Charles, *The Story of the Empire*, Collins, 1924

Lucey, Dermot J., 'Cork Public Opinion and the First World War', M.A. thesis, University College Cork, 1972

Macardle, Dorothy, *The Irish Republic*, Corgi edn., 1968

Macdonald, C. A., 'Lloyd George and the search for a post-war naval policy', in A. J. P. Taylor (ed.), *Lloyd George: Twelve Essays*, Hamish Hamilton, 1971

Mackinnon, A. C. B., 'The Moplah rebellion 1921–22', *Army Quarterly*, viii (1924), pp. 260–77

MacNaught, Kenneth, *The Pelican History of Canada*, Penguin Books, rev. edn., 1973

Macready, Sir Nevil, *Annals of an Active Life*, 2 vols, Hutchinson, 1924

Majumdar, R. C. (ed.), *History and Culture of the Indian People, vol. XI: the Struggle for Freedom*, Bombay, 1969

Malleson, Sir W., 'The British military mission to Turkestan', *Journal of the Central Asian Society*, ix (1922), pp. 95–110

Mansergh, P. N. S., *The Commonwealth Experience*, Weidenfeld and Nicolson, 1969

Mansergh, P. N. S., *The Irish Question 1840–1921*, rev. edn., Allen and Unwin, 1965

Marlowe, J., *Anglo-Egyptian Relations 1800–1953*, 2nd edn., Frank Cass, 1965

Marlowe, J., *Late Victorian: the Life of Sir Arnold Wilson*, Cresset, 1967

Mason, Philip, *A Matter of Honour. An Account of the Indian Army, its Officers and Men*, Penguin Books, 1976

Maurice, Sir Frederick, *The Life of General Lord Rawlinson of Trent*, Cassell, 1928

McLean, Iain, 'Popular protest and public order: Red Clydeside, 1915–1919', in R. Quinault and J. Stevenson (eds.), *Popular Protest and Public Order*, Allen and Unwin, 1974, pp. 215–242

Middlemas, R. K., *The Clydesiders*, Hutchinson, 1965

Moore, R. J., *The Crisis of Indian Unity 1917–40*, Clarendon Press (Oxford), 1974

Morgan, Kenneth O., *Consensus and Disunity: the Lloyd George Coalition Government 1918–1922*, Clarendon Press (Oxford), 1979

Morison, J. L., *From Alexander Burnes to Frederick Roberts: a Survey of Imperial Frontier Policy*, British Academy, 1936

Mowat, C. L., *Britain between the Wars*, Methuen, 1955

Nicol, Graham, *Uncle George: Field Marshal Lord Milne of Salonika and Rubislaw*, Reedminster, 1976

Nicholson, G. W. L., *Canadian Expeditionary Force, 1914–1919*, Queen's Printer (Ottawa), 1962

Nicolson, Harold, *Curzon: the Last Phase 1919–25*, Constable, 1934

Nicolson, Harold, *King George V*, Constable, 1952

Nitti, F. S., *Peaceless Europe*, Cassell, 1922

Norman, Edward, *A History of Modern Ireland*, Penguin edn., 1973

Norris, D., 'The British navy in the Caspian, 1918–19', *Journal of the Central Asian Society*, x (1923), pp. 216–40

Philby, H. St. J. B., 'The triumph of the Wahhabis', *Journal of the Central Asian Society*, xiii (1926), pp. 293–319

Philby, H. St. J. B., 'Trans-Jordan', *Journal of the Central Asian Society*, xi (1924), pp. 296–312

Preston, Richard A., *Canada and 'Imperial Defense'*, Duke University Press (Durham, North Carolina), 1967

'Q.L.', 'The Transcaspian expedition', *Journal of the Royal United Service Institution*, lxiv (1919), pp. 478–89

Rawson, J. O., 'The Role of India in Imperial Defence beyond Indian Frontiers and Home Waters 1919–39', D.Phil. thesis, Oxford University, 1977

Reynolds, G. W., and A. Judge, *The Night the Police went on Strike*, Weidenfeld and Nicolson, 1968

Riddell, Lord, *Intimate Diary of the Peace Conference and After 1918–23*, Gollancz, 1933

Rumbold, Sir Algernon, *Watershed in India 1914–1922*, Athlone Press, 1979

Spear, Percival, *A History of India*, vol. II, Penguin Books, 1970 edn.

Spender, J. A., *The Life of the Right Hon. Sir Henry Campbell-Bannerman*, 2 vols., Hodder and Stoughton, 1923

Stanley, G. F. G., *Canada's Soldiers*, rev. edn., Macmillan Canada (Toronto), 1960

Stern, J. A., 'Britain, Italy and the Versailles Settlement, 1917–22', Ph.D. dissertation, Cambridge University, 1970

Sykes, Sir Percy, *History of Persia*, 2 vols. 3rd edn., Macmillan, 1930

Taylor, A. J. P., *English History 1914–45*, Penguin Books, 1970

Taylor, Rex, *Assassination! The Death of Sir Henry Wilson and the Tragedy of Ireland*, Hutchinson, 1961

Tod, J. K., 'Operations in Trans-Caspia, 1918–19', *Army Quarterly*, xvi (1928), pp. 280–303

Townshend, Charles, *The British Campaign in Ireland, 1919–21*, Oxford University Press, 1975

Troeller, Gary, *The Birth of Sa'udi Arabia: Britain and the Rise of the House of Sa'ud*, Frank Cass, 1976

Ullman, Richard H., *Anglo-Soviet Relations 1917–21*, vols. II and III, Princeton University Press, 1968 and 1972

Ward, Alan J., 'Lloyd George and the 1918 Irish Conscription Crisis', *Historical Journal*, vol. 17 (1974), pp. 107–29

Wavell, Viscount, *Allenby in Egypt*, Harrap, 1943

Wilkinson, R. J., 'The influence of oil on imperial organisation', *Journal of the Royal United Service Institution*, lxviii (1923), pp. 109–114

Wilson, Sir Arnold, *Mesopotamia, 1917–20; a Clash of Loyalties*, Oxford University Press, 1931

Index